D1563894

Aging in Today's World

PUBLIC ISSUES IN ANTHROPOLOGICAL PERSPECTIVE

General Editors: William O. Beeman and David Kertzer, Department of Anthropology, Brown University

Aging in Today's World

*Conversations Between an
Anthropologist and a Physician*

Renée Rose Shield, Ph.D.
and
Stanley M. Aronson, M.D., MPH

Berghahn Books
New York • Oxford

First published in 2003 by

Berghahn Books

www.berghahnbooks.com

Library of Congress Cataloging-in-Publication Data

Shield, Renée Rose.
    Aging in today's world : conversations between an anthropologist and a physician /
Renée Rose Shield and Stanley M. Aronson.
        p. cm. -- (Public issues in anthropological perspective ; v. 4)
    Includes bibliographical references and index.
    ISBN 1-57181-420-5 (cloth : alk. paper)
    1. Aging. 2. Aging--Anthropological aspects. 3. Aging--Physiological aspects. I.
Aronson, Stanley M., 1922- II. Title. III. Series.

HQ1061 .S467 2003
305.26--dc21   2002027713

British Library Cataloguing in Publication Data

A catalogue record for this book is available from the British Library.

Printed in the United States on acid-free paper

Contents

Acknowledgements

B ooks don't write themselves, nor do they navigate through the intricacies of internal consistency and the shoals of editorial revision without substantial, and frequently anonymous, assistance. The authors of this text therefore happily acknowledge the support and love of their families, and the tolerance, good grace and enormous editorial help rendered by William Beeman, Marion Berghahn, Vivian Berghahn, Caroline Graf, David Kertzer, Christine Marciniak, and Janine Treves-Habar. We wish to express our heartfelt thanks to these wonderful folks as well as make the customary disclaimer that errors in the text, regretfully, are our own.

to Paul, with my love
— Renée

to the blessed memory of
Betty E. Aronson, M.D.
— Stan

Chapter 1

Introduction

(RRS)

A ging is something we do, although it remains a mystery to all of us, those who study it as well as those who undergo or endure it. That's everyone.

> *Wait: not quite everyone, since close to 80 percent of those born alive will never taste the fruits of aging. Even in the most advanced nations of the world, there are still many, perhaps one in four, who will not reach their seventieth birthday. [SMA]*

> *Hold on, Stan. I mean aging in the sense that one ages from the moment of birth onwards. I do not want to assign an arbitrary age to the beginning of aging and prefer to see aging through the life course as a continuing process. [RRS]*

Because aging is often viewed with dread and is associated with death, it carries many loaded assumptions. This volume is offered as a way of peeling the skin off some of these assumptions and encouraging better communication, scholarship, and understanding about aging.

The two authors are a cultural anthropologist (RRS)—age mid-fifties—and a physician (SMA)—age about eighty—each with long-term interests in the relationship between aging and society. We have carried on both a professional and personal dialog with one another for close to twenty years about how age, culture, and health interact. We find that we operate under different assumptions, and our conversations have helped to clarify the areas we have taken for granted and the areas we feel need explaining and defending. While we inevitably revisit our core beliefs, we have agreed to continue the argument in order to sharpen each other's defenses and hone our overall understanding of this human process.

This book continues our conversation. The reader will note, from the first paragraph above, that we engage in discussion, repartée, and retort as we pursue our wish to understand. We hope to draw the reader into the issues and questions that we find compelling. We intend for it to help chart a way for professionals as well as anyone interested in aging to think about the variously humbling, enriching, bewildering, and humanizing experiences of aging. We do not intend this book to be an exhaustive text of the subject since these are available elsewhere; most of all we hope to inspire readers to enter into their own active thinking and discussions about age and aging.

The format of this book reflects the thrust of the dialog. Each chapter has a primary author, the initials of whom appear in parentheses. Chapters end with a commentary from the other author. By and large we each stand in the wings waiting for the chance to respond at the end of the chapter. Here and there, however, we cannot wait, and the italicized interruptions are the result. In this manner, the dialog often goes back and forth within the chapters.

The reader of these pages will sometimes encounter, indented and italicized, yet another voice added to the voices of the two authors. This third voice that intrudes upon the text from time to time, and is identified with the initials "OM," represents the imagined thoughts of an eighty-seven-year-old male resident of a nursing home in Providence, Rhode Island. Though OM would prefer to maintain his anonymity, OM's occasionally wry words are not entirely fictional. One of the authors [SMA] chaired the board of trustees of a large home for the aged about a decade ago, and it was his custom to wander through the halls and chat with many of the residents who appeared unoccupied. OM's comments represent a distillation of these countless conversations.

We believe, given the constraints of the structure of a book, that this format mimics the realities of earnest conversation. Furthermore, our intent is to deliberately *not* meld our separate perspectives into a unified voice. Such a voice would result from a reconciliation of our different approaches, and the reader would be spared the uneven edges of ongoing reflection, thought and discussion. Preserving the differences in our voices, we believe, retains and underscores the lack of resolution and the continuing need for more conversation on the important subject of aging in today's world.

SMA wishes to add some thoughts here:

There are notable differences in the way anthropologists and physicians are separately trained to address problems, and then to fulfill what they each consider to be their professional responsibilities.

The physician, in theory, is trained to observe distressed persons one at a time; to engage such persons, through deliberate conversation, so that they may clarify the historic origins and dimensions of their distress; and then to determine the extent to which this distress translates to disability; to employ technical means by which one or more underlying pathophysiological processes may be identified; to describe to the distressed person, now a patient, the likely natural evolution of this pathophysiological process; or, if no specific treatment is available, to offer, at the least, palliative interventions so as to reduce the patient's suffering; and to periodically revisit the patient to retest the accuracy of the diagnosis and to ascertain the effectiveness of the therapeutic interventions. All of this is subservient to the oldest of medical aphorisms, primum non nocere, first do no harm. The physician's four-fold role (diagnosis, prognosis, therapy, counseling), undertaken within a framework of medical ethics, is ideally proactive. It fails, by definition, if there is no meaningful intervention or if it is confined solely to observation. Both the patient and the medical profession demand: "Don't just sit and observe; do something! Change things for the better."

In recent decades there has emerged a branch of medicine which regards the entire community, rather than the isolated patient, as its client. Public health physicians, strongly abetted by the discipline of clinical epidemiology, now seek out possible causes of major disease (such as lung cancer or coronary artery disease) within the environment or within the lifestyles of the affected members of the community. This form of medicine changes the fundamental covenant from the physician waiting passively until the suffering patient seeks his/her help, to the socially concerned physician pursuing a more proactive role. [SMA]

In the next chapter I [RRS] explore some of the differences between our disciplines' various perspectives to help promote the dialog we're trying to foster. [Here let me add that the objects of anthropological study—unlike people who go to doctors—rarely, if ever, present themselves to anthropologists asking to be studied or otherwise "understood."] By definition, anthropologists impose themselves on those they study wishing to understand some essential questions of their humanity. Anthropologists are seeking to be illuminated. We try not to change people's lives though we are aware that our mere presence necessarily affects those we view and those with whom we interact—a social Heisenberg effect. Those we study are not usually seeking advice on how to change how they are conducting their lives. However, the process of talking with and observing people in action—asking people to reflect on their lives and to give thought to what and why they do and think what they do—sometimes (perhaps often) has the effect of clarifying areas of discontent and discomfort. Sometimes this reflection mobilizes people to act. Furthermore, anthropologists who work in impoverished or third-world societies, are often asked for help when they are identified as people with access to power, medicine, money, transportation, and the like. Anthropologists also have a code of ethical standards that requires them to "do no harm" to their informants or the group studied. Ethical dilemmas are complex and unavoidable, however.

"Applied" anthropologists explicitly attempt to change a situation by applying what they have learned about the group. After observing how school children interact on a playground, for example, they might recommend an intervention designed to reduce bullying. Or an anthropologist studying the culture of a nursing home might issue recommendations about how the lives of the nursing home residents could be improved.

In general, anthropologists try to "stand there" and not "do something," at least while they are trying to understand the people they are studying. [RRS]

The reason that we believe this conversation is an important one to pursue is that aging is a huge and complex subject about which there is not a lot of agreement. Is aging inevitable? Is it a bad thing? Is it a burden or a gift? What is successful aging? Why are some people "better" at aging than others? (By which most people mean, why do they seem to age "more slowly.") Where does aging begin? What is responsible for it? How does aging vary among individuals, within groups, between groups, cultures, societies, and over the centuries? What can we understand about the social context of aging? Why are there so many old women in contrast to the paucity of old men? Why are most of the caregivers female? Are old people "useful?" How do we define useful? Is, it, finally, a process of progressive enrichment? Or alternatively, a form of irreversible degeneration?

In the next chapters we tackle a number of subjects that touch on and develop various of these concerns. We hope that by the example of our dialog we encourage more discussion about aging in general and in particular. Since aging matters to all of us and we live in a world with greater and greater numbers of old people, it is necessary to make bridges between disciplines and actively debate the many questions that the phenomenon of this demographic imperative raises. Together, we seek ways to better understand this increasingly important period in the life span.

Interlude
Death Be Not the Enemy
(SMA)

If this commentary were to discuss schistosomiasis, cholera or even malaria, it might hold some intellectual interest. The problems created by these wretched diseases are indeed immense, destroying the lives of millions of people and hampering the economies of entire nations. Yet, in truth, they affect the health of very few in the United States.

In contrast, issues concerning the end of life, sooner or later, involve all of us throughout the world. We readily acknowledge the universality of death and there is no paucity of books on the subject. Yet, despite this we do not have authoritative voices to instruct us on the subjective intricacies of dying. None of us has passed through the terminal months of a wasting disease and can then reflect back upon the experience saying, yes, we were there and can now clarify its nature for the rest of us who are still in the midst of life. Except on television, dying is not something that we endure, only to discuss it retrospectively at the next church picnic. On the other hand, dying is something that we cannot avoid; it is part of our inevitable human destiny, our ultimate fate.

In an epidemiological sense, we are all terminally ill. We differ only in the imminence and velocity of our departure and the degree to which we cling to thoughts of immortality. Children, and perhaps first-year medical students, believe that human existence is a simple matter, with people readily assign-able to one of two categories called either life or death. To those innocents, the role of physicians is equally clear: they are to sup-port life relentlessly, strengthened in their resolve by no thought other than the preservation of life. Death, then, becomes the implacable enemy, and its arrival is sure evidence of failure. Those with such simplistic thinking give precious little thought to that twilight zone, the terminal months of life when we real-ize—by what we have been told and by what our body tell us—that life is now concluding.

In this past century, American families have gradually relinquished their personal control over such critical life-events as birth, sickness, care of the elderly, and dying—yielding the management of these chores of passage to society and its com-plex institutions. Death, in particular, has been so effectively sanitized and disembodied that few will experience the sounds, sights, and odors of the final few minutes in the lives of their beloved ones. For more Americans in this decade, the first true intimacy with death will be their own.

In the past, medical practitioners watched but could do lit-tle to modify their patient's final trajectory towards death. Death, then, was a more natural event, typically taking place in the home. Before the emergency rooms and intensive care units became the primary venues for most, older physicians will remember when death had the decisive hand. And when it approached, the physician's skills were reduced to an easing of the dying process and a reduction of any accompanying pain. It was, in truth, a non-heroic encounter often with nurses, clergy, and family as intimate witnesses, sharing in a respectful accep-tance of reality.

When confronting the critically ill patient, the newer physician in the U.S. now has access to a lengthy menu of med-ical interventions in a variety of technical settings. Life will often be prolonged, but sometimes at great moral cost. There are instances when modern technology has been subverted to maintain humans in a vegetative state for weeks or months; and in the naïve thinking of some Americans, death has been reduced to an option rather than an inevitability.

The displacement of death from the family bedroom to some windowless cubicle in a large medical center has its consequences. In the past the family, including the children, were witness to the last respiratory struggles of the dying person. The time of day was carefully noted and for the rest of their lives, each living soul present in that room will have remembered the passing of a cherished relative. Few Americans have that privilege of immediacy today since society has intervened, allegedly to shield us from the discomfort and anxiety of watching the passing of a loved one. The actual departure of this relative, therefore, often takes place in some inner institutional chamber; and we learn the fate of our loved one only after a nurse or physician announces the event minutes or hours after death has been documented, the messiness of the agonal events having been safely hidden.

Physicians trained in the twenty-first century, though, are learning not to be mindless slaves to their own wondrous capabilities; they are trained now to temper these technical interventions with compassion and sensitivity. If this were the first school day for a class of new medical students, one might envisage a dean welcoming the incoming students with words such as these:

Before you begin your intensive medical training, hear this: Death is inevitable; and from this uncomfortable fact you will each be required to dissect out certain inescapable realities. As a profession, we have been immensely successful in prolonging life, diminishing the burdens of contagious, cardiovascular, and neoplastic disease. But, ultimately, medicine fails. At best we ease the way; increasingly, too, we lengthen the years of life, sometimes efficiently, sometimes painfully. We may substitute one cause of death for another, one date of death for another, one place of death for another. But finally, we will indeed fail. And should you, in the years ahead, employ your energies and your authority to deny these realities you will then be incapable of offering to your patient those unique professional gifts that only you can bestow.

You stand at a privileged intersection of those who know the secret dynamics of human sickness, and those who are privy to the secret passions and wishes of the patient. Others may offer comfort, but you can offer both comfort, meaningful intervention and the approximate truth regarding your patient's future. You do not know the future well, but you know it better than do others.

And when, finally, all of your therapies fail, you must then not walk away, but with summoned courage and tenacity you must stay with your patient, hopefully in the company of his loved ones, to his last recorded gasp of breath. Do not permit his final companionship in life to be solely with machines.

Chapter 2

Examining Our Assumptions

(RRS)

There is no cure for birth and death save to enjoy the interval.
— *Santayana*

The fact of aging, the mechanisms of aging, the probability of old age for most of us and the certainty of death for all of us seem to be natural facts, obvious and basic. But how natural are the facts, how obvious and basic? We know that even core biological processes are profoundly mediated and affected by non-biologic factors embedded in culture. And certainly the process of aging, the most visible component in the core biologic act of living, is immensely sensitive to cultural forces and societal imperatives.

Here I review various ways that the subject of old age and aging has been treated by medicine and other disciplines through the years. Myths about aging are tenacious and universal (though the myths are hardly the same!), and different societies believe and behave with much variety toward their older members. It is necessary that we examine our basic assump-

---

Notes for this section begin on page 39.

tions about what is allegedly natural regarding aging—and what is culturally contrived—so that we can see it with fresh eyes and enrich our understanding.

The Hope and Disenchantment of Modern Medicine

In 1973 Michel Foucault's *The Birth of the Clinic* challenged the basic idea of medical objectivity. Attempting to brush away centuries of faith in the so-called progress of accumulated knowledge in western science, his book is an overarching critique of the role of medicine in modern life. By narrowly focusing on what is observable, Foucault maintained that Western medicine discounted other forms of experience and expression in its claim for mastery of the mysteries of health and disease.[1]

> What was fundamentally invisible is suddenly offered to the brightness of the gaze, in a movement of appearance so simple, so immediate that it seems to be the natural consequence of a more highly developed experience[...]It is as if for the first time for thousands of years, doctors, free at last of theories and chimeras, agreed to approach the object of their experience with the purity of an unprejudiced gaze (1973:195).

Foucault believed that the way of thinking and talking about disease and the afflicted changed radically at this point. He claimed that Western biomedicine adopted a superior stance toward its subject. Medicine seemed immune to culture and relativism. Its status as objective tended to shield it and make it sacrosanct. While healthcare policy and individual practitioners could be criticized, few challenged the methods by which Western biomedicine studied its subjects and issued its conclusions. Medical claims continue to exert a powerful force within Western society.

But, of course, Western biomedicine is a product of its culture. Increasingly, it is challenged by other forms of healing that hail from varied societies or spring from diverse systems of knowledge. We are in an interesting time at the beginning of the new millennium. Optimism about medical progress and biomedical technology is at an all-time high peak at the same time that increasing numbers of people are skeptical of the presumed authority of medical knowledge. As more people in the United States and Europe are disenchanted with traditional biomedicine and its shortcomings, especially in relation to chronic diseases, the way death is treated, and pain management, awareness of other methods and philosophies of healing is growing, and these alternatives have appeal.

> *I would contend that the disenchantment with medicine is more with its tendency to "underutilization" and depersonalization rather than with the clinical results. [SMA]*

> *Certainly, I agree that the way we finance healthcare in the United States fundamentally relates to how healthcare is perceived and received. Specifically, millions of Americans do not have health insurance and thus cannot receive regular medical attention. The clinical results are part and parcel of this flaw in the American system. Depersonalization is another problem that I would also contend intimately affects the clinical outcomes of care—and it is also related to the financing problems underlying the structure of healthcare. [RRS]*

Western biomedicine has driven consumer expectations to spectacular heights. The technological array of diagnostic and treatment mechanisms and tools available to modern physicians in the West is staggering. The forté and focus of this medical competence have been significantly limited to those diseases and conditions that are acute, however. When a child falls off the uneven bars doing a gymnastics routine and breaks her elbow, for example, the surgical and rehabilitative technology and knowledge to fix this discrete part of this child's anatomy is superlative. Many areas in medicine have benefited by increasing knowledge and better tools, whether they are diagnostic, therapeutic, or pharmacologic. However, Western biomedicine is much less successful in dealing with chronic conditions, and more and more people, particularly the elderly, have chronic ailments. They are a result of medicine's great success in keeping vast numbers of physiologically impaired people alive.

More people in Western society survive with diseases and conditions that would have guaranteed them much shorter lives decades ago. Many babies survive after being born with astonishingly low birth-weights, but their later lives are often complicated by multiple and complex impairments. Older adults increasingly survive into advanced old age, often coexisting with simultaneous multiple ailments.

> *For example, about one adult in eight suffers from diabetes mellitus and most diabetics will survive for decades. A century ago, before the isolation of insulin, the diagnosis of diabetes foretold a grim and brief future. [SMA]*

Many of the available therapies can ameliorate though not cure these conditions. Degenerative processes are amenable to some of the therapies, but sometimes the best that can be hoped for is a slowing of the degeneration rather than a reversal. Many more diseases, such as AIDS, are becoming chronic diseases that can be effectively managed but not cured by drug therapies. For all these reasons, increasing numbers of people, both young and old, are burdened by chronic conditions, often accompanied by pain or disability, that do not yield to cure.

People who are dying and those who have untreatable conditions are often failed by the current biomedical system, although there are persistent and growing efforts to change the situation. Since the 1960s, numerous researchers have noted how dying persons are considered failures, and as a result they are less well attended to.[2] Despite physician attempts to be humane and care for their patients as best they can, the technological imperative of treating the treatable often drives the system philosophically, practically, and financially. For example, specific procedures and treatments are paid for whereas activities such as spending time, being supportive and caring are not. This situation leaves those who are dying or uncured in limbo, not quite alive and not quite dead. Too often these patients are told that there is nothing else to be done for them. Hospice care fills some of the need, but not all. Furthermore, attempts to reconcile dilemmas of medical care often neglect the determining cultural contexts from which they spring.

Alternate and complementary modes of healing, with sources from throughout the world, have marched into this seeming lapse in Western healthcare. They have panache in this day and age, seem consumer-friendly, appear to consider the whole person as opposed to a discrete organ or symptom, are often less expensive, and seem to offer views of disease and illness that are more suited to chronic conditions and pain in general. Greater numbers of people are using these therapies, often without informing their physicians of their practices. Increasingly, established insurance companies are reimbursing a number of these therapies. As there is more openness toward these therapies, Western medicine is feeling the impact. Some of these treatment philosophies counsel those suffering from chronic diseases toward better ways of adapting to the condition (see Goldstein 1999).

It is no coincidence that the unredeemed hope about and subsequent disenchantment with Western biomedicine arise at a time when the number and proportion of old people is greater than ever. The sheer numbers of old people surviving into advanced old age confounds some of our most cherished prejudices about aging. Much of the reason for the aging of our population is due to fertility decreases in this century, thus diminishing the input of newborns into the population mix. As the numbers of healthy old people become our models and offer more hope about our own futures, they also illustrate the limitations of medicine, the finiteness of human life, and the difficult underside of aging that coexists with the privilege of entering the senior years. While we witness the vitality of increasing numbers of people in old age, we are also participants in the problems in the healthcare system and we see firsthand both the limitations of the body and of medical science. Increasing numbers of Americans attempt to fill the holes in the system of community supports and services, and more and more of us try to help our aged loved ones as they experience multiple chronic impairments that come with old age. Spoiled by success, we are frustrated both by the limitations in healthcare and our ultimately vulnerable human bodies.

To refresh our discussion and enhance our understanding, it is important first of all to see that both the perception of medicine and its clinical agenda are embedded within culture.

Acknowledging this makes it possible to discuss the contributions that anthropology, medicine, and other fields devoted to aging offer to one another to help illuminate the mysteries surrounding aging and old people. Rapp aptly writes that "We as a science-seeking nation have much to learn, in all our diversity, from emergent epidemiologies which stress the social, not only the more narrowly biomedical, when thinking about health, illness, and effective interventions" (2000:315).

Nature and Culture

One of the themes of this book is the distinction between nature and culture. Though a favorite subject of anthropologists, it is a topic less often considered by physicians.

> *Physicians generally hold that their activities are more science than art; that they are sufficiently objective and that culture may determine their conversations or manner of dress but not their therapeutic regimens. [SMA]*

> *Do you ever ask us old ones what kind of doctor we want? Yes, we get impressed with, and maybe frightened by the modern doctor with his fancy machines and his nose in the chart. And yes, we know that the doctors manage to keep many of us alive. But that doesn't answer the question of what kind of doctor we seek. We want somebody who looks at us rather than our chart, maybe even enjoys seeing us. Someone who sits down, tells us his problems, really listens to our belly-aching, and doesn't promise miracles. Someone I can tell a joke to. Someone who's heard of the Red Sox. Above all he should be a mensch—but that's a word you've never heard of. [OM]*

In recent years, however, physicians are increasingly attending more to the social contexts of disease. There is a growing awareness of the impact that sociocultural factors have on illnesses. Furthermore, the increasing ethnic diversity of Western society means that most doctors now come face to face with patients whose backgrounds and beliefs are different from theirs, and doctors themselves are more diverse than ever, coming from all over the world.

> *As a compelling example of this diversity, of the 628 newly licensed physicians to practice medicine in Rhode Island in the last two years, 183 were born and educated in places other than United States or Canada, and 34 percent were from Asia, principally India and Pakistan (Deary et al. 1999, 2000.) [SMA]*

Tangible as well as subtle manifestations of culture influence physiologic dynamics. These factors include attitude, ideas, and beliefs about illness and healing, finances, family structure, nutrition, among others. We will try to address some of these in our discussions.

An anthropological article of faith is the following: if something is considered natural, it is probably cultural. A simple example: a cultural belief in American society is that it is only natural that mothers do the child rearing. This belief has undergone considerable rethinking in the last couple of decades. It was a taken-for-granted truism around World War II, but is contested today. Before feminists challenged this notion in the 1960s, few Americans would have agreed that the idea was cultural rather than immutably natural. Hrdy's (1999) review of motherhood in humans and primates should put to rest the idea of a fixed way to be a mother. Her book thoroughly demonstrates not only the vast diversity of ways that infants and children are nurtured and reared, but how the mother continually strategizes to make critical choices to ensure her and her offspring's survival.

The normality or deviancy of homosexual behavior is widely debated. As more "normal"-seeming individuals declare themselves gay, American assumptions about sexuality and sexual orientation are challenged and modified. As this closet-clearing increases, notions about discrimination and fairness and the relationship between nature and nurture are necessarily debated. School boards and political factions fight it out in community meetings and at the ballot box. The Boy Scouts are under fire for discriminating. Even biologists and psychoanalysts disagree, with most now arguing that a continuum of sexuality and intersexuality is normal in the animal and human species. Anthropologists point to the diversity of behavior and attitudes regarding sexuality and its expression worldwide, underscoring its immense cultural variety, acceptance and plasticity.

In short, civil rights, feminism, consumerism, and gay rights are twentieth-century movements that have challenged older ways of thinking in the United States. Population dispersals that create waves of immigration combined with the greater exposure to diversity because of globalization adds to this process. Little by little social values in American life begin to reflect the different and changing sources of knowledge.

In less dramatic ways, but equally as firmly rooted, people and cultures hold views about aging that appear natural and uncontested to them, but on examination are found not to be shared by others.

Even life expectancy—a statistical or actuarial concept to describe how long defined populations, on average, survive—has changed dramatically in the twentieth century. This neutral measure has yielded to the impact of medical and cultural factors, such as sanitation and nutrition. The life expectancy number varies relative to country and socio-economic status today. As life expectancy has changed, so too have definitions of old age. Changing definitions in turn affect how laws are written and modified and what behaviors are expected of and considered appropriate for groups of individuals.

> *The arithmetic means of life expectancy have changed—certainly. But not its meaning (which is culture-free) or the procedures by which it is determined. [SMA]*
>
> *Yes, I agree with you. [RRS]*

Whether or not you are considered old at a given age varies according to the culture and epoch in which you live. In many places in the world a girl is old enough to marry after her first menses, and is therefore, at that age, a culturally-determined "adult." In traditional Ireland, in contrast, a man in his fifties was not considered fully adult until his father had died, and this expectation still exists in parts of rural Ireland.

In some places old age begins with the marriages of children and the birth of the first grandchildren, as in India (Vatuk 1980). Lamb describes her experience in West Bengal:

The family heads initiated their transition to being "senior" by gradually—often with years of ambivalence, arguing, and competition—handing over their duties of reproduction, cooking, and feeding to "junior" successors, usually sons and sons' wives. When their children married, women would also start to wear white saris, which signified their increasing seniority and asexuality (2000:44).

Menopause (Kerns 1983) or widowhood (Lopata 1973) are often common markers of old age for women, or when the death of a man's father happens as in the Lango culture of Uganda (Curley 1973). Nason noted that the end of child-rearing among the people of Etal, a Micronesian atoll, generally occurred close to the time that a person became less able to do the rigorous work of gardening and fishing and began to substitute such physical roles with other valued social and educational ones (1981). Glascock and Feinman sampled worldwide data to derive generalizations about the beginning of old age (1981). They found that being "old" was associated with a change in a person's economic or social role, being between the ages of forty-five and fifty-five, as well as changes in physical characteristics (as noted in Sokolovsky 1997:3).

The celebration called *kanreki iwai* has been a traditional way of commemorating the beginning of old age in Japan during a person's sixtieth year, but as Plath argues, many today consider sixty too young to be called old even if he or she is eligible for healthcare and social benefits (1998:194). In a Mexican peasant community that Sokolovsky studied, old people begin to be called *culi* after the birth of several grandchildren has taken place. When they show evidence of decreased strength and can work less hard at their old tasks, the label *culi* is more consistently applied to them (Sokolovsky 1997a).

We get an inkling of some of the evolutionary and plastic aspects of age in the United States when we realize that the definition of old in United States society has been undergoing profound change in only the last several decades. Since the Depression, for example, a person was usually defined as old when he or she retired from work. In the twenty-first century, however, more and more people are retiring to second careers, new educational pursuits, vigorous leisure activities, and the like. Retirees experience unprecedented good health and are often compared to the prior generation's forty-somethings. Today's fifty-year-olds are appalled when they are prematurely (in their judgment) offered membership in the American Association of Retired Persons (AARP). Eighty-year-olds push weights and run marathons.

> *A grandmother running down the street no longer means that she is seeking a policeman or a fire alarm box. [SMA]*

It seems that we are fairly safe in considering an eighty-five-year-old "old" nowadays, but we are likely to offend a sixty-year-old by the same designation. Our reluctance to ascribe the old label to people in their sixties is a recent development that attests to the malleability of the concept. Advertising for age-related products such as denture cleaners has succumbed to the demographic imperative by showing older models with graceful, athletic bodies, and tasteful smile lines that exemplify wisdom and experience rather than frailty and closure. Note, however, the ageist slant to the bottom line: it is tolerable, but still not desirable to be considered old.

We worry about the dire impact of the graying of the population—and in particular, the aging of the baby-boomer generation—yet we do not seem to completely appreciate the boon of how much more healthy and active our aging population has become.

The plasticity goes along with a general loosening of age-norms in United States society. We witness eighty-year-olds receiving college degrees, increasing numbers of women becoming mothers in their forties, other women becoming grandmothers as early as age thirty-five or as late as seventy, while seventy-year-olds enter the Peace Corps, and the public debates the suitability and appropriateness of post-menopausal women having babies (which interestingly disregards the morality of old fathers bringing new babies into the world). No longer can we assign simple age-appropriate roles with assurance that they represent a true picture of what Americans are experiencing in their lives. As Gail Sheehy has written of these non-normative ages:

> Consider: Nine-year-old girls are developing breasts and pubic hair; 9-year-old boys carry guns to school; 16-year-olds can "divorce" a parent; 30-year-old men still live at home with Mom; 40-year-old women are just getting around to pregnancy; 50-year-old men are forced into early retirement; 55-year-old women can have egg donor babies; 60-year-old women start first professional degrees; 70-year-old men reverse aging by 20 years with human growth hormone; 80-year-olds run marathons; 85-year-olds remarry and still enjoy sex; and every day, the "Today" show's Willard Scott says "Happy Birthday!" to more 100-year-old women (1995:3-4).

On the other hand, in contrast to the opportunities afforded by better health, we also know that many poor people age in a physical or health-related sense more rapidly than do those who are economically more secure. In an epidemiological context, wealth and privilege cushion people from many precipitating conditions that give rise to disease or in other ways foreshorten life. Wealthier people have doctors and consult them when they are ill. Usually sharing similar socio-economic characteristics, these patients and their doctors can therefore communicate with one another more effectively. Such patients have access to the Internet that connects them to sophisticated ways of getting help.

Poor people throughout the world unfortunately often face a confluence of factors that make daily life difficult, predispose them to disease and/or injury, limit their access to healthcare, and hasten death (Farmer 1999). Poor people in the U.S. who live in crowded, unsanitary surroundings, often have little or no access to primary care physicians, vaccinations, and regular preventive care. With insufficient, dangerous, physically wearing work, or no work at all, they often live in areas of high crime, in older and more hazardous buildings. They are more likely to have asthma, lead poisoning, tuberculosis, hepatitis, and other serious infectious and environmental diseases. They are more vulnerable to violent crime and experience more injuries in work that is usually more physically dangerous. Each of these risk factors predisposes individuals to shorter and/or more disease-prone lives. The rural poor face additional challenges generated by physical isolation and separation that can be just as serious (Rowles 1983; Salber 1983).

Greater affluence brings health benefits that ameliorate some of the effects of aging. More education, higher income, better healthcare, higher rates of compliance with medications, lower rates of smoking, substantially lower rates of obesity, and overall healthier lives are factors that are often correlated with one another. Overall, as the saying goes, it is better to be wealthy and healthy than poor and sick.

In the United States the inequities between rich and poor perpetuate and grow worse, and overall provide an ironic commentary on the nation's unprecedented prosperity. This disparity has far-ranging health and life expectancy effects that are serious and significant for the nation as a whole.

> *The National Mortality Survey of 17,014 deaths in the United States for 1966/68 was studied to determine the existence and character of relationships between family income and mortality rates. Selected causes of death were assigned to three major diagnostic categories: infectious diseases, cardiovascular and cerebrovascular diseases; and certain neoplastic (tumor-producing) diseases.*
>
> *In general, the disease-specific mortality rates were inversely proportional to the stated family income. In each diagnostic category the income differential was most evident in the youngest age groups, progressively diminishing to a statistically nonsignificant difference in those dying beyond the age of seventy-five years. Within this sample, the sensitivity of mortality rates to family income was most apparent in those deaths caused by infectious disease and least apparent in those dying of neoplastic disease. When, however, the neoplastic disease deaths were segregated into those neoplasms held to be caused by environmental factors (e.g., cancer of the lung, upper respiratory system and urinary bladder) and those cancers not shown to be caused by tangible external factors, a differential sensitivity to family income became evident: The environmentally oriented neoplasms were more sensitive to family income.*
>
> *Mortality is undeniably 100 percent. But being rich delays this inevitability somewhat (Frenkel and Aronson 1986, National Center for Health Statistics 1966-68). [SMA]*

Not only do people age at varying rates, but the signs of age mislead. The presence of wrinkles and gray hair seems to herald advancing age incontestably, but not always. These signs mislead because they can be cosmetically altered or may vary because of genetic predisposition, nutrition, disease, smoking, exercise, stress, exposure to excessive sunlight, or other as yet unknown factors. The presence of these signs may signal advancing years when in fact the person with them is relatively young. These taken-for-granted signs of age cannot be assumed to cue us accurately to a person's chronological age. When Gloria Steinem still looked beautiful and "young" on turning fifty, her exclamation, "This is what fifty looks like!" became a ringing cry for baby boomers convinced that they too could beat the aging game. They plan to defy mortality through fitness, diet, and the spirituality fads that currently reign in U.S. culture.

Nature and culture interact in complex ways. The more we can recognize the factors that are involved separately and together, the better we can attempt to understand aging.

While the assumptions of what is natural and what is right are often silent in disciplines that concern themselves with aging, they exert a powerful influence on their adherents and practitioners. They determine the parameters of what is understood, the questions that are asked, the expectations that are desired, and ultimately the ways in which the results are used.

Gerontology and Geriatrics

The field of gerontology and its medical counterpart, geriatrics, arose at the end of the nineteenth century with an objective of making old age as disease-free as possible. Prior to the eighteenth century old age in America and Europe was understood as "an existential problem requiring moral and spiritual commitment" (Cole1992:xxiv). Moral ambiguity surrounded the mystery of aging during ancient and medieval times. While aging was lamented, it was suffused with religious and metaphorical meanings that perhaps in another life promised redemption and renewal. These attitudes provided some emotional sustenance and enveloped aging and the inevitability of death within an accepted philosophical framework that helped to soften the experiences.

These resigned and comfortable attitudes were soon to change. Benjamin Franklin, for example, wished he had been born later in order to reap the advantages of scientific accomplishment in which "all diseases may by sure means be prevented or cured, not excepting even that of old age, and our lives lengthened at pleasure" (quoted by Cole 1992:xxiv).

Old age had developed associations with loneliness, loss of productivity, and dying in nineteenth-century Protestant America, and these notions led to the idea that aging was a problem that could be "managed" by professionals. The development of the fields of gerontology and geriatrics was a powerful response to the anxiety that Puritan and Victorian America had about isolation, age, and death. The growing prominence of science and medicine launched a new set of hopes and expectations about the wonders that could be accomplished. Geriatrics set out to distinguish "normal" aging from pathological disease processes that originate with age, or at least are statistically associated with aging, and set itself the goal of eliminating as much disease as possible.

> *The goal of eliminating the degenerative diseases of the elderly will likely not be achieved in the lifetimes of the writers—or the readers—of this text. Only children, newspaper reporters, and avid fans of science fiction believe that diseases of senescence will be conquered as readily as was the control of infectious diseases. The Bible talks of man being granted 120 years of life; and there are no verified post-deluvial instances of humans exceeding this limit. If, for the immediate future, man will not accept this chronological limit, then Nature will remind him. The words of Emily Dickinson are worth remembering. [SMA]*
>
> > *Because I could not stop for death,*
> > *He kindly stopped for me;*
> > *The carriage held but just ourselves*
> > *and immortality.*

Gerontology joined geriatrics in seeking to abolish the mystery surrounding aging, confident that its problematic nature could be answered, understood, and ultimately overcome. The numbers of poor and old had been growing, and geriatrics and gerontology responded to the pessimism with a vision of scientific hope. Accompanied by the idea gaining prominence that science could ultimately solve all questions and cure all ills, these fields outlined a vision of physical salvation through increasing knowledge and study.

The hope has extended to this day, and to many it seems excessive. There were always people, and there remain people to this day, who believed that aging and death can one day be conquered, that the finitude of the human life span can be overcome. These hopes, though understandable, are not likely ever to be realized.

> *Most diseases of the elderly are intractably chronic. They are "here to stay" as long as the elderly patient lives. Which is not to say that much cannot be done to relieve their symptoms and to lessen their anxiety concerning the underlying nature and progression of the disability. The elderly person with, for example, severe arthritis, has no illusions of total cure; he or she is frequently satisfied with palliative interventions, steps to prevent the disease from progressing too rapidly, and advice on how to get around some of the obvious disabilities. Amongst the many therapeutic interventions, gentle humor should not be ignored. When geriatric medicine is successful, the disease lingers but the illness abates. [SMA]*

> *The hospice nurse attending a woman dying of brain cancer whose increasing agitation prevented her from falling asleep gave her patient wine at bedtime. This intervention transformed the onerous bedtime struggle into a pleasant social ritual that the woman looked forward to. She was able to relax and fall easily to sleep. [RRS]*

But what exactly is gerontology?

The term "gerontology" was coined in 1904 by Elie Metchnikoff, the Nobel Prize-winning founder of modern immunology (Cole 1992:195). The American Heritage Dictionary of the English Language defines gerontology as "the scientific study of the biological, psychological and sociological phenomena associated with old age and aging" (1992). One popular textbook terms gerontology the multidisciplinary study of the biological, psychological, and social aspects of aging, and gerontologists hail from fields such as biology, medicine, nursing, dentistry, psychology, psychiatry, sociology, economics, political science, and social work (Hooyman and Kiyak 1993:2). Professionals from anthropology, nutrition, architecture, law, physical and occupational therapy are also much in evidence within the field.

Predominantly consisting of researchers, the field also includes clinicians involved in hands-on care with elderly persons.[3] Each specialist approaches the subject of age from a specific point of view. In practice, the specialists utilize their particular perspectives to consider a patient. In many nursing home care-planning meetings, for example, the professionals gather to present information about their interactions and interventions regarding each individual. Federal law requires that each discipline submits paperwork justifying therapies, recommending treatments, and proposing goals, and these treatment meetings are efficient ways to pool information from each caregiver. Perpetuated in these meetings also, however, are the unspoken and possibly unacknowledged assumptions underlying the field of each practitioner. The resulting agreement among the professionals can remain superficial since these assumptions are rarely discussed and reconciled.

Since aging is such a multifaceted subject, it lends itself to analysis by people of diverse backgrounds, all valid. But like the old elephant that the blind professionals are trying to understand—one specialist examining the feet and concluding one thing about aging, another tackling the trunk and coming away with a different view—the two can scarcely have a conversation since their inquiry has tackled such radically different aspects of the beast that the connections between the animal's foot and its trunk are not grasped.

In addition, gerontologists often presuppose the problematic nature of the subject in question. Thus, the name *caregiver stress* is applied to the supposedly negative condition that burdens the caregivers of the elderly. Similarly, the language of dementia research is littered with words that richly describe the anguish of the brain disease, the burden of the caregiving, the endless death, and so on. Distracted by their sympathy to suffering and plight, some of the researchers have unfortunately missed more holistic aspects of the subjects they study. The label *caregiver stress* disguises and sometimes erases what can be the real and sustaining gratifications of caregiving—albeit along with the burdens. When labels are freighted with pejorative meaning, self-fulfilling experiences tend to follow, and distortion creeps in.

Moreover, aging requires an overview understanding, an appreciation of the forest and not just the trees. Bringing varying specialist points of view together requires an interdisciplinary approach. The fact that we discuss the assumptions structuring our respective disciplines in this book means that we struggle to perform an interdisciplinary as opposed to a multidisciplinary endeavor. Here is where anthropology comes in: while often theory-laden to the extreme, this field tries to balance the insights that gerontology has contributed because it also asks its informants—the old—to speak for themselves.

Anthropology and the Study of Age

Anthropology arose within the colonial structure of an imperialist, expansionist world in the eighteenth century. Explorers and Christian missionaries were the first *de facto* anthropologists. Understanding other peoples went hand in hand with converting them to Western religion and Western ways of life. First it had to be determined whether the natives were real human beings. If they were deemed to be marginally human, then began the attempt to transform them into reputable human beings (aka Christians). All the while anthropologists tried to preserve them as scientific evidence or as survivors of a more rudimentary social organization. Early anthropologists categorized peoples of the world into an explicit evolutionary framework, from the simplest (i.e., primitive) to the most complex (i.e., modern, Western society).

Societies were classified according to their complexity of organization. The unchallenged assumption was that Western society was the pinnacle of the evolutionary framework, and simpler societies represented stages on the way to the predetermined end-point that Western social organization represented. In critiquing these tainted anthropological roots, Johannes Fabian

(1983) noted how the discipline considered Western realities a standard against which "the other" was made alien. Anthropology was couched in an implicit philosophy of judging others ("the rest") against Europe and the United States ("the West").

Anthropologists were also intent on understanding other ways of life in other cultures as a way of turning the mirror back on those doing the looking. This reflexive aspect of anthropology continues to drive much of the impetus of the comparative method. The who-are-they questioning leads to who-are-we introspection that helps to clarify our overall understanding of human similarity and variety. Old people figured into this dynamic since anthropologists talked to them in the field.

Anthropologists typically credit Leo Simmons (1945) as perhaps the first anthropologist to apply methodological rigor to the endeavor. Prior to Simmons anthropologists benefited by talking to the elderly members of the societies they were investigating. Aged individuals usually had the most time to talk with the anthropologist so that reality made them a virtual captive audience. In addition, the elderly had the most in-depth information about the subjects the anthropologist was interested in, whether it was kinship, migration patterns, folklore and mythology, and ecology, for example. Furthermore, in many so-called primitive societies, the old were the ones closest to the ancestors. They had the wisdom of experience to negotiate disputes among members, knew precedents firsthand, could remember where the sources of water had once been located, were less motivated by material or sexual conquest, and in general and by definition, held the long view.

> *Ask most people to picture, in their minds, the wise old tribal elder and the image that emerges is that of a wizened elderly male. Since there were far more female than male survivors in the senior decades of tribal life; and certainly in the less industrialized communities of the world the female possessed this crucial knowledge of such things as agricultural skills, why this male image persists remains a puzzle. Is this a problem in perception—or is this how it was in reality? [SMA]*

> *You document in the demography chapter that women lived less long than men in earliest times. Nonetheless, women have a hard time being well represented in the scientific record or in the popu-*

> *lar imagination. The baskets they wove to collect berries and tubers rarely survived to be excavated, so when we don't find them, we cannot credit these and other similar kinds of contributions. [RRS]*

Anthropologists began to study aging in earnest in the 1960s and 1970s in part to disprove the reigning psychological and sociological theories of activity, disengagement, and modernization. In general, anthropologists were intent to describe rather than prescribe approaches to aging, but combating myths and stereotypes was always an implicit if not explicit mission.

The "activity" theory promoted by Havighurst (1963) and others claimed that continued activity and the replacement of old roles with new roles was the key to successful aging. In contrast, Cumming and Henry (1961) theorized that it was "natural" for old people to become gradually less interested and involved in their work, family, and other activities as they aged, and that this "disengagement" happened to coincide with society's gradual relinquishment of them. The "modernization theory" postulated a direct relationship between the well-being of older people and how "traditional" their societies were. Each of these theories contradicted the others to some degree, and each relied on the authors' intuitive common sense to a considerable degree.

Anthropologists were provoked by what they saw as the over-reliance on assumptions about behavior which remained unproven. As they were quick to show, the how-aging-should-be-done prescriptive bent fueling psychological and sociological theories needed to be supplemented with cross-cultural descriptions of how aging really happens. What was needed was cross-cultural research to document who the elderly actually are and the variety of ways in which they are regarded.

Margaret Clark and Barbara Anderson (1967) led the way by criticizing the ruling assumption that aging was irretrievably associated with such negative "D" words as dependency, decay, deterioration, dementia, disease, and death. These researchers seemed to wake up a generation of anthropologists who were intent on discovering who were the old people in cultures worldwide. It appeared to anthropologists that old people were being maligned by simplification and stereotype. They responded that disengagement was a sorry excuse for societal neglect of older people. They criticized the apologist stance that inherently justified the status quo (see especially Hochschild 1976). Recently Luborsky wrote:

> The enticement to study aging springs from old yet familiar roots in our field. The shattering of dearly held but little-examined stereotypes, overgeneralizations, and biases has always been a touchstone of cultural inquiry. Anthropology's ancestors, for example, labored to change the dominant demeaning stereotypes about the natural inferiority of non-European peoples, societies, and women that validated their mistreatment ... In a corresponding way, anthropological interest in old age and aging was piqued by a similar discourse about old people, a discourse that resonated with familiar assertions about the elderly's "primitive" mentalities and lifeways. A few decades ago, elderly people were presumed to live healthier, more valued lives in other societies and in earlier eras ... These sentiments linger today in popular thought and biomedical research (Luborsky 1995:277).

Since then a fervent contingent of anthropologists has weighed in. Many of the myths about aging in other parts of the world as well as in our own part of the world have been shown to be false (see below). As Luborsky hints, it is not necessarily true that old people in more traditional societies live longer and have more fulfilled lives than those in complex societies. It is also a myth that Americans abandon their elderly to a greater degree than other societies, and that multigenerational families were commonplace and harmonious in the American past. Anthropologists attempt to describe how real people deal with aging and how they view those who are old. Necessarily, a rich portrait of a complex and multifaceted domain emerges from such research.[4]

The anthropological focus on cross-cultural research corrects myths and adds vital information to our knowledge of aging. Such research describes how aging in the United States compares with other places, examines potential models and solutions to problems associated with aging, and suggests general hypotheses about aging (Sokolovsky (1997:xxiii).

The training of the anthropologist predisposes him or her to observe without changing the situation insofar as that is possible. Anthropologists try to understand a given situation minus the intervention, understanding full well that their mere presence is inevitably a compromising factor. Their purpose is weighted toward understanding as opposed to fixing. Physicians, on the other hand, are trained to act and to help.

> *Sometimes they act before they fully understand. [SMA]*
>
> *You said it, not me. But sometimes, or perhaps often, they must do something to try to help. [RRS]*

Their training socializes them to diagnose problems that suffering individuals bring to them in order that they be alleviated or cured. In practice, of course, the oppositions often break down: anthropologists also act and physicians also listen, wait, and watch.

Anthropologists try to withhold judgment until they have heard enough informants speak negatively of their experiences—then they may call for action. Because anthropologists collect the views and experiences of a range of old people, they are usually impressed with the variety of responses to aging and the multitude of strategies that old people and others devise for these many situations. The variety of responses create a more complex composite picture that advocates caution rather than action.

Myths of Aging

Rarely is age mentioned in a neutral, nonjudgmental manner.

> *Nor is it simply linear or exponential. Aging tends to plateau much of the time, with inevitable ebbs and flows. The visible deterioration seems to arise only after some intercurrent infection or trauma. The loss of abilities, physical or cognitive, is never linear; rather it is a series of irregular punctuated downturns. [SMA]*

Myths have flourished about our understanding of aging. The myths solidify beliefs that people entertain both about themselves and about those in other cultures. Our myths and our beliefs are often exaggerations of ideal or negative notions about our society and other cultures.

Though Americans take care of their elderly, often at great cost and effort to themselves, the myth persists that Americans neglect their elderly family members and dump them in nursing homes at the first opportunity. Why we hold onto this myth is unclear. Maybe we feel inferior to other cultures, ethnocentric bravado to the contrary. Regarding our ideas about aging, we tend to idealize other cultures for allegedly honoring their elderly when, indeed, they often do not. We also idealize our own eighteenth and nineteenth century past and the happy extended family, picturing harmonious family ties between generations.

> *Is there not truth in the "myth" that grandma always had a warm seat by the hearth? [SMA]*
>
> *I'm not sure, but I think grandma was often digging roots, picking berries, weaving baskets, caring for children, ordering daughters-in-law, and the like. Sometimes grandchildren are sent to live with their widowed grandmothers temporarily to keep them warm. In some times and some places the old lady bosses the younger women of the household and they are afraid of her power. Sylvia Vatuk tells us that though the older widows in India fulfill the ideal cultural value of living with their children, this living arrangement tells us little about the quality of relationships within the actual households, which are often less than ideal and fraught with conflict (1980). There's a reason witches and hags in much folklore are old females. Roald Dahl's children's books are full of really mean grandmothers. [RRS]*

Our myths tend to be polarized into us versus them, or now versus then. Anthropological study has shed light on the diversity of experiences that old people have, often undermining sweeping generalizations. To describe how social policy swings have been justified on the basis of either a negative or a positive view of history, Kertzer has written the following about the polarity:

> A romantic view of the past has produced images of a time when the old were treated with respect, when they occupied positions of power by virtue of their control over family holdings, and when they were surrounded and supported by married children and

grandchildren ... On the other side...we find a revisionist view, one that sees a far grimmer story of old age, in which old people crowded meager public charitable facilities in search of a miserable lodging, or a piece of bread, to allow them to survive in a society that gave no quarter to those lacking the brawn or the health to earn their daily living (1995:364).

Anthropologists have helped to demystify some of the myths that have hampered the authentic understanding of aging. A great deal remains to be done.

> *Are there no statistical reports on how the elderly—rare as they were—were cared for a few hundred years ago? [SMA]*

> *Kertzer and Laslett's volume (1995:47) provides some clues. One finding is that in England in the nineteenth century, old people tended to continue to live on their own rather than in multigenerational families. Laslett (1995:48-49) reports that as early as the seventeenth century the English Poor Law provided pension-like support to widows. "From time immemorial" the elderly were allowed to glean after the harvest[5] and benefited from other indulgences in England. Various arrangements, including institutional care, were made over the years to care for incapacitated elderly. Laslett writes, "The impression must not be given that the modestly placed 70-, 80-, and 90-year-olds of the past were ever anything but badly off in comparison to their juniors, and the historian is often puzzled that they managed to survive in the numbers that they did" (1995:50). [RRS]*

The old are "other," and this distance that we maintain helps to explain the ease with which myths about the elderly are established and perpetuated. Though Keith's *Old People as People* (1983) was written as a way to explain that, yes, old people are like everyone else—that is, people—an assumption of otherness still guides the exploration of who old people are and what old age is. Too often we make the attempt to understand age and aging as if it is foreign, distant, not us, somehow removed.

> *Are you scientists so sure that we old ones want to be merged with all of the younger groups? We feel different and not merely because we are a few years older; and whether or not you assign us to something that you call "a continuum of aging" we demand to be considered different. Being different gives us some visibility and*

individuality; and remember, we have damned little else to feel
individual about. [OM]

We study old people as if they are objects. Those who are
young or middle-aged or who resist the label of "old" do not
seem to understand, fundamentally, that we are all becoming
old. As Simone de Beauvoir wrote years ago, understanding ourselves as aging entities is perhaps the most difficult task we face.
She said:

> When the time comes nearer, and even when the day is at hand,
> people usually prefer old age to death. And yet at a distance it is
> death that we see with a clearer eye. It forms part of what is
> immediately possible for us: at every period of our lives its threat
> is there: there are times when we come very close to it and often
> enough it terrifies us ... Age is removed from us by an extent of
> time so great that it merges with eternity: such a remote future
> seems unreal. Then again the dead are *nothing*. This nothingness
> can bring about a metaphysical vertigo, but in a way it is com-
> forting—it raises no problems. "I shall no longer exist." In a dis-
> appearance of this kind I retain my identity (1972:12-13).

Barbara Myerhoff (1979) took whatever reluctance she
had in hand when she decided to study elderly Jews in California, switching her focus from the Huichol Indians because she
expected to become a "little old Jewish lady" one day rather
than an elderly Huichol woman (see Myerhoff 1979).[6] Moody
(1988) has said that researchers of aging have a "triple
hermeneutic" (Giddens 1976). Not only is there an interpretive
element in both the relationship of theory with fact and the
relationship of meaning and behavior, but because the researcher
is aging while doing the research, this third hermeneutic has to
be first acknowledged and then examined.

Scientific principles of inquiry constitute the most fundamental assumption held by researchers of aging—and they can
distort. These Western tenets of scientific study determine our
efforts at understanding, presupposing that there is a knowable
object that rational methods will neatly uncover. We use questionnaires and problem checklists, note symptoms and complaints, and scrutinize old people and their caregivers with

sympathetic condescension—but as though they are foreign from us. We are likely to misunderstand, predetermine, distort, and make others over in our own image when we remain unaware of this powerful assumption.

In short, so-called "primitive" cultures may not treat their elderly any better than our more modern and sophisticated ones in the West. Some may argue whether it is better to be placed on an ice floe or in a nursing home. Foner (1984), as well as others, rejects a straightforward relationship between modernization and the treatment of the elderly. Ethnographic research has shown a mixed picture. Modernization can be good for the old when poverty is decreased, social welfare systems enhanced, and medical care and access improved. On the other hand, when industrialization and modernization decreases the worth of the skills that the elderly formerly held, which in turn decrease their respect and status, the elderly are often less well off.

Palmore's rosy picture of respect for Japanese elderly in Japanese society (1975) as compared with what he considered the decline or lack of respect in U.S. society provoked criticism both in Japan and in the U.S.[7] Respect for Japanese elders was not as ideal as Palmore stated, the critics claimed. The rate of suicide among East Asian elderly in industrialized areas, including Japan, as reported by Y-H Hu (1995), for example, is extremely high compared to the rate in Western nations. Sokolovsky's (1997) edited volume of cross-cultural aging offers examples of the great diversity of situations in which the elderly live in the world, providing proof of the complex factors that determine the fate of old people, including the myth of the "geriatric utopias" of long-lived peoples. It appears that the numbers of people living over 100 years of age as well as the incidence of dementing diseases seem to be similar throughout the world as compared to the U.S. (see Sokolovsky 1997:xxv; Beall 1987; Palmore 1984).

Gender and Age

"The privileges of age are so closely linked with the privileges of gender," Foner has written (1984:249). Much research on aging now attempts to distinguish the complicating strands of age and gender, as interwoven and difficult to disentangle as they are. Research often describes older women—inadvertently or not— possibly because the majority of the elderly as well as their care-givers, informal and paid, are generally female. But there are numerous accounts of aging men, as well. Anthropologists in the 1930s and 1940s, primarily, gave us descriptions of age-sets, usually in East African societies, where males of a certain age occupy defined age statuses—each with set roles attached—and move with their cohorts over the life course to eventually become "elders." Though men in various societies may accumu-late wives, power, and some material resources as they achieve great age, the resulting strains on their relationships with younger generations complicate the picture. One of the benefits of anthropological research is that it reminds us not to imagine that older men in non-industrialized, "traditional" societies are unequivocally powerful individuals (see Foner 1984).

Men also lose roles and statuses as they age. Some retire-ment research in the U.S. has focused on the rolelessness of retired men after they cease working. In my work with wholesale diamond dealers in New York City, the desire of men to continue working into their eighties and nineties—as well as the repug-nance many of them feel for a life without work— is a clear goal, one that many of them manage to fulfill (Shield 2002). The plight of homeless men in urban centers of the U.S. has been described by some (for example, see Sokolovsky and Cohen 1997). Here the struggle and perils connected with everyday survival are illus-trated through the poignant portraits of three very different men.

Until the last few decades, little rigorous attention was paid to the overwhelmingly female character of old age in the twentieth century, especially in the West. As women live longer than men in most (all?) societies, survival into extreme old age has an increasingly female cast.

> *The greater life expectancy for females is not universal. Men live longer than women in most Moslem nations. [SMA]*

The 2000 census reveals that over two-thirds of poor people in the U.S. are women over the age of fifty-five and that discouraging percentage increases with age, prompting John Rother of AARP to comment, "Almost any way you look at it, women as they get older are disadvantaged compared to men" (*Providence Journal* 1 November, 2000). Loss of a spouse leads to different outcomes for men and women: men remarry a great deal more often than do women, and widowhood for women results in a lower status for them much more often than for men.

In addition, the caregivers of old people throughout the world are traditionally women, and the work of caregiving is usually overlooked, poorly compensated, and socially undervalued (cf. Abel 1991, Ray 1996). Nonetheless, when the burden of the work of caregiving is acknowledged, the further assumption of *"caregiver stress"* is presupposed, thus denying the experiences that female caregivers of older people actually have. As Abel points out:

> ... the current research agenda on caregiving ... has focused almost exclusively on the issue of stress ... But this preoccupation with stress has denied us a full understanding of the experience of caregivers. Furthermore, studies that view caregivers as objects without consciousness foster policies that treat caregivers in an instrumental manner (1991:8).

Women are also patients, and in general, are more subservient and less powerful than men.

Widowhood can be an especially painful part of life, and it seems to be a greater burden for women than for men. Research with widows has demonstrated how these women are diminished in status as well as income in the U.S. as well as in other places of the world (Lopata 1996). Widows in some parts of India used to have to shave their heads, observe food restrictions, maintain celibacy and sleep on the ground—whereas widowers were expected to remarry (Lamb 2000:213). The custom of *sati*, or widow-burning, in India, is an extreme reaction to widowhood, rooted in both religion and economics (see Hawley 1994; Weinberger-Thomas 1999).

Nonetheless, after menopause, and sometimes even after widowhood, women can become increasingly powerful in some places of the world. There is an interesting body of work that demonstrates the greater assumption of power by women after their reproductive years are past (e.g., Brown and Kerns 1985; Cattell 1997). Freed from child work responsibilities as well as the tainting taboos surrounding menstruation, they can move about the society more freely and in some cases take on an expanded repertoire of roles. Sokolovsky reports such a "loosening of social restraints" of older women in a Mexican peasant village that he studied. There, older women could be seen "guzzling" beer in public, a behavior not condoned in younger women. In addition, old women sometimes became healers, midwives, and entrepreneurs in their later years (1997a).

How free women actually are depends importantly on who is doing the reporting as well as the specific circumstances and perspectives of those involved, as Lamb makes clear from her work in West Bengal:

> When I first began to study the experiences of aging among those I knew in West Bengal, what struck me immediately was how different the shape and feeling of social relations and gender constructions looked to me through the eyes of the elderly women and men I sought out. The accounts I had read of South Asian social life had been based predominantly on the perspectives of younger and middle-aged adults. For instance, South Asian women are commonly depicted as requiring veiling and modesty; but I saw white-haired women who left their homes to roam village lanes, not only with their heads and faces uncovered but bared to the waist on hot days, without regard for showing their long-dry breasts. I had read younger adults' views of older women as having the power to limit a daughter-in-law's movements, to interfere with a son's marital intimacies, and the like; yet the older women I knew spoke of feeling that *they* were losing in the contest for a son's affection, loyalty, and favor. Studies of Indian widowhood rarely distinguished between the consequences of widowhood for a woman in her youth and for a woman past menopause, although I found striking differences. And what of all the people who told me that older women were, in important ways, "like men," implying that what differentiates a "man" from a "woman" is not constant over the life course? (2000:2).

Menopause is differentially experienced in diverse cultures, as well. Margaret Lock showed how hot flushes are considered less of a difficulty in Japan than among North American women. Her study revealed that Japanese women report hot flushes about one-third as often and do not have a term that directly translates to the English term (1993). The recent emergence of a loanword, *hotto fusasshu,* used increasingly in Japan, however, changes the context of what menopause means and how it is experienced, Zeserson reports. She credits the emergence of the term to the increase in middle-aged and elderly women in the population as well as the growth of obstetrical and gynecological medicine that markets hormone replacement therapy as a way to alleviate symptoms of menopause. Her research indicates that "the expressions people choose to use vary according to their reasons for communicating and that their motivations for verbalizing symptoms (hot flush, in this case) depend on the priorities and sanctions of the society in which they live" (2001:189).

The gerontology texts often view women, like other minorities in the U.S., as doubly jeopardized in old age. Stigmatized first by their secondary status as women (or African-Americans, Latinos, etc.) and secondly by their diminished state as elderly, they suffer greater rates of poverty and isolation than their male counterparts (Hooyman and Kiyak 1993).

Exposure to the cross-cultural range of roles, statuses, and experiences of the old is critical to understanding the elderly of the world. These accounts help to counter our intuition about how we imagine the world of the old to be. We must remind ourselves that the things we consider most natural in our personal and professional lives are often the most cultural, and therefore, not natural at all. If they are cultural, then there is a certain arbitrariness to them. Whether beliefs and behaviors about aging have arisen because of certain historical, political, economic, geographical or other factors, it is helpful to understand that these assumptions are embedded and fixed with a kind of immutable certainty that our rigorous, questioning scrutiny should attempt to review. The job at hand is to critically examine the assumptions that underlie our work so that we can arrive at new and refreshing insights about how we age and what the experiences are of people who are old.

And yet by reviewing the natural aspects of the menarche, menstruation and menopause while simultaneously decrying their "medicalization" we tacitly infer that aging may also be natural; and further, if we discard the "medicalization" of the senescent process, we will somehow bring back a serene, tranquil element to aging. [SMA]

I don't think so. I think that medicalization is the almost automatic thinking that stems from the great success medicine has had in ameliorating and sometimes curing ailments that attend so-called natural processes, such as childbirth, menopause, and aging. I object to medicalization when it unnecessarily "problematizes" experiences that are not necessarily pathological. Determining whether or not something is pathological is difficult, and often the criteria used are unacknowledged cultural ideas about normality and pathology. I'm not going to say that aging is serene—with or without intervention.

But we're getting ahead of ourselves. This is a preview. See chapter 4 for more on medicalization and the "problem" of aging. [RRS]

Notes

1. I continue the anthropological tradition of differentiating the terms "disease" from "illness." Disease is the term many researchers use to indicate the specific biomedical dysfunction. Illness refers to the kinds of responses individuals have to this state. Disease is generally thought of as a more objective term that describes the condition, while illness is understood to be more subjective (see Fabrega 1975; Kleinman 1980, for example).
   Medicine also distinguishes between the word, "disease," and the word, "illness." A disease is defined generally as a specific pathophysiological departure from the accepted norm and is characterized by defined metabolic and structural alterations and specific clinical signs and symptoms. Illness, on the other hand, is a more subjective state reflecting the victim's perception of changes within his/her body and his/her ability to function. [SMA]
2. Much is written on this subject. Some good sources are Koenig 1988; Sudnow 1967; Muller and Koenig 1988; Kaufman 1998, 2000; Callahan 1987, 1993; Teno 2001.

3. Gerontology programs and certificates in gerontology at the college level help prepare students for working with older people in different settings, but standards and accreditation criteria are not uniform (Selzer and Kunkel 1995; Johnson 1995). The development of theories about aging seems to be secondary (Bengtson, Parrott and Burgess 1996).

4. This does not mean that anthropologists do not criticize one another. As an example of this Cohen (1994) argues that the cultural study of age has neglected to examine the assumptions that fuel it. Labeling them as so many "tropes" categorized as proselytizing, conversion, anger, exploration, and ambiguity, he asserts that there is no truly critical examination of the ageist and sexist assumptions implicit in the work. He objects that while some anthropologists have "discovered" aging (over and over again), others are attempting to proselytize a particular point of view against some received wisdom of commonly accepted views of age, and still others argue for an acceptance of the varied textured, ambiguous quality of aging, to take the "good" with the "bad." He takes those anthropologists who advocate "critical gerontology" (e.g., Moody 1988; Luborsky and Sankar 1993) to task because their critique of the social and political status quo that most research takes for granted does not in itself go far enough because it conforms to Western scientific models of reliability, validity and so forth.

5. as was ordained in Mosaic Law. [SMA]

6. Sadly, she died at the age of fifty.

7. Palmore collaborated with a Japanese researcher in a revised edition, but their statistical study of household patterns offered a similarly idealized view (Palmore and Maeda 1985).

Commentary:
Understanding Aging
Being Old Helps

(SMA)

O ld people will tell you that most assumptions about the
elderly are little more than errant presumptions. The
elderly will contend that such scholarly assumptions are frequently uncritical; and that the attitudes, agenda, and priorities
assigned to the elderly are more accurately descriptive of forty-
year-olds. The old, after all, have the dubious advantage of being
able to look back with understanding to younger days, since they
had already been there. The younger ones, not having been
there yet, can only speculate about what elderliness is like.

When I was thirty, married, and deeply immersed in my
profession, I recall hearing my parents, then in their early seventies, declaring that it was not possible for me to understand,
nor certainly appreciate, their inner feelings concerning their
passage into the senior decades. I had assumed, then, that their
statement reflected something more than the customary gener-
ational gap. They had been born overseas, came to this nation as
frightened, destitute immigrants, began work at age twelve and
had then struggled through a lifetime of bewildering, contentious,
and dismaying happenings. And in over six decades within this
nation they had never really overcome their initial feelings of
being strangers in a strange land.

My parents became citizens shortly after their arrival in the last decade of the nineteenth century. They did all the things that proper patriotic citizens were expected to do. Yet, to the day they died, they were never free of that subtle sense of estrangement which many foreign-born know so intimately. For example, they scrupulously obeyed each civil law, active or obsolete, motivated in part by a subconscious fear of being deported. They had arrived here, lived here, but believed earnestly that they were then tolerated rather than absorbed.

I did not understand my parent's interpretation of elderliness, but I was convinced that my lack of understanding arose solely because my childhood had not been parallel to theirs. I had never undergone that profound feeling of alienation and disruption which people experience when they are removed from one culture—even an oppressive one—and dispatched to another. Yet, when I reached my seventies and had children in their forties, I too was certain that my offspring could not possibly know the inner feelings that I experienced as a senior citizen even though both my children and I had been born in the United States, all of our subsequent moves had been voluntary, and our trajectories in life were similar.

Could it be, then, that the immigrant elderly and the native-born elderly experience a converging set of emotions as their lives decelerate? Could there be a group of feelings unique to the elderly which are unknown, as well as unknowable, to younger folk? Immigration or childhood trauma, alone, certainly could not account for the distinctive emotional character and context of elderly thinking.

Over the centuries the social sciences have managed to overcome cultural barriers separating the observer and the observed. Anthropologists, by immersing themselves in cultures other than their own, have been able to offer authentic descriptions of the lives of certain primitive peoples despite the fact that they themselves had never grown up as primitives. (But, the elderly might counter: "Histories are written by the conquerors; and anthropology texts are assembled by members of the cultural majority. Do aborigines ever write learned texts about their resident anthropologists?")

We do have some efforts at this reversal in anthropology. Increasing numbers of anthropologists derive from cultures outside the West. Their presence has been making an impact. [RRS]

Male psychiatrists have, with only limited success, described the inner complexities of female thinking. And notable texts on pre-adolescent male aggression have been written by women scientists. But to render an objective account of the inner complexities of another culture, another gender or another age, requires the observer to abandon a lifetime of preconceptions and biases. It requires that there be an open, creative mind armed only with an appreciation of the scientific method.

Given the expanding roster of pains, ailments, and irreversible disabilities that burden most elderly, one should never assume that the will to live, in the eighty-year-olds, is as uncompromisingly powerful or as compelling as it had once been. Certainly the desire to survive must have been robust to reach the age of eighty. Getting to be old, it has been said, is not for sissies. For the average forty-year-old, there is no conceivable alternative to life. To an eighty-year-old, the will to live, of course, persists—but now with numerous codicils and provisos in fine print.

And it would be presumptuous, wouldn't it, to always label such qualifications a malady called "depression"? [RRS]

Grief is an unwanted accompaniment at all ages. It is certainly never a stranger to adults who must be prepared for the increasing likelihood of additional sources of grief. But while the accumulation of grief can be limitless, the capacity to tolerate grief has its limits. Some older people, in a perverse way, seem to nurture their grief; but most elderly prefer not to dwell on their losses. They encourage themselves, therefore, to forget their heartbreaks. Not all forgetfulness amongst the older ones, it should be remembered, is attributable to organic changes such as Alzheimer's disease. Many elderly infinitely prefer forgetfulness or even sleep to the pall of unrelieved anguish. Theirs are no longer the grievings of financial reverses, loss of jobs or even unrequited loves. Their laments have slowly coalesced and have been slowly transformed over the decades to an ill-defined, dimensionless but pervasive sadness that has neither name nor specific etiology. Theirs is a sadness, distinguishable from reactive depression, that arises from a pervasive fatigue, a sense of point-lessness, and a deep awareness that death does not arrive, suddenly and unbidden, some late Thursday night; death, for decades, has become their increasingly covetous companion, taking bits of life away in piecemeal fashion while returning nothing.

> *I know a 79-year-old man with lung disease who recently lost his wife to cancer. Sharing his deceased wife's religious faith in the hereafter, he tells me that he hears his wife calling him to join her "up there." He is weary of life, confined to bed and an oxygen container. He has no fear of dying and seems instead to welcome it though I don't think he would take measures to hasten it. [RRS]*

It becomes understandable, then, that many elderly become preoccupied with death, praying that it will be swift and without warning. Even a young Woody Allen had once declared that he was not afraid of death—only the process of dying.

> *I think I recall his saying he preferred not to be there when it happened! [RRS]*

It would also be a mistake to assume that those situations or interpersonal relationships that satisfy young adults will necessarily provide comparable gratification for the elderly. The personal fulfillment experienced by younger adults in acquiring things, in confronting new challenges, in entering new situations, even in trying new foods, loses much of its exultation for the elderly. For them, newness may be more of a threat than a promise.

> *Should we be surprised that many older adults do not prefer to move to housing that also includes young families complete with crying babies, roller-blading eight-year-olds and skulking teens? Many would rather live without such immediate evidence of raging youth. [RRS]*

When one gets older, the youthful urges for expansion and acquisition abate and are then supplanted by the need for fewer surprises, fewer new excitements, certainly fewer adventures, even sexual adventures, with undetermined outcomes. [You know that you are old when you won't take yes for an answer.]

The elderly strive to simplify their lives, moving from larger dwellings to smaller apartments, retreating from many social encounters and throwing things out—even objects once thought to be indispensable for life. Precious objects are given away; and a curious, inexplicable feeling of calm descends upon them when a closet no longer overflows with relics of the past.

The language employed by the elderly is similarly simplified. Despite older myths of garrulousness, most elderly become quiet, laconic, their sentences more childlike in structure. But this is not a second childhood; this is a first elderhood.

The world of the elderly is a contracting world. Things get smaller, desires diminish, needs become more modest. Standards, and even definitions, change with increasing age. Age sixty-five had once been considered the dividing line between vigorous adulthood and declining seniority, but this too is changing. Geriatricians now regard age seventy-five as the entrance into their domain of competence. There is a story about Justice Oliver Wendell Holmes, a spry eighty-eight-year-old. He enjoyed a daily walk near the Supreme Court Building. And one day he spied a beautiful young woman walking on the other side of the street. "Oh, to be seventy-five again," he exclaimed.

If a cookbook were to contain a recipe for making tiger soup, the initial instruction would likely be: "First capture a tiger." And to begin to understand the elderly, then, one must first capture their world, a smaller world than ours, less confrontational, less noisy yet more disconcerting, fragmented, and decelerating. One must maintain a strong desire to live, but tempered now by an equally robust appreciation of the impermanence of life and a greater sensitivity to the hazards that may imperil it. One must begin to give up that most unique of human attributes, egocentricity, and the companion belief that the world was created expressly for us humans. And finally, one must become accustomed to a hushed sadness that never departs, a lessening of hungers, an acceptance of a shrinking, finite existence, and a sensitivity to the utter humor and irony of life.

Chapter 3

The Historical Demography of the Very Old

(SMA)

Youth is a blunder; manhood a struggle; old age a regret.
— B. Disraeli[1]

The four stages of man are infancy, childhood, adolescence and obsolescence. — Art Linkletter[2]

Is not wisdom found among the aged? Does not long life bring understanding? — Job 12:12

An eighty-seven-year-old widower was admitted to a Providence, Rhode Island assisted living facility on an uncomfortably humid day in August. First came a few days of acclimatization during which time he rearranged his furniture, checked out the bathroom, hung a picture of his departed wife on the wall, memorized the location of the elevator, and became acquainted with his new roommate. Then, on the third day, he was interviewed by one of the resident social workers.

Notes for this section begin on page 60.

"The food alright?"

"Not too bad; I guess it's okay."

"Your arthritis troubling you?"

"No more than usual."

"You look deeply disappointed. Care to discuss it?"

"Yes, I'm disappointed. It took me a long time to get to be eighty-seven years; and somehow I thought it was a big deal when I finally reached this age; that maybe I'd be the only one at this age. Maybe there would be a celebration; fireworks, maybe. But I look around this place and all I can see are AKs[3] older than eighty-five. My roommate, for example, he's older than me. Nobody visits him and he doesn't talk very much, spends most of his time looking out of the window ...
   Where did all of these shuffling old folk come from? And why are there so many of them?" [OM]

The golden age of eighty-five years does not suddenly arrive without a prior life of struggle and unceasing confrontation with loss. This particular eighty-seven-year-old, indeed many seniors older than eighty-five, must have experienced a sense of disappointment, if not dismay, upon learning that he was hardly unique. As a child he had been taught the singular rarity of those living to advanced ages. Furthermore he was sternly instructed that the very old were to be venerated; and in keeping with scriptural commandments, they were to be respected and lovingly cared for. But for many seniors the current reality has been grimly otherwise, particularly when they see so many of their elderly colleagues no longer with their families but consigned to facilities not of their choosing, and to sites barely removed from nineteenth century warehouses. In a youth-worshipping society, old age seems to have become more an embarrassing transgression than a gift.

So many of the elderly reaching their eighty-seventh year of life are both sullen and dismayed. When they were forty years of age, the thought of living to eighty-seven seemed to be a unique achievement, if not a miracle. But with increasing age came only diminishing authority, diminishing capability, diminishing satisfaction—and chronic pains. Instead of being congratulated many felt that they were being punished for crimes the character of which had never been revealed to them. Kafka, who died in early middle age, had a sure understanding of punishment without specified criminal charges.

The old ones living in nursing homes complain. But they do not complain about the issue that distresses them the most, namely, the tragic realization that they failed to live up to some unspecified standard, and that it is now too late to do much about it; and further, that life has failed them as well. Instead, they complain about marginal issues such as the quality of their meals or why they have not heard from their children in weeks. And even when their children, now well into middle age, visit them, the old ones complain bitterly because the children have the temerity to complain also about the physical limitations that accompany their own advancing age. We have lost most everything, the elderly claim, at least let us keep a monopoly on grumbling about aging.

Better and more comprehensive medical care, public health enactments, and improved nutrition have jointly conspired to make the old even older and have converted the terminally ill into chronic invalids; and to such a degree that in developed nations of the West, substantial numbers of the very old and infirm are now commonplace. About one American in eight is elderly (defined as sixty-five years of age or older), and about one in eighty is very elderly (defined as eighty-five years of age or older). Many persons in the economically developed nations have achieved this senior status only to encounter a society ill-prepared, and even reluctant, to provide them with compassionate, individual attention. You kept me alive, say many old ones, so why didn't you also take away the joint pains and make me see better?

Survival in Ancient Populations

To the extent that older vital statistics records and demographic inferences concerning older civilizations may be relied upon, the phenomenon of substantial numbers of very elderly is an extremely recent happening. No historical interval prior to the late twentieth century has been required to provide for substantial numbers of elderly. Indeed, the number of U.S. residents eighty-five years or older first exceeded one million only in 1965.

Preliterate societies, by definition, do not provide us with documentation of survival patterns or life expectancy figures. But the emerging science of paleopathology can examine ancient human bones and, with some measure of reliability, date them in terms of era lived in and gender; and then offer approximations of their chronological age and even make educated guesses as to certain occupations, life experiences (such as participation in combat), and causes of death.

In the absence of dependable evidence concerning average life expectancies, one must therefore rely upon the relatively meager data yielded by bone analysis. There are, of course, the fantasies of ancient populations wisely governed by sage octogenarians surrounded by adoring great-grandchildren; or, alternative fanciful scenarios offering grim Malthusian fantasies of a depraved savage community in fierce competition within its ranks over inadequate sources of food and shelter while regularly abandoning its elderly to the forces of feral nature.

I have a feeling you're talking about the Inuit. Anthropologist Joel Savishinsky has this to say: "Perhaps the most stereotypic cultural image of the end of work, and life itself, has been that of the Eskimo (Inuit) elder left to die on an ice floe. The larger world has both overstated and misunderstood this practice. In their aboriginal way of life, older Inuit men and women tried to remain productive for as long as they were physically able by participating in such activities as making tools and clothing, minding children, and performing rituals. The rare solitary death took place only under conditions of great adversity and starvation, and when it did happen, it was as likely to be an act of altruistic suicide by the old as one of abandonment by the young. Furthermore, believing in reincarnation, and in the identity of a person's soul with his or her name, Inuit elders faced death with the knowledge that they would soon be reborn in the person of the next child to carry their name" (2000:7-8). [RRS]

Paleodemographic studies of prehistoric populations can now offer cautious, defensible estimates of the gender and age within settlements based solely on analyses of skeletal remains (Hassan 1981). Morphological criteria of human aging, such as dental eruption, closure patterns of cranial sutures, morphology of erupted teeth and osseous maturation, are generally regarded as reliable. Mann (1975) has concluded that these structural criteria assigned to various age categories are about the same whether in australopithecine or in contemporary *Homo sapiens* bones.

How large were these early hominid settlements? Based upon such measurable factors as artifacts recovered, food remains, the number of human bones, the spatial arrangement of nuclear dwelling units, the size of each dwelling unit and evidence suggesting continuity at the camp site, some reasonable guesses are possible.

Bar-Yosef (1970), Marcus (1976) and others have encountered no prehistoric groupings exceeding an estimated forty-eight inhabitants, most numbering about twenty-four adults, probably representing little more than extended families. Until deliberate farming had been established as a dependable source of food, settlements rarely exceeded a few score individuals. The size of paleolithic settlements assumes importance when attempting to identify the relative weights of disease-causing elements and their relative effects upon survival.

Weidenreich (1943), Vallois (1960), and Angel (1972) have offered estimates for average age at death in each of the major archeological periods. In most analyzed sites there seemed to have been an underrepresentation of infantile and juvenile osseous remains suggesting that pre-adult deaths were not accorded customary burial rites. These estimates, therefore, represent the arithmetic means of the death-ages of those skeletal remains estimated to be fifteen years of age or older. These paleontologists have found few skeletal remains of elderly. The oldest bones examined, or cited by Weidenreich, were derived from males estimated to be about sixty-five years of age. The average age of death, throughout the Lower, Middle and Upper Paleolithic were between twenty and 22.8 years. Only in bones recovered from Neolithic settlements does the average age at death reach 30.5 years.

Angel (1972) has also accumulated data from numerous published sources summarizing the average ages at death of adults (judged to be fifteen years of age or older) living beyond the neolithic period and spanning the interval from the Bronze Age to the early decades of the Industrial Revolution (table 3.1).

Table 3.1

Historical Period	Average age at death of adult males	Average age of death of adult females
Late Bronze Age	39.4	36.1
Early Iron Age	38.6	31.3
Rome, 120 AD	40.2	34.6
Medieval Era, 1400 AD	37.7	31.1
Europe, 1750 AD	40.2	37.3

The crude estimates of the average age at death in table 3.1 suggest that while humanity may have made monumental gains in mathematics, the physical sciences, and the applied technologies during these four millennia (i.e., from the Late Bronze Age to the mid-eighteenth century), such advances did little to improve average life expectancy.

The average settlements, in preliterate communities, rarely exceeded a few hundred people and usually numbered fewer than thirty. It is therefore likely that major communicable diseases had no measurable impact upon morbidity or mortality in such small and often isolated communities. Many of the pestilential diseases of viral origin (e.g., smallpox, measles, influenza) require a densely settled population of many thousands in order to be maintained indefinitely as endemic infections. In smaller, isolated communities, either the pathogen never reaches the settlement or, alternatively, it enters the community and kills most of its residents. Thus, because of a lack of new susceptibles, the pestilence typically disappears since most human viruses have but one natural host (e.g., smallpox) and cannot survive outside of a susceptible body. Only when large numbers of newborns are repetitively added to a densely packed urban population will a viral disease such as measles or smallpox be sustained; and only then will it exert a negative pressure upon life expectancy within the community. Long before the germ theory had been proposed, long before the keeping of accurate vital statistics was envisioned as an important research tool in public health, long before the kinetics of epidemic spread were reduced to mathematical formulae, observers had noted that major epidemics were far more destructive in big cities than in rural communities; and that if a pestilence descended upon a small agricultural settlement, it typically wrought its damage within days and then ceased to exist as a communicable threat.

Causes of death in preliterate communities of modest size, therefore, tended to be dominated by such non-infectious factors as starvation or subacute malnutrition (leading to such avitaminoses [diseases caused by vitamin deficiencies] as scurvy, rickets, and beri-beri), civilian trauma and its consequences, warfare, ritual murder and obstetrical complications. Infectious disease emerged as the principal cause of mortality only with the development of great cities and constant mercantile communication between large population centers.

Women tended to die at an earlier age than did men (see table 3.1), with a gender discrepancy of three to seven years. This gender difference did not diminish or reverse itself until the twentieth century. Two factors are responsible for this gender-related disparity. First, female infants did not survive the rigors of infancy and early childhood as readily as their male siblings because they were deemed a less valuable commodity for the family. And second, many adult women succumbed to the complications of repeated pregnancy. When, however, infant and maternal mortality rates were diminished by gender equity and rational hygienic and medical interventions, the innate biological superiority of females over males became apparent. The force of this superiority is evident even in Stone Age civilizations. Yanomama women of Brazil, surviving beyond the antifemale bias of infancy and the perils of the childbearing years, manage to live somewhat longer than the males of their community.

Thus, in the interval between the ancient Mediterranean cultures and later medieval Europe, two opposing historical forces became operative: the first was the progressively improving living standards that tended to increase life expectancy. Under the rubric of improving living standards are such elements as a more abundant, and increasingly diverse, food supply; greater literacy and increased understanding of rudimentary hygiene; establishment of hospitals and hospices; facilities for the aged and infirm; better housing; increased medical knowledge. But opposed to this were the devastating effects of the pestilences, particularly after the fourteenth century, when rat-borne bubonic plague first arrived in southern Europe, during the fifteenth century, when epidemic typhus first spread through Europe; during the sixteenth century when syphilis became a major source of morbidity and mortality, and the nineteenth century when cholera spread from its endemic center in India to afflict all of Europe and the Western hemisphere, and also in the nineteenth century, when tuberculosis spread through the crowded tenements of the urban world. These were the better known pestilences of the fourteenth through the nineteenth centuries; but the major sources of morbidity and mortality, during this half-millenium interval, continued to be such banal contagions as infectious diarrheas of childhood, upper respiratory infections, and measles.

Only when rational public health measures took hold in the late nineteenth century did the average duration of life begin to show a significant increase, accompanied, in stabilized societies, inevitably by an increase in the numbers (and proportions) of the elderly. These public health measures included effective sewage systems, protected sources of drinking water, vaccines, insect vector suppression, improved maternal and pediatric care, and better nutrition.

Average life expectancy, during the second half of the twentieth century, increased substantially in the developed nations of the world. Indeed, between 1950 and 1975, more average years of life were added to the lives of Americans than during any comparable interval in recorded history. Epidemiologists ascribe this bonus in life to a clearer understanding and a better medical control of such common cardiovascular risk factors as hypertension, diabetes mellitus, hazardous lifestyles, and obesity.

"So, the food is satisfactory?"

"No, just okay. Sometimes hot foods come up hot; sometimes the food tray waits in the corridor and then the food gets cold. Yesterday was supposed to be a special treat. They served us Norwegian salmon. Awful. I'm not sure whether the salmon was imported or deported from Norway. Maybe it's me rather than the food. Nothing tastes the way it used to taste. Something is lost. I'm getting old.

 Some of us in this place live only in the past, and some of us don't live anywhere. Mrs. Horowitz, down the hall, spends every afternoon looking through her albums of photographs. She cries a lot over her small collection of memories. But some, like my roommate, live neither in the past nor in the present. He shuffles around but I wonder sometimes whether he is still alive. He no longer remembers the past and he doesn't play pinochle. You know it's tough being nostalgic if you don't remember anything. At least, though, he doesn't cry like Mrs. Horowitz." [OM]

Variables Affecting Life Expectancy

Place of birth and continuing residence, race, gender, socio-economic status, and occupation, separately and collectively, are the major factors that modify life expectancy. The most significant of the many factors in influencing the likelihood of survival into the senior years is the country of one's birth and continued residence. Geography, in this equation, must be presumed to be a surrogate for standards of living. Table 3.2, below, indicates life expectancy, at key ages of life, as recorded in various geographic locales. For example, a child from sub-Saharan Africa, born in the year 2000, will live to an estimated age of fifty-five years, but if born in one of the nations with developed economies (e.g., United States, western Europe) will live to seventy-seven. The differences in life expectancy between these two socio-economically disparate regions diminish as age advances. Thus, someone aged sixty in sub-Saharan Africa may anticipate another fifteen years of life; a sixty-year-old in western Europe may anticipate another twenty years, a difference of only five years.

Table 3.2   Life Expectancy, Year 2000

Region	At age 0	At age 5	At age 15	At age 60
Sub-Saharan Africa	55	59	51	15
India	61	63	54	16
China	71	69	59	18
Latin America, Caribbean	71	70	60	19
Eastern Europe*	74	70	60	19
Established Market Economies**	77	73	63	20
World	67	67	57	17

Source: Data in tables 3.1 and 3.2 are derived from the World Health Organization (Investing in Health Research and Development 1996).

* Nations formerly under socialist economies.

** Nations such as the U.S., with established market economies.

Table 3.3   World Population Structure and Dynamics

Region	Population, in millions	Number of live births, in thousands	Life Expectancy in years	Adult male mortality per 100,000	Adult female mortality per 100,000
Sub-Saharan Africa	510	251.8	52	381	322
India	850	258.1	58	272	229
China	1,134	251.3	69	201	150
Latin America	444	124.6	70	228	163
Eastern Europe*	346	52.9	72	281	112
Established Nations**	798	104.0	76	147	73
World	5,267	1,427.1	65	234	169

* Nations formerly under socialist economies.

** Nations with established market economies.

A second major factor in influencing life expectancy is social status and occupation. Comprehensive studies in France have shown a consistent concordance between social status (as determined by occupation) and longevity (table 3.4).

Table 3.4 Expectation of life by occupational status, France, 1971

Occupation	Expectation of life (years)
Unskilled worker	67.9
Agricultural worker	69.9
Tradesman	71.6
Public sector employee	72.2
Middle echelon supervisor	73.5
Catholic clergy	74.5
Professionals (e.g., law, clergy, medicine)	75.5
Teachers, primary school	75.9

Source: Data from France, 1971 (WHO Investing in Health Research and Development 1996).

Causes of death also vary according to one's profession. In individuals between the ages of thirty-five and forty-four years, the mortality rate for unskilled workers is 681.9 per 100,000, while the mortality rate for those in the professions, in the same age group, is 169.0 (a ratio of 4.0). By age fifty-five to sixty-four years, the mortality rate for unskilled workers rose to 3,038.1; and for professionals, to 1,333.0, the ratio of difference now diminishing to 2.3. Specific causes of death such as suicide, tuberculosis, and vehicular accidents are substantially higher in the unskilled cohort accounting for the bulk of differences between the two socio-economic groups.

African-Americans are at a disadvantage in average life expectancies. A male African-American infant, born in 1998, may anticipate 67.8 years of life while a male white infant will live 74.6 years. A female African-American infant born in 1998 will live an estimated 75.0 years and a female white infant, 79.9 years. The discrepancy in years of survival between white Americans and African-Americans has been consistently greater in males than in females (6.8 years vs. 4.9 years).

> *"Do you like to watch television or go to the movies?"*

> *"I remember seeing a Western movie many years ago with actors, famous ones, that I bet you never heard of. It was about an Indian tribe fleeing from white settlers. And in their midst, before the tribal campfire, sat a very old Indian who was the local wise man. Problems were brought to him; he responded and the younger ones listened carefully; and they always fed him his favorite foods. When I was a kid in Brooklyn that's what I thought growing old would be like. I was wrong. Nobody brings me problems to solve and so my brain doesn't do any work anymore. It just sits and forgets things, except maybe old movies."*

> *"Next week is Labor Day. How would you like to celebrate it?"*

> *"I bet that you didn't know that it is also my eighty-eighth birthday next week. I wonder if they'll give me a birthday cake. I remember a movie comedian named Bob Hope. Anyway, Hope once said that you are really old when the candles on the birthday cake cost more than the cake. Did you ever hear of Bob Hope? I wonder if he played pinochle?" [OM]*

The Numbers of Elderly

In late 2001, Nancy Gordon, associate director for demographic programs at the Census Bureau, held a press conference outlining some of the data and projections based on the year 2000 census. The worldwide sixty-five-and-older population, she declared, rose from 131 million in 1950 to 420 million in 2000. This increase she observed, amounts to about a 2 percent increase each year. In the United States the 2000 Census showed about 12 percent or about 35 million, of the nation's 281.4 million people to be sixty-five years of age or older. By the year 2030, one out of every five Americans, she forecast, will be over sixty-five. Only nations such as Japan and Italy will have larger proportions of their population in the aging category. And in developing nations such as Malaysia, Colombia, and Costa Rica, the sixty-five-and-over population is expected to triple by the year 2030.

"Why do you sit alone?"

"Good question. Because I don't want to hear the others complaining. And if I sit with others, I am forced to see their faded and sagging faces. And that reminds me that my face must be just like theirs. Maybe we should all wear masks and talk only about happy things."

"I haven't seen you smile much."

"I used to play a lot of pinochle in the old days, but no more. Sometimes you win, sometimes you lose; but when you lose game after game, then you don't smile much. Life is like pinochle: you can only play with what they deal you; and there is nobody to appeal to when you lose the game." [OM]

Table 3.5 summarizes the estimated numbers of inhabitants sixty-five years of age or older in certain geographic regions as determined for the decades between 1950 to 2000. The world population of the elderly is currently increasing by about twenty million per year.

Table 3.5   Size of the Elderly Population (in millions)

Region	1950	1980	1990	2000
Sub-Saharan Africa	9	17	23	32
India	20	42	59	76
China	41	73	101	132
L. America	9	21	31	43
Eastern Europe	26	45	57	67
Est. Nations	69	127	145	163
Other	26	46	72	149
World	200	371	488	662

Source: World Health Organization, see above. Elderly is defined here as those sixty-five years of age or older.

How many aged are there in the United States? For comparison, there were 849,000 Americans sixty-five or older living in this country in 1860. Table 3.6 summarizes census statistics since the onset of the twentieth century. And while the sixty-five years and older population has increased three-fold, the very elderly, eighty-five years of age or older, have increased six-fold in the last century. The year 2000 will see about two-thirds of a billion elderly.

Table 3.6   United States Census Data on the Elderly (in thousands)

Year	Number 65+	Percent 65+	Number 85+	Percent 85+
1900	3,080	4.1	122	0.2
1920	4,933	4.7	210	0.2
1940	9,019	6.8	365	0.3
1960	16,560	9.2	929	0.5
1980	25,550	11.3	2,240	1.0
1990	31,079	12.6	3,021	1.2

Source: U.S. Census

The National Institute of Aging, of the National Institutes of Health, in a news bulletin issued in December of 2001, declared that every month, the world's population of persons aged 65 and older grows by 800,000 individuals. Eight hundred thousand new people over age sixty-five every month.

"Do you read much or watch television? And how about a little physical exercise?"

"I used to read books, but no longer. I don't seem to have the patience to go through twenty chapters to find out if some stranger either died or reached his goal. And books on philosophy I don't even open.

Exercising? You mean waving the arms and legs with those old ladies in the auditorium? I don't have the energy or maybe the will for physical activity. My wife, Rachel, when she was alive, used to say that old men combined the wisdom of youth and the strength of the very aged."

"Do you think, perhaps, that you are depressed?"

"Is that what you call it? I feel useless, tired all of the time but can't sleep well at night, and there is nobody who knows how to play pinochle. I'm slowly dying and I guess that is what you call being depressed. It used to be when you began to die, you died.

Now with modern medicine, dying takes forever, sometimes many years. And this is confusing. I don't know when to laugh and when to mourn."

"And so, how are you feeling now?"

"I'm feeling alright—but don't ask for details." [OM]

Notes

1. From *Coninsby*, Book 3, chapter 1.
2. From *A Child's Garden of Misinformation*, chapter 5.
3. *Alter kocker.* Yiddish expression, of vulgar origin, denoting the decrepit elderly. *Leo Rosten's* The Joys of Yiddish *includes the following notes:* "A.K. is a testimonial to the ineradicable earthiness and vigor of Yiddish. (My mother never let me use such a phrase, or employ such vulgarity.) A.K. is as often used in mild, fond condescension as it is in derision: 'Let him alone: He's just an A.K.' 'He lies in bed all day, like an alter kocker.' I make no special plea for alter kocker, but I certainly prefer A.K. to its English equivalent, 'old fart.'" (1968:14) [RRS].

Commentary
What Are Some of the Implications of So Many Old People?
(RRS)

Recent years are witness to a skyrocketing in the numbers and proportions of elderly throughout the world. These numbers vary among countries and have various cultural determinants. In general, the levels of fertility and mortality define the population aging within nations. When a nation's fertility rate is very high, its proportion of elderly tends to be low. When there is high infant and childhood mortality in a society, the numbers of people surviving into old age is likewise low. The improvements in combating infectious diseases, particularly those infections of early childhood, allow more people to survive into the senior decades of life.

What are some of the implications of an aging world? There are important gender differences, for one thing. As a biological constant, there are more male than female births throughout the world. Male mortality at all ages, however, tends to be greater than that of females. The result is that the numbers of females in the population through time increase relative to males. Though the proportions vary among countries, there are usually many more women than men among the elderly. Furthermore, by the time they are old, most men are married while most women are widowed. (This is also because most men marry and remarry women younger than they are, and most women generally marry men older than themselves.)

The diversity of the aged population is one of its most important characteristics. As the numbers of elderly grow, however, the unfortunate tendency to stereotype and generalize about the elderly also increases. This is an ironic outcome since human beings express their individuality more and more as they age. If one has any reservations about lumping together children from birth to age eighteen in one category—obliterating their vast uniquenesses from one another—it is almost absurd to talk about "the elderly"—together they span three or more decades—as some kind of homogeneous group. The weight of years and experiences have forged individuals with profoundly complicated and separate histories. After long years, the elderly are more different from one another in their seventies than they were in their teens because of the array of choices, events, and circumstances that have intervened during those years to make them who they are.

Diversity in the elderly population is composed of many factors. Gender, race, religion, disability, ethnicity, and sexual orientation combine to create a pool of people distinct for many reasons and in myriad ways. In cases in which a person has experienced discrimination because of these identifying characteristics in younger years, the stigma often persists into old age. Often, age, coupled with disadvantaged minority status(es), combines to create double (or triple) jeopardy for the person. Overall, these individuals experience higher rates of poverty and poor health. Gays and lesbians often face additional hurdles of having to fight for basic legal rights, such as visitation, access to medical records, privacy with their partners, and inheritance. Sometimes these fights are against biological family members who have rejected them.

On the other hand, some stigmatized groups of people also develop strategies for coping that turn out to serve them well in older years. Having learned to deal with discrimination or disability over their lifetimes, for example, they have often found supportive friends, and acquired flexible and adaptive methods for handling adversity. These techniques and attitudes help them as they get older. Becker (1980) describes some of the strategies that deaf elderly have developed. According to Quam and Whitford (1992), gay men and lesbians become more self-affirming and more accepting of changes in role status as they age. Having learned not to rely automatically on family members for support, for example, they develop stronger networks of friendships than they might have. Both Becker and Quam and Whitford stress the advantages associated with being highly involved in their deaf and gay and lesbian communities respectively.

As the proportion of the population over the age of sixty-five and the even greater proportion of that figure over the age of eighty-five increases, certain societal implications follow. The progressively fewer younger people in relation to the elderly raise troubling questions. How, for example, will Social Security and Medicare in the U.S. be financed when there is a smaller proportion of people in the population who work and contribute to these funds? The age cohorts of the U.S. and other nations in the world used to look like a pyramid when drawn in schematic form. The youngest age groups (at the bottom of the pyramid) contained the most people and the oldest group had the fewest. Now the population pyramids of the U.S., and other developed nations, and even the less industrialized nations, approach a rectangular shape as the numbers of young, middle-aged, and old become equalized. Who will take care of the elderly as more people become old? Will societies become more tolerant of their elderly members and more proactive in planning for greater numbers of dependent people? Or will intolerance increase as fewer people support more retirees and young people continue to deny that they will one day grow old?

Women, for example, can expect to spend more time caring for a dependent parent than for a dependent child. This probability will exert a significant impact on their participation in the workforce. What role will government play as a result?

Another implication of an aging world is the increasing proportion of older people living alone because of changing gender roles and expectations, delayed marriages, increased divorce rates, and greater mobility. Many younger people continue to provide care for elderly family members. However, many elderly survive with multiple chronic disabilities, thus straining the resources of both the healthcare system and family caregivers.

In the U.S., for example, the health needs of the elderly stress a healthcare system ill-equipped to manage the growing demands of those elderly with increasing disability and morbidity. While Medicare, designed to alleviate the costs of acute medical and hospital treatments for the elderly, has reduced the numbers of elderly living in extreme poverty, the system is inadequate for the chronic and disabling conditions with which many elderly are increasingly burdened.

Our system of care subsidizes medical treatment for acute illness, but provides only limited funds for rehabilitative care. An individual disabled by chronic disabilities, such as Alzheimer's disease, will receive no government assistance for care except when an acute illness or injury supervenes. Individuals struggle to care for family members with dementia—in many cases, missing work or leaving jobs to do so. Caregivers wear out. The person with dementia falls and breaks her hip because the resources of supportive care in the community and the home, if they exist, are generally sporadic, uncoordinated, and inadequate. The broken hip must be fixed in the hospital; after extensive rehabilitation in a nursing home, the person with dementia is usually more confused and less able to survive unassisted: often the result is an extended nursing home admission. An ironic result of our healthcare system is how people often end up in the most expensive sites of care (hospitals and nursing homes ultimately subsidized by government funds) when their less expensive custodial needs cannot be paid privately and will not be paid publicly.

Gerontologists argue over the characteristics of the future elderly. Will they observe healthier lifestyles—eating prudent foods, exercising more, eliminating smoking, and curbing their alcohol intake—so that they avoid disabling chronic illnesses and live relatively unencumbered by disease until the final disease that kills them in advanced old age? Will more people do crossword puzzles and other cerebral exercises to keep their brains as energetic and limber as possible? Or will this idea of the "compression of morbidity" (Fries 1984) be overrun by the competing idea: that more people will live longer with more deeply embedded disabilities? Will the ideology of life at any cost continue to drive the technologies that enable extremely frail and disabled individuals to prolong life beyond hope of a reasonable existence? What trade-offs will societies make as their populations age? Some demographers attempt to calculate the "active life expectancy" of individuals as a way to predict the descriptive shape of our years in the future.

It is unclear whether the challenges of an aging nation, such as the U.S., can be met by new ideas about work, productivity, and retirement, and whether the healthcare system can adjust appropriately to care for more chronically ill, aged individuals. It remains to be seen whether more people will age older and healthier or whether increasing numbers of elderly will endure with multiple chronic ailments. Ethical dilemmas about the quality of life, not just the quantity of life, are certain to focus more of our energies as more of us survive to live longer and longer lives.

In settled communities with available shelter and food for its citizens, the majority will live into the senior decades of life. People, of course, want to survive indefinitely considering the alternative. And yet, according to Oliver Wendell Holmes, Jr., a person is always startled when he hears himself seriously called an old man for the first time. [SMA]

Chapter 4

Is Aging a Problem?

(RRS)

Today, among other junk mail, there was a questionnaire from some research outfit, addressed apparently to a sampling of senior citizens and wishing to know intimate things about my self-esteem. It is their hypothesis that a decline in self-esteem is responsible for many of the overt symptoms of aging …

I looked at some of the questions and threw the thing in the fireplace. Another of those socio-psycho-physiological studies suitable for computerizing conclusions already known to anyone over fifty. Who was ever in any doubt that the self-esteem of the elderly declines in this society which indicates in every possible way that it does not value the old in the slightest, finds them an expense and an embarrassment, laughs at their experience, evades their problems, isolates them in hospitals and Sunshine Cities, and generally ignores them except when soliciting their votes or ripping off their handbags and their Social Security checks? And which has a chilling capacity to look straight at them and never see them. The poor old senior citizen has two choices, assuming he is well enough off to have any choices at all. He can retire from that hostile climate, or he can shrink in his self-esteem and gradually become the cipher he is constantly reminded he is. Stegner, The Spectator Bird *1976:116.*

Notes for this section begin on page 97.

The Problem with Problems

For decades aging has been viewed as a problem in the U.S. In similar fashion, adolescence is a problem, pregnancy and childbirth are problems, active boys are problems, shyness is a problem, and the list goes on. That aspects of these time periods and experiences in human life have their difficulties is not in doubt; what needs to be re-questioned is whether certain categories of people and various conditions are problems.

Seeing aspects of life as problems prejudges groups and experiences in a way that strips individuals of their uniqueness and robs groups of their idiosyncratic membership. Until feminists and consumers raised serious questions about how childbirth was treated by physicians, for example, women were medicated unconscious and amnesiac during labor. Medications had been given to laboring women to reduce the problems attendant in childbirth as well as to ameliorate the pain of labor and delivery. However, new medical knowledge and techniques aimed at delivering healthier babies and reducing mortality of both mothers and babies were too often accompanied by paternalism in the physician. Furthermore, these interventions sometimes created unintended negative consequences that women reacted against.

Unanticipated difficulties related to the position of the prone women in labor, the [at times] overuse of labor-inducing and pain-reducing medications, and the use of forceps, surgical procedures, and the like, became more widespread with the general use of these methods. The medical tide may be turning against the general use of episiotomy—the routine cutting of the perineum to prevent tearing of the women's tissue as the baby is born. Just the routine of "confining" women for one or two weeks following childbirth because it was thought that bed rest was best turned out to create difficulties for the new mothers who were weakened from the forced inactivity.

The intentions were good; some of the consequences were not.

Yes, delivering babies today is safer and more "physiologic" than ever before. But I doubt that the impetus for these changes came solely from the midwives or the leaders of the feminist movement.

They came about, as I recall, as much from the obstetricians as the others. [SMA]

That's not the way a lot of women remember what happened. But there had to have been a good number of physicians who thought the changes were necessary. However, it has always puzzled me why no one campaigns against the use of analgesia and anesthesia for other kinds of painful procedures, such as root canal therapy or impacted molar extractions. Don't we want to fully participate in and be aware of these experiences? [RRS]

The ways in which pregnancy and childbirth have been treated constitute an example of a phenomenon that has been called medicalization by those who study the cultural context of medical systems. Medicalization is characteristic of how some domains of life have become encompassed under the purview of Western biomedicine and social policy in the twentieth century, and of how increasing areas of our lives are considered to be in need of solution. Though it would be foolish to claim that problems were nonexistent until Western biomedicine and governmental agencies provided "solutions," it is fair to say that definitions of what constitutes normality have narrowed while the scope of what constitutes problems has broadened accordingly.

What is the problem with that? Is it not preferable that things that are broken get fixed? Should a caring society not look after all its citizens and work to ensure the best health and situation possible for its members?

Of course. However, as the medical and social "gaze" has focused on various domains of life and these domains have become medicalized, they have become pathologized as a result. Thus, the medical problems that accompany some pregnancies and some births become linked with pregnancy and birth in general, and pregnancy and birth come to be seen as a problem in and of itself as well. The attitude has increasingly fanned out to the social domain. Solutions have been devised for people whose characteristics or living situations do not conform to the recommended optimum.

The reason this trend is worrisome is that as a society we necessarily forfeit some of the vigor of the diversity that comes from the fact that many people do not fall within prescribed boundaries of what might be considered normal. Individuals vary along a very broad continuum of behaviors and attributes, and this variety should remain robust. There is reason to worry about the limitations we indirectly place on such diversity. Should "cosmetic" drugs, such as Prozac, be prescribed for conditions such as shyness when psychological traits like assertiveness are increasingly preferred in the society? (see Kramer 1993).

Consider the notion of dementia as another example. "It is important to note," sociologist Karen Lyman writes, "that only premature senility was considered an illness earlier in this century. Senility was considered normal" (1993:15). Her research among 150 Californians with dementia in several daycare settings also revealed that some of the strategies that caregivers devised to deal with stressful situations actually exacerbated the situations that in turn made the work of the staff more difficult. The unintended consequences of these interventions themselves caused problems. As research, funding priorities, and public awareness have intensified regarding Alzheimer's and other dementing diseases, a curious phenomenon has occurred in recent decades. Dementia is viewed as pathological disease, but at the same time it has become so common as to be perceived almost as part and parcel of advanced aging (see Gubrium 1986). Is it normal or not?

> *There is a grave risk in considering an age-related departure from the average as signifying a "normal" state if it is statistically quite common. It is also a mistake to consider three words in the preceding sentence (i.e., average, normal, common) as interchangeable.*
>
> *If, for the sake of discussion, senile changes are encountered in 60 percent of a sample of ninety-year-olds, this does not, per se, make these changes normal; common perhaps, even average, but not normal—as long as there are some (in this case, 40 percent) who are free of these burdensome changes. And if we still feel obliged to call the people with these changes "normal," how then do we designate those ninety-year-olds who do not have these senile changes? Super-normal?*
>
> *About 70 percent of urban American adults are now obese. Should we now accept obesity as non-pathologic? A disease is a disease, whether it is rare or frequent. [SMA]*
>
> *You have a very good point, I must admit. Yes, certain pathological conditions are pathological, no matter what—"objectively"*

speaking. The question perhaps centers on how objective the criteria can always be. Who is judging what is pathological and what is normal? How much do cultural preferences come into play in defining the differences between normal and pathological at any given time and across cultures? While a certain number of plaques and tangles in the aged brain are "normal," too many indicate Alzheimer's disease. Who makes the cut-off? If a person had no symptoms of dementia, but upon autopsy is found to have plaques and tangles, was he demented after all?

It used to be that children who were left-handed were taught (or forced, as the case may be) to write with their right hands. Being left-handed was not okay—perhaps it was considered pathological? [RRS]

I respond to this both as a left-hander and the father of two left-handed offspring. For biased reasons, I regard left-handedness (found in about 9 percent of the general population) as a normal variation, not a deviation. Nonetheless, there are good scientists who now provide compelling epidemiological evidence that left-handers—consistently—are at greater risk for a variety of auto-immune and neurological diseases (e.g., Alzheimer's disease). The decision as to whether something is a normal variant, a deviant or an objective risk factor rests finally, not upon collected anecdotes, but with carefully designed, objective cohort studies. [SMA]

Oliver Sacks has devoted a good part of his career to writing about the vagaries of his practice in neurology. His books richly describe the continuum in neurological diseases that manifest themselves in different ways. He raises fascinating philosophical questions about what it is to be human and what constitutes definitions of normal and abnormal. Perhaps his main point is that the brain, a uniquely flexible organ, learns to adjust to many of the deficits that it sustains. The adaptations can lead to beautiful results at times, and his books catalog the unique achievements that some gifted individuals with neurological deficits are able to make. He describes the gifted surgeon with Tourette's syndrome and the painter with color blindness, among others. Introducing this idea he writes:

> Thus while one may be horrified by the ravages of developmental disorder or disease, one may sometimes see them as creative too—for if they destroy particular paths, particular ways of doing things, they may force the nervous system into making other

paths and ways, force on it an unexpected growth and evolution. This other side of development or disease is something I see, potentially, in almost every patient; and it is this, here, which I am especially concerned to describe (1995:xvi).

And further:

This sense of the brain's remarkable plasticity, its capacity for the most striking adaptations, not least in the special (and often desperate) circumstances of neural or sensory mishap, has come to dominate my own perception of my patients and their lives. So much so, indeed, that I am sometimes moved to wonder whether it may not be necessary to redefine the very concepts of "health" and "disease," to see these in terms of the ability of the organism to create a new organization and order, one that fits its special, altered disposition and needs, rather than in the terms of a rigidly defined "norm." Sickness implies a contraction of life, but such contractions do not have to occur. Nearly all of my patients, so it seems to me, whatever their problems, reach out to life—and not only despite their conditions, but often because of them, and even with their aid (1995:xviii).

So too with age.

When we define the range of normal within increasingly narrow boundaries, those who fall outside the normal range are then viewed as abnormal. A case could possibly be made for the observation that more diversity of behavior among individuals was tolerated in the past in the U.S. than is perhaps tolerated at the present time. Those who fall outside the normal range are perceived as having something wrong with them. If this trend is true, it also occurs at a time when the opposite is also true: more effort is made to correct, bring into the fold, and indeed save those who in the past would have been allowed to die, placed in institutions, neglected, forgotten. Acceptance of all kinds of diversity may also be increasing.

There is something eminently appealing about the thought that some higher authority, as an expression of pious compassion, attempts to bestow added capabilities upon those already burdened with genetically determined diseases not of their own making. Sacks does talk eloquently of certain compensating attributes in those, for example, with Tourette's syndrome. But I would urge that hereditary neurological deficits not be romanticized.

*Yes, there is a gifted surgeon with Tourette's syndrome; but I sus-
pect that his diagnostic skills and manual dexterity were achieved
despite, not because of, his inborn disorder (and I suspect, further,
that Sacks's series of gifted surgeons with Tourette's syndrome consists of one case.) The great majority of those with Tourette's syndrome expend most of their energies in trying to overcome their
illness and have little remaining energies for creative display. In
this case it is not nature but Oliver Sacks who is displaying compassion in publicizing a notable but isolated accomplishment.*

*People may perhaps point to Franklin Delano Roosevelt whose
outstanding political career in elective offices began only after an
attack of acute poliomyelitis left him with paralyzed legs. He was
elected governor of New York in 1928; and beginning in 1932 was
elected for four consecutive terms to the presidency of this nation
before a cerebral hemorrhage brought his astonishing career to an
abrupt close. Did the enduring paralysis mold his character and
thus prepare him for the daunting tasks of world leadership? Or,
alternatively, might his career have been ever more auspicious had
he not been impeded by paralysis?*

*It is pointless for people to speculate on what Roosevelt's career
might have been like had he not contracted poliomyelitis as
a young man. But nature has a curious way of demonstrating
certain causalities.*

*Consider, for example, a uniformly fatal disease of infancy
called Tay Sachs disease (TSD). The disease arises only when a
newborn inherits a certain defective gene from both parents. Inher-
iting the gene from only one parent produces no apparent defect in
the offspring; but that person with a single TSD gene now becomes
a carrier who may subsequently pass on the actual TSD disease to
his/her newborn if his/her partner is also a carrier. The question
then arises: will society be better off if there were fewer TSD carriers ? It would seem so. The question, however, no longer rests in
the realm of the hypothetical since there now exist reliable laboratory tests to identify these otherwise unidentifiable carriers.*

*But now that the population of carriers can be identified (num-
bering about one in 250 in the general American population) are
they in anyway different than others who are not carriers? Careful
studies have demonstrated that these TSD carriers are endowed
with an extraordinary resistance to the germs of tuberculosis
(Myrianthopoulos and Aronson 1966). Geneticists call this compensatory capability a biological advantage. They point to the fact
that carriers of the gene for sickle cell anemia also show an amazing biological advantage: they are resistant to the pathological
effects of the parasite that causes malaria. And there are yet other
instances in which homozygosity (i.e., carrying both defective
genes) produces a mortal disease while carrying only one gene (the*

carrier state, or heterozygosity) confers an enhanced resistance to some infectious agent.

But—and this must be stressed—these compensating blessings arise only within the context of inherited diseases of infancy and childhood, and are played out solely by affecting the survival rate of the carriers and the number of offspring they produce for the next generation. Diseases of the elderly, inherited or not, do not in any way influence fertility and are not then participants in any Darwinian struggle for gene survival. I know of no compensatory biological advantage conferred upon those with Alzheimer's disease, related forms of dementia or vascular diseases of the heart and brain, and I therefore see no hidden advantage in bearing these diseases. [SMA]

While I agree with these last statements completely, I take exception to the wholesale prejudging of individuals with disorders. While it is clear that they labor under a burden of disability that should not be romanticized, it is also true that individuals respond differently to the diseases and disorders with which they are beset. It seems to me that it is the variety of responses to neurological deficits—some of which become creative assets—that Sacks wants to reveal and in some cases, champion. [RRS]

Women have long been medicalized and/or pathologized by Western biomedicine, and both feminists and anthropologists have attempted to reestablish the normalcy of such physiological thresholds as menarche, pregnancy, childbirth, menopause, and other uniquely female experiences.[1] In attempting to understand menopause, for example, Lock (1993) compared the cultural construction of menopause in North America and Japan—in other words, she noted the differences in how menopause was understood, talked about, and experienced in the two places. She demonstrated how the historical development of Western medical science has managed or reinterpreted our fundamental ideas about this part of the female life cycle. She writes:

A scientific approach to the body, while it offers an extremely powerful paradigm for assembling knowledge about biology, produces a fragmented and partial picture. It uncovers and reifies, isolates and decontextualizes pieces of information, abstracting them from time and space. A person, however, is clearly not an abstract entity, but a conscious being perpetually in a state of change, whose body is the center of ongoing dynamic interactions among physical and social surroundings (Lock 1993:371).

Through a combination of questionnaire, survey data, and numerous long narratives of Japanese women describing their lives in considerable detail, Lock shows how (so far) the symptoms of menopause (roughly, *konenki*) in Japan are much fewer than in North America.[2] Lock furthermore shows that even in North America, the *experiences* of women undergoing menopause are far less severe than the mythology that surrounds it would have us believe. As Davis has recently observed about the increasing numbers of large-scale studies of menopause that: "... menopause is most remarkable for being unremarkable" (1997:17).

Look how the scope of dentistry has widened. I would contend that in the progressive medicalization of dentistry in the U.S., many conditions that used to be considered fine are now considered pathological and in need of a "fix." Dentists used to pull teeth that were rotten. Until the eighteenth century specialist tooth-pullers removed teeth because of pain. They had little ability to do much more than that. While false teeth had been made for centuries, their generally poor fit was not improved until the advent of wax, plastic, and rubber. With the advent of dental hygiene and the development of preventive dentistry techniques, increasing numbers of potential dental problems could be identified, prevented and/or fixed. Orthodontia devised ways to correct mismatched teeth and jaw alignments that also had a functional reason for intervention.

Increasingly, dentistry and orthodontia have added cosmetic areas to the corrective applications of the traditional dental/orthodontic arsenal, such as bleaching teeth, applying orthodontia for non-functional reasons, bonding teeth to enlarge or decrease them so they will appear more attractive. In so doing the purview of dentistry and orthodontia has widened. Increasing numbers of people are now considered proper candidates for procedures that would have been relegated to the strictly cosmetic in the past. Procedures previously considered frivolous are now more common and expected. In this way thereby, the category encompassing what is considered a dental or orthodontic "problem" has been broadened accordingly.

Focusing on dentistry highlights how this one field has over the last centuries both refined its techniques and expanded its scope of intervention, concomitantly enlarging the problem areas and blurring the line between cosmetic and functional dentistry. But the role of dentistry is also pertinent to the subject of aging. Dental concerns of the elderly have often been ignored or lightly treated. In nursing homes with inadequate staffing, the inability of residents to eat properly because of dental or other problems can lead to malnutrition if the residents are not properly aided (Kayser-Jones 2000, Harrington et al. 2000). Attention to dental needs prolongs lives and offers great promise. An example from natural history offers a dramatic illustration of this phenomenon. Whereas polar bears in the wild normally live about forty years and die of starvation because of periodontal disease, a polar bear in captivity who receives regular dental check-ups is currently around sixty years old (Wetle 2000). The impact of this relatively minor intervention raises the question of what the "normal" life span of a polar bear is. What do interventions do to us humans?

Interventions

Anthropologists and physicians often differ in how they define problems and in when and how they decide to intervene regarding something they view as a problem. The knowledge and understanding from the different professions can illuminate the reasoning and provide insight into alternatives as the various practitioners decide whether interventions are appropriate and will have the desired consequences.

There are hazards to interventions. Sometimes professionals intervene in the lives of old people without understanding that an elderly person has more resources than was thought. For example, many old widowed women in American society live alone. Most of these women do not remarry, largely because the pool of potential spouses is so small, but also sometimes because of preference. Many of these women also resist social worker attempts to bring them "into the system." They look frail, they are isolated, they often have cats. They seem like a homogeneous group. Though they may worry the neighbors, they often refuse official help.

Is this a bad thing? Is this a catastrophe waiting to happen? Or is not intervening a sign of respect for their individuality, their autonomy? Maybe we need to tolerate our own uneasiness when people prefer to live in ways that we judge unsafe or unsound.

Furthermore, it is important to understand that we may know far less than we think we do. The little old lady (the common medical acronym is LOL) who seems to be entirely isolated may be less lonely, less frail, and less helpless than the professionals perceive, and even if she receives help from an agency, the ethical issues are still complex (Wetle 1995). She may have contacts that the professionals know nothing about. Perhaps the little old lady has an arrangement with an eight-year-old neighbor who takes out her garbage twice a week and gets a cookie and conversation in exchange. Perhaps the postal worker is keeping a watchful eye to ensure that mail is indeed being picked up. Postal workers, electrical meter checkers, and others in the community whose routes take them into neighborhoods where they develop a sense about their customers and the area are often clued in when things have gone wrong. Sometimes, maybe often, the women isolated in their tiny apartments in the impersonal apartment complex may have worked out their own system to let one another know that they are all right and to signal when they need help. Most do well on their own.

> *You talk about the LOL who is less helpless than the professionals perceive. Possibly so—if she is cognitively intact. [SMA]*
>
> *OK. [RRS]*

To find out what one group of women like these were actually like, one researcher systematically studied and talked with forty-three American widows from parts of the Midwest and Southwest who lived in an apartment complex in San Francisco (Hochschild 1973). She expected a great deal less community than she found. Judging from external appearances and accumulated preconceptions, she and others might have assumed that the women were isolated and lonely, and in need of "help" from the system. However, she discovered from talking with them that theirs was a community that functioned, "as a mutual aid society, as a source of jobs, as an audience, as a pool of models for growing old, as a sanctuary and as a subculture with its own customs, gossip, and humor" (1973:xiv).

She called the group of women an "unexpected community" because she had not expected the level of cohesiveness and cooperation she found. The women had developed strategies. For example, they let one another know that they were all right by opening their curtains in the morning. Closed blinds alerted the others that something was awry and needed immediate attention.

Other expectations that the researcher had were similarly corrected. For example, though one of the old women told Hochschild that she did not "neighbor" much, it turned out that she regularly received about six daily visits from neighbors and friends. The women were not only signaling one another about danger, they were encountering one another with some regular frequency. This particular woman used the term "neighbor" to mean sharing meals rather than the short encounters she was having (1973:5).[3] It was necessary for Hochschild to be among the people, talking, observing, and participating, in order for her to find out what was actually going on in the women's lives and, most importantly, how they viewed it.

> *That frail, elderly, widowed matron in a plain gray dress, sitting alone by the window in her two-room apartment, does manage to move us deeply and generate feelings ranging from earnest sympathy to rampant guilt. And so many organizations from "Meals on Wheels" to "Friendly Neighbors" have been established as our surrogates in answer to the perceived needs of the disabled and lonely elderly of our community. In truth these Samaritan organizations do fulfill a notable and important societal function, not only for those receiving the visits or meals, but also for those delivering them.*
>
> *In so many instances, though, that elderly widow has as many visits per day, from neighbors and others, as she can tolerate. And rarely do records reflect two further sources of significant companionship for the elderly in our society.*
>
> *First are the multitude of pets that bring noise and responsiveness to an otherwise quiet apartment. Cats, for example, have provided congenial company for millions of otherwise lonely widows. These pets listen while their owner may repeat the same story, perhaps embellished, of the significant episodes in her life; they respond eagerly to a caressing hand; and they are quiet when*

quietness is sought. Cats eat little, keep themselves clean, demand little and enjoy the tranquility that comes from watching, from the kitchen window, the comings and goings of a hectic outer world. Only cats and the elderly understand the profound gratification that comes from mere window-watching. And talking of interactions with dumb animals, have you ever seen the look of utter contentment on the face of a senior citizen when he feeds pigeons or seagulls?

The second source of companionship for the elderly person living alone is not apparent to the hurried clinician or the clip-board carrying sociologist. At particular intervals each day the elderly person repairs to a comfortable chair, turns on the television set and enters the world of the soap opera, those continuing sagas of human action and interaction. Only after gaining the trust and confidence of the elderly person does the social worker begin to appreciate the extent to which this elderly woman has become part of the happenings on screen as she inserts herself into the travails, the ambiguities, the mysteries, the interpersonal frictions, and on rare occasions, the resolutions of the many vexatious problems plaguing the characters. There is a palpable reality to soap opera which only an elderly person, living alone, can possibly understand. These television actors, along with their multitudes of problems, have become an integral part of this elderly woman's family.

And finally, there is the blessing of solitude. Being alone, to an adolescent, means being rejected or even ostracized by one's peers. To an adult, being alone is a frightening experience associated with such catastrophes as divorce and losing one's job. But for a very old person who has weathered a lifetime of contention, rejection, periodic loss and interactions, both pleasant and unpleasant, the opportunity to sit without an agenda and without time constraint is a rare gift allowed only for the old. During these reveries, the thoughts are not profound; nor are fundamental issues of life and death ever confronted; the mind's eye may follow the moving shadows of a tree as the sun moves across the sky. A happy recollection from earlier years or perhaps the fragment of a poem memorized in childhood may intervene; but mainly the thoughts are unfocused, formless, and without direction.

The elderly person is deprived of so many things: internal organs that function effortlessly without constant maintenance checks, freedom from pain, an assignable role in a busy society. But there is always a forgiving, yielding solitude that tempers the sorrows of the day much like a warm security blanket.

The busy clinician misinterprets the widow's lengthy intervals of silence thinking it to be evidence of senility. He is, of course, seeing a tired person seek refuge in a place that demands little and allows for unlimited reflection and peace. [SMA]

I love what you've written here! So I must comment. First of all, you remind me how nursing homes used to prohibit pets because they were trying to maintain a sanitary (i.e., sterile) environment. Imagine! In recent years, however, reformers have been able to vitiate this "cordon sanitaire" in order to introduce pets (and plants and children even) to these too-often forbidding places. The fear of germs has finally given way to some common sense in order to make these places more human. Wasn't it a mistake to be more concerned about sanitation than the comfort and quality of life of the individuals in nursing homes?

Or think of the pressure put on some of the frail elderly to move to assistive housing—that happen not to allow pets. Why are we surprised that the old person becomes despondent and listless without his or her quiet companions?

Your passage also reminds me of a recent occurrence. In a visit to my mother-in-law in the backyard of her assisted living complex, she was so entranced watching two little girls play with their dog that she had little interest in chatting with me. So while the sun warmed us and we had glasses of juice, the two of us sat and watched and enjoyed the children and the dog carrying on. It was a lovely interlude. [RRS]

Gay Becker's important book, *Growing Old in Silence,* is testimony to the idea that what the dominant community perceives as a major problem or deficit is not perceived as such to those experiencing it. Her thesis goes further, however, in demonstrating that the skills needed to cope with a profound deficit like deafness during a person's lifetime help to prepare him or her for difficulties likely to be encountered in old age. She found that the deaf people she studied formed communities that provided help and support to its members. She notes that many hearing old people have never encountered the devalued status that often accompanies old age until they are old. In contrast to them, she writes,

> When low status occurs early in life, as with the aged deaf, the individual has a far better chance of learning to cope with it over a lifetime than does the individual who acquires such a status late in life. It is likely that coping with the stigma attached to low status early in life helps one to cope with old age, particularly if the previous status is more stigmatizing than that of old age (1980:115).

It seems that there are two strongly competing trends in this country that are at loggerheads when it comes to this question.

One impulse attempts to address the social and medical ills of the population, raise and maintain a community standard within the country, put a floor beneath people, attach a durable safety net into which frail individuals can be cushioned from a fall and not be hurt. This perspective drives the social policy imperative to improve the wellbeing of the nation's population as a whole. This imperative fueled the moves to create Social Security, Medicare, and Medicaid.

The other impulse, from the policy perspective, is to allow individual choice for people to live their lives the way that they see fit. If little old ladies live alone, perhaps they prefer it that way, and furthermore, perhaps it is for the best. One should not presume mental illness or otherwise pathologize what might be to them their personal preference. This latter laissez-faire ideology presumes on the one hand a respect for individual variation. On the other hand, it might imply a Social Darwinist assumption. This thinking equates a person who is poor, or living in substandard housing, or living alone in advanced old age or unable to find a job, with the lot he or she is in. It draws the conclusion that because the situation is the way it is, it is just and fair that it be so. Likewise, a person who is rich and successful is presumed to be worthy of those achievements. Or, as former Governor of Texas, Ann Richards, acidly said about the senior George Bush, a person who is born on third base should not conclude that he has just hit a triple.

The first stance reflects the more liberal, traditionally Democratic view that holds that a more active federal government is necessary to create a uniform standard of living that benefits the entire nation as a whole. The other stance is closer to the Jeffersonian notion that the best government governs least, a view that has been a frequent war cry of mainstream Republicans in recent decades. In practice of course, the stark distinction is usually never bright and clear.

In any case, my purpose here is to illustrate that interventions are not always a good thing. The injunction to new physicians to "first, do no harm" is an important aphorism of the profession. This dictum has profound implications, especially in our technologically driven world. The impulse to "do something" is very strong in medicine and stands in sharp contrast to the behaviors of those of us who would watch and wait. Koenig (1988) has described how routine medical practices enable physicians to perform procedures largely because they are possible to do. This "technological imperative" predisposes practitioners to use the methods they have at their disposal. With so many technologies available and with monetary reimbursement providing incentive and tacit legitimacy, it becomes hard to resist using them. But sometimes they need resisting.

Should an eighty-five-year-old woman with a past history of breast cancer now undergo a full mastectomy followed by chemotherapy to prevent the possibility of a recurrence to be on the safe side? Is this the best idea when the patient has a history of heart disease, is anxious and fearful of surgery?

> *Renée, how often do you see eighty-five-year-olds, with heart disease, undergoing mastectomy? Maybe fifty years ago—but not today. You may be beating a dead—or at least moribund—horse. [SMA]*

> *Honestly, it's true. Luckily, in this case, the surgery didn't happen. However, the doctor recommended such an option to the patient and her children. Though the family felt pressured, they said no. [RRS]*

Should a seventy-nine-year-old nursing home resident with dementia brought to the emergency room because of a suspected stroke undergo an MRI when the treatment for her condition will remain unchanged with the new information? This story is also true.

> *More often than not because the family demands it or implicitly threatens malpractice litigation. [SMA]*

> *In this case I think the doctor thought the family wanted him to pull out the stops and do all the tests. After a protracted conversation to clarify options and recommendations, the family and the physician decided to forego the MRI. I understand that malpractice fears can be the motivation for the excessive testing. In this case, the family members reassured the physician that they were in agreement that they considered the testing to be excessive and that they would not hold the physician responsible since they were requesting the tests not be performed. [RRS]*

Because she could not express her wishes, family members believed she should return to the familiar environment of the nursing home, judging that her quality of life today was more important than the presumed advantage of extra information. Would the doctor have automatically ordered the MRI had they not been there to review the options for her and challenge him?

On the other hand, an opposite story: an unassuming eighty-two-year-old man felt unwell and decided against going to a family party. Among the guests at the party were a few physicians, who hearing of his symptoms (including some difficulty in breathing), immediately went to his house and persuaded him to go to the hospital where his pneumonia was diagnosed and treated. He was released a few days later. The hospitalization probably saved the man's life since pneumonia in the elderly can progress rapidly and be life threatening.

The wish to treat the elderly can be seen as a relatively new phenomenon. A geriatrician involved in the establishment of a nursing home ethics committee in the 1980s wanted to counteract the medical tradition in which he had been trained whereby nursing home residents were often considered too old to be treated for various conditions (see Shield 1995). This physician felt it was important to treat many kinds of conditions in the nursing home resident if treatments improved the resident's life.

By the time the nursing home ethics committee was established, however, the pendulum in mainstream medicine seemed to have swung in the other direction. Nursing home residents, family members, and various nursing home staff members were now protesting that too much unwanted treatment was being foisted on unwilling and/or unknowing frail individuals, with often undesired consequences. The ethics committee was established in order to make sense of the competing forces in attitude and treatment choices as modern medical possibilities proliferated. How were decisions made whether to treat or not to treat? Who should speak for the elderly nursing home residents who could not speak for themselves?

In past decades dementia was considered a normal consequence of growing old, and the pneumonias and influenza viruses that healthy, younger people withstood easily would naturally kill the frail and the old. Pneumonia was in fact referred to as the "old man's friend," and was a common cause of dying in old age. The attitude that old age carried inevitable consequences pervaded medicine. Old patients who complained of vision and hearing problems, joint pain, difficulties walking, sexual dysfunction, memory loss, and so on, were often told by their doctors that this was normal and to make the best of their aging condition. "What do you expect?" was a frequent refrain, and patients agreed, shrugged their shoulders, and adapted.

A joke upending this assumption goes as follows: an old woman visited her doctor for her check-up. After the examination that confirmed the usual list of this and that, the doctor asked if she had any further questions or problems. Rather sheepishly, she ventured that she did. It seemed that she and her husband were having some sexual difficulties, she confided shyly. The doctor reassured her and clucked, "Well, after all, Mrs. Goldberg, you *are* ninety-three and your husband *is* ninety-five. Not to worry." Mrs. Goldberg gently persisted, however, and said that this problem was bothering her and it was fairly recent. The doctor then asked her, "When did you first notice this?" and she responded, "Last night ... and again this morning."

Along with civil rights movements for women, African-Americans, other minorities, and the disabled came the Gray Panthers and similar groups to mobilize support for elderly rights and to protest "ageist" treatments and practices, including how old people were viewed by the medical establishment. Furthermore, gerontology and advances in treatments have conditioned the public to reject resignation about the limits of medical interventions to alleviate discomforts or cure various ills. But finding the right balance for the individual as well as for society remains hard to achieve.

At the extreme edges of life, decisions are sometimes made to extend life and to do one more procedure or technique because it is possible to perform them. This reasoning has been questioned both because of the dubious benefit to the dying patient as well as the extreme costs to the medical healthcare system. As Callahan has written, "Medical powers and possibilities have become the constant companion of the self in its effort to live with mortality" (1993:25). It is important not to confuse medicine's effort to restore a person to health with prolonging his or her life without restoring health. Callahan (1987) is one of the voices arguing that age is a legitimate consideration in allocating scarce medical resources. His voice is one of many in a growing chorus that believes that the prolongation of life in old age is not always desirable. Whether it is or not is a question still intensely debated and not likely to be resolved soon.

The children of a nursing home resident wanted their mother to move to a larger and nicer room in the nursing home. The resident was demented and needed a great deal of guidance and help. The children arranged the move and felt good about the upgrade. Unfortunately, however, the nursing home resident was accustomed to her slippers placed on the left side of her bed. Because the orientation of the new room reversed that of the former room, her slippers were now on the other side of the bed. The nursing home resident did not see the slippers and tripped over them and fell. She had trouble finding other things in her room and was generally more disoriented in her new room. As a result she was upset, had trouble sleeping, and was disruptive to the other residents. So on balance, was it a good thing that the room was changed? Did the resident herself derive anything positive in the move?

Rather than argue against all interventions, it is nonetheless necessary to point out that interventions have consequences, sometimes unintended, that are not necessarily obvious or intuitive. Intuitive, after all, is what seems natural to the person having the intuition, and what seems natural to one person is not necessarily shared by others.

In a book about impoverished elderly women in the U.S., the gap between objective and subjective poverty proves important. Past expectations were salient indicators of how the old women viewed their present situations. What seemed to be more important to them was the quality of the personal interactions that the women experienced, as opposed to financial ones. "Rather," the authors wrote, "deprivation was often equated with an emotional, relational or spiritual lack" (Black and Rubinstein 2000:14). Had the researchers prejudged what was important to these women, they would have missed the mark.

Furthermore, stepping into the life of a person who has not asked to be helped introduces significant ethical dimensions into the decision. The presumption that a benevolent outsider who wants to provide aid knows better than the person being helped is a shaky premise for action. Who makes the judgment about the worthiness of the proposed intervention? Why should another's judgment and interpretation of events be considered superior to that of the person involved? What assurance is there that the intervention will achieve the desired goal? What is the likelihood that negative consequences might result instead of or alongside the expected positive consequences? In real life most factors cannot be controlled. In short, it presumes a great deal to enter a situation from the outside intending to do good but with the distinct possibility of inflicting harm instead. Sometimes it is more important to understand that a person who wants to be of the most assistance should not, "just do something" but should instead "stand there" until more information about how to proceed makes the decision clearer.

> *It is difficult to respond to anecdotes detailing insensitive medical care and needless technical interventions in the elderly, particularly when the tale is told by one observer without the impressions of the hospital or the physician of record. [SMA]*
>
> *Granted ... [RRS]*
>
> *The majority of malpractice suits, in years past, were prompted by claims that a diagnostic intervention had not been undertaken, or that some test might have revealed some arcane disorder amenable to therapy.*
>
> *Hospitals and physicians have responded to these pressures, in a clearly defensive manner, by mandating that certain tests be undertaken when confronting certain signs or symptoms. An MRI test for an eighty-five-year-old with progressive dementia may be both expensive to the community, an utter waste of technical skills, and very upsetting to the patient. It seems, at first glance, to be either a mercenary or idiotic intervention. Yet bitter experience has shown that a certain form of hydrocephalus in the elderly simulates a global dementia, and further, that this form of hydrocephalus is quite treatable resulting in appreciable cognitive recovery. [SMA]*

Yes. Full disclosure: I was involved in such a group decision, and because the affected person was not complaining about her condition, I was hesitant about agreeing to surgery that would change her situation and jeopardize her equanimity. She seemed to understand the procedure and gave her consent, but she had to be reminded about it as the time grew nearer. As it turned out, the procedure was done and she improved dramatically. The balance of risks and benefits should always be weighed and considered carefully. [RRS]

Furthermore, I know of no institution that would undertake such procedures without informed consent. When, as happens sometimes, some relatives beg that their beloved grandmother be spared inhuman testing while other relatives, frequently the more strident ones, demand immediate intervention, problems will be inevitable. And the situation then becomes anecdotal proof of either callous negligence or insensitive, needless intervention depending upon who is doing the talking [SMA].

Often, thoughtful discussion of difficult decision-making cannot be conveyed to outsiders. I hope that nuanced discussions are taking place, and that doctors and family members are listening to one another. But these conversations require time—an increasingly scarce commodity—and the fast pace of the hospital shrinks the time that is allowed for thoughtful discussion. And when the afflicted person is unable to speak for himself, it becomes less evident that his wishes are being honored. As most clinicians know, uncommunicative patients and quarreling family members are not uncommon in the institutional setting. [RRS]

The Stigma of Age

The current situation with the Palm Beach County ballot and the confusion many had using it bears out an opinion I have held for quite some time. I am not dismayed at all that many votes of the elderly were disqualified because those casting them had stupidly voted for both Gore and Buchanan. Senile people should not be voting in the first place. Today's elderly have repeatedly voted themselves an exorbitant amount of largess (sic) from the U.S. Treasury in the past, thus creating a dismal economic future for their progeny. They have essentially stolen the prosperity of their grandchildren by voting for socialist politicians who repeatedly rob the productive tax-payers to expand benefits for the non-productive elderly. Any who are soon destined to die should not vote in an election. The elderly voters will not be burdened by the calamity of their choice; the consequences of the foolish elderly vote are borne by the young. It is time that the nearly dead step aside (letter to the editor, *Providence Journal*, 11/16/00).

This letter to the editor sums up some of the worst stereotypes that stigmatize the elderly. Notwithstanding the fact that the letter-writer leaps over logic to claim his moral high ground, his assertions caricature some of the common misunderstandings about the elderly that plague the ways they are perceived. The letter-writer equates old age with the "nearly dead" and the "senile" and conflates these falsehoods with the idea that the elderly are a homogeneous greedy bunch who should be entirely disenfranchised. This letter is a demonstration of a certain kind of stigma that pesters those who are old.

In Stegner's novel, *The Spectator Bird* (excerpted at the beginning of the chapter), the protagonist contemplates his own aging with growing mortification. He has contempt for the body that encases him and steadily limits him. He notices a society so caught up in its adoration of youth that it necessarily degrades old people. He rejects the rejecting society, but at the same time is repelled by the aging he witnesses in himself. He has incorporated the social repugnance for old age and he reflects it. As he thinks about his own past and considers how he has come to this point, he reveals how devalued he feels by the betrayal of his body. But he is protesting: he seems to be saying that his bodily limitations are one thing, but the social contempt is another. He can manage his own aging and negotiate how to deal with his constraints on his own terms. He can adapt and he can struggle. But to also be the object of social scorn by younger people and to see derision reflected in their eyes is unacceptable and reprehensible to him.

The incorporation of social values into one's own assessment of self is key. The sociologist, Erving Goffman, termed this "spoiled identity" crucial to stigma. "By definition, of course, we believe the person with a stigma is not quite human," he wrote. "On this assumption we exercise varieties of discrimination ... we tend to impute a wide range of imperfections on the basis of the original one" (1963:5). Though Goffman referred mainly to stigmatizing conditions such as deafness and physical disability, the attribute of old age also has stigma clearly attached. Becker's (1980) discovery that the deaf old have benefited from a lifetime of adapting to not hearing and its stigma serves as a corrective to this concept.

One of the major ways older patients have been stigmatized by physicians has been through medical humor. Physicians typically go into medicine out of a genuine desire to do good and to help relieve people's suffering. The rigors of medical training and the difficulties of hospital practice are well known. More of a secret, perhaps, is the ambivalence physicians often hold toward their patients and medicine.

From the frustrations of dealing with difficult patients and diseases that are resistant to cure to the implacable third party payers who deny treatment decisions and the impossible socio-economic disparities that underlie so much disease, the reasons that physicians hold conflicting feelings about their work are numerous and complex. Medical humor is an effective outlet known for its rough and often bitter edge. Like all humor it contains important elements of truth that are transformed by intentional hyperbole into the ridiculous and raunchy, rendering it less painful and dangerous. At the same time, some needless medical humor is directed against patients and much of that humor and scorn is directed at old patients. It is a special form of blaming the hapless victim (see chapter 5).

Elderly patients have borne the brunt of much medical prejudice and contempt. The bestseller *House of God* (Shem 1981) brought the slang term "gomer" (get out of my emergency room) into general parlance. It introduced the public to the disparaging attitude many physicians, especially those in training, display toward the elderly patient who has been rushed from the nursing home to the emergency room—yet again. The following painful incident, for example, was described as "less cheering, but somehow humorous" by the self-critical medical student who wrote about it years later:

> He [a 95-year-old demented nursing home patient being evaluated at the hospital for a possible colon cancer] lay in a more or less fetal position in his bed, a few wisps of white hair askew on his

head, and said over and over again, "Why you do this to me? What I did to you? I never did nothing to you. Why I have to have this? Why you do this to me? What I did to you?" This demented speech, given in common-sense, if distressed, tones, made a constant background refrain in the life of the ward (Konner 1987:292).

Konner, an anthropologist who went back to school for this medical training, confessed that he saw the above as evidence of a funny and ironic failure of communication. If Konner wrote this book today, I believe he would realize that the demented nursing home patient he was attempting to treat did not merely represent a failure of communication, but was indeed an abject failure of the healthcare system. What possible reason did these medical practitioners have to waste precious resources and inflict discomfort on this frail man in order to find out whether colon cancer existed in his troubled body along with everything else?

It is sometimes said that old people make frustrating patients for physicians because they often fail to respond to the life-saving treatments that doctors utilize. Though doctors have always understood how limited they were in preventing death and disease, modern technological advances ironically seem to have made doctors less able to understand death as anything but failure writ large. Since one of the incredible successes of modern medicine is that death is increasingly relegated to old age, doctors see death embodied in old people and cringe. Humor compensates.

At the end of the discussions one senior physician shook his gray head, sighed, and smiled. "As George Burns says," he mused aloud, "not many people die after ninety." This was to become a favorite remark during morning rounds for the rest of the month, uttered ritually by the residents in chorus, whenever we left the bedside of a patient over ninety. The more hopeless the patient, the funnier the line (Konner 1987:287).

Of course today in the twenty-first century, more and more people die after ninety, and increasing numbers of people live past 100. So who is the joke on now?

The fight against non-human status that the stigma of age and physical limitation confers on individuals has been expressed by others, such as Murphy (1987), an anthropologist who described his own quadriplegia, and Laird (1979), an anthropologist self-styled "survivor" who recounted her frightful stays in several nursing homes. As Murphy pointed out, disability places a person in a category neither here nor there, in a limbo status that seems dangerous to others, that culturally removes a person from the realm of others who are "normal."[4] In talking about the disabled, the following remarks could also apply to how the elderly too often find themselves in our social order:

> The long-term physically impaired are neither sick nor well, neither dead nor fully alive, neither out of society nor wholly in it. They are human beings but their bodies are warped or malfunctioning, leaving their full humanity in doubt. They are not ill, for illness is transitional to either death or recovery. Indeed, illness is a fine example of a nonreligious, nonceremonial liminal condition. The sick person lives in a state of social suspension until he or she gets better. The disabled spend a lifetime in a similar suspended state. They are neither fish nor fowl; they exist in partial isolation from society as undefined, ambiguous people (Murphy 1987:131).

Old people have a long time in which they gradually notice themselves becoming old, but being old is a status that is often denied and shunned by them rather than acknowledged and embraced. The signs come on us in middle age or earlier.

The timelessness with which the elderly fashion and understand themselves over time has been analyzed by Kaufman in *The Ageless Self*. She wrote,

> Identity is created and recreated over time as a person progresses through the life span. The structure and meaning of one's identity is established as experience is layered on experience and is simultaneously reflected upon, evaluated, adjusted to, and incorporated. But rather than being constructed to follow the rise and fall of an external trajectory through time, identity is built around themes, without regard to time, as past experiences are symbolically connected with one another to have meaning for a particular individual ... Continuity of themes is thus a key element in the ageless identity of this particular elderly population and, I suspect, in the elderly in general ... The individual *actively seeks* continuity as he or she goes through ordinary daily existence and interprets the circumstances with which he or she deals (1986:151-152).

All of us participate in the lifelong process of self-creation. We are jarred by the lack of resonance between the external signs and our internal sense of who we are. I notice the lines and the sags, and I am frankly puzzled: had I not vowed that my body was not going to go that way? I am aware of the ways in which I am not as resilient or strong as I used to be. There are some improvements with age, ways in which I am more efficient and experienced because I am older, but for the most part, I catch myself in the mirror and see the undeniable evidence of years and wonder, "how come?" People talk about the strangeness of the sudden recognition of the signs of their own aging. How could it be? a person seems to protest. Certainly not me. And the shock is felt as an insult. I am who I am so how did these changes come and stake me out? It seems that somewhere along the way permission should have been granted. It is a disruption in our notion of our selves to see ourselves gradually transformed into the creatures we call old. We thought they were "other," but they are us.

Becker (1997) has discussed a variety of ways in which lives can be unexpectedly disrupted, and this disruption has a significantly disorienting effect. In examining the lives of stroke victims, people with infertility, and others who have experienced important disruptions in their lives, she shows how people find meaning and the glimmers of understanding in their new situations. Like Bateson's idea of "composing a life," (1989) she sees the struggle to find coherence and order out of chaotic and disrupted experience to be a uniquely human impulse. We strive for a sense of coherence and resist when our lives do not make inherent sense to us, or when our bodies do not conform to our notion of ourselves. We deal with stigma, with disruption, with difficulties of all sorts, and in all kinds of ways, and then we construct a narrative for ourselves that allows us a way to fashion coherence and significance from the disparate ingredients that make up our long, messy lives.

The stigma of age creates problems separate from those of aging. Being attuned to some of the assumptions that underlie this stigma helps distinguish which is which.

Social Policy as Problem

On the broader, societal level, the elderly as a group has been constituted as a problem, and ironically perhaps as an unintended consequence of programs explicitly designed to help the problem. Passage of Medicare and the Older Americans Act as part of Lyndon Johnson's Great Society initiatives of the 1960s have largely spurred the development of the fields of gerontology within sociology and geriatrics within general medicine. While Medicare was designed to pay for hospital and physician services for the elderly, the Older Americans Act of 1965 had ambitious social goals for the elderly, including the best possible physical and mental health and retirement in health, honor, and dignity.[5]

Together these programs are largely responsible for the significant gains the elderly population has made in American society. But far from eradicating poverty, discrimination, and social ills, their establishment paradoxically created their own problems and inadvertently perpetuated some of the other problems.

Over twenty years ago, sociologist Carroll Estes delivered one of the first and most critical accounts of the way in which the Great Society programs designed to alleviate the difficult conditions for the elderly in the U.S. had the effect instead of defining the elderly as a problem. In her classic analysis of how policy creates reality, or the "social construction of reality," she began her book by stating flatly that:

> The major problems faced by the elderly in the United States are, in large measure, ones that are socially constructed as a result of our conceptions of aging and the aged. What is done for and about the elderly, as well as what we know about them, are products of our conceptions of aging. In an important sense, then, the major problems faced by the elderly are the ones we create for them (1979:1).

This was Lyman's point in the daycare settings for elderly with dementia (1993). Interventions created to assist those with dementia often caused the stressful situations they were meant to prevent. Estes went on to say:

I hope to call particular attention to how the aged are often processed and treated as a commodity in our society and to the fact that the age-segregated policies that fuel the aging enterprise are socially divisive "solutions" that single out, stigmatize, and isolate the aged from the rest of society (1979:2).

Her critique was one of the first to demonstrate how the programs and policies created an industry of helping organizations that had, and still have, a vested interest in understanding the elderly as needy and problematic. This stilted way of looking at the elderly has become its own industry. It is important to remember that one of the major ways that Medicare passed Congress and received the support of the country was by publicizing the desperate straits of many older Americans. They had to come into public consciousness as a recognizable group needy of help and distinguished from the rest of us (presumed to be normal). As programs and policies are created to fix the ills, and people are trained and hired to fill the positions to help clients get services, an environment of entitlement and dependency begins. Rather than solving the problems, the problems perpetuate. The people hired to fill the positions do not want to see their programs eliminated. Some degrading assumptions about the elderly lay beneath the premise of the laws and agencies created and maintained to help the elderly.

I tend to agree with your reasoning, realizing that any argument vis à vis aging is easily defeated. If you favor an "industry to take care of senile ones," you are perpetuating a cynical business where those with jobs will do everything to keep their nursing home jobs. And if we take a libertarian point of view (as did Ayn Rand), you are then accused of being indifferent and insensitive to the frail elderly. You are little more than a twenty-first century Ebenezer Scrooge.

Dickens had such a talent for devising names with phonetic messages! And if you ask an elder citizen, he'll immediately say, "Of course I got problems! And of course I am a problem. Don't make me into a forty-year-old who happens to have white hair. I think differently (when I think at all) and inside of me I function differently. So don't take away my 'problem' status. When you are eighty-five years old, Mr. Professor, you can then have it taken away." [SMA]

The problem is that seeing age (or labor and childbirth or adolescence or ...) as a problem predisposes people, including the elderly themselves, to expect problems, to anticipate the negative. These self-fulfilling prophecies generate their own momentum in which both young and old expect age to be the core problem.

This may be an important reason that despite the *fact* that the vast majority of people over the age of eighty live independently in the community, the popular perception exists that most old people live in nursing homes. Perhaps this is why many Americans believe that as a society we tend to neglect our elderly family members when in *fact* most Americans are in frequent contact with their elderly family members, visit them often, and help them in substantial ways. We do a disservice to the older members of our society by assuming and anticipating problems for them. Life is hard enough without social preconceptions of distress attributed to this or that group.

In our society in general, age, the neutral counting of passing time, is encumbered with a host of dizzyingly, discouraging attributes. Disease, dependency, decay, deterioration, dementia, depression, death, decline, decrepitude, distress, degeneration are some of the common terms that frequently make up this vastly skewed list. Why do these terms so greatly overshadow other words we could as easily use to describe age, such as wisdom, experience, sagacity, tenacity, endurance, perseverance, fortitude, resolve, determination? Age is clearly a loaded subject about which North Americans have many negative preconceptions.

Incorporating the Perspective of the Old Person: an Alternative Formulation

A simple principle that can be a wise corrective to instituting ill-conceived interventions is to keep the old person central in the considerations. It is vital to try to discern the person's perspective whenever possible. It is good to ask the person what he or she wants. How does the person see the situation? Does a change need to occur? Is the proposed change a way to help the caregivers feel useful or will the intervention actually benefit the person? It is incumbent upon us to sort out these factors whenever possible.

Keeping the old person central is the unifying criterion connecting the best physicians and anthropologists. This means that it is necessary to try to elicit the central concerns of the person. Most importantly, it is critical to try to understand as well as respect that the person is different from you and unique in his or her right.

A woman marveled at her mother's ability to compose a beautiful letter to a new mother despite her increasing forgetfulness. This act was a dramatic demonstration of some of the marvelous capacity that the brain has to preserve itself, adjust and compensate for the injury and insult of disease, and maximize the possibilities of what remains.

It would do this fine woman a disservice to see her in terms of her clinical diagnoses: the well-nourished middle-class white woman of eighty-nine, with moderate dementia, and a history of diabetes and anxiety. In describing the presence of disease these labels make her unique history and personality fade from view. The labels place her in categories with others similarly labeled, each of them likewise stripped of their quirky and wonderful idiosyncrasies, their individualities disguised. The labels do not reveal her preferences, her passions, or what separates her from other old white women with dementia, heart disease, diabetes, and anxiety.

The best physician understands that she occupies an artificially derived medical category that aids certain medical decision-making. The best physician understands that knowledge of this category provides merely the scantiest baseline information needed to be effective. Knowing who this particular woman is, including her preferences, passions, and uniquenesses, will help the physician provide excellent care for her.

Geriatric assessment of older patients is only lately beginning to incorporate something of the patient's point of view in the process. Too often the old person's views are left out of these exercises undertaken for the purpose of assessing the deficits and strengths of the person.

> Too often assessment measures fail to do justice to the person who is assessed ... [I]t reflects more on measurement design and training and illustrates our own values about the role of the client in the assessment process. For example, even experienced practitioners sometimes fail to consider the client as an important source of information, instead relying on caregivers or their own judgment (Geron 1997:10).

What an oversight!

Patrick Mullen described the lives of nine elderly individuals in southern Ohio, each of whom had positive attitudes about their lives despite various serious problems (1992). Mullen attributed some of their positive attitudes to the fact that these individuals were actively passing on folk traditions of various kinds. It is also likely that they represent countless others—perhaps the vast majority, or perhaps all of us—who in our own ways, pass on our own private traditions, and attempt to muster whatever strengths we have to go on. Others have written eloquent accounts of ordinary and extraordinary old people telling about their lives (e.g., Myerhoff 1979, Blythe 1979, Kaufman 1986), and these stories are moving. These books chronicle the lives of old people in which the struggles, the difficulties, the pleasures, the defeats, as well as the deficits are selected and woven by the old person into a narrative that helps filter and shape the person's life into a coherent meaning. This is a process that is creative and inherently regenerative.

There is a disconnect between what we see and understand as outsiders and what the internal perspective may be. The demented woman in the nursing home who rarely responds and offers little clue of her experience looks to us, as interested outsiders, as the product of severe brain dysfunction. There is little more that we can see. The strokes and senile plaques have caused damage to her neurons and synapses, and effective connections between them are diminished. But that tells us nothing of the person's internal experience. What does she see? How does she feel? What does she make of us gazing at her? How does she understand herself? How does she value her life? What does it feel like to be her?

Cotrell and Schulz have noted how the patient is often relegated to the status of object rather than a legitimate contributor to the research process. They wrote, "The inherent message is that individuals with dementia are important actors responding and adapting to the disease, rather than passive individuals who are succumbing to deficits (1993:206). Lyman (1993) has stressed the negative effects that come as byproducts to the assessment and treatment of those with dementia, largely because social factors are so often eliminated.

Assessment is not neutral, language can hide as well as reveal, medical labels can obscure as well as enlighten, and the elderly person's perspective is critical. Furthermore, the person is often part of a family that is in turn embedded within a community, an ethnic, religious, racial group that helps to define him or her.

Like the best physicians have known for ages: it is important to understand not the disease the person has, but the person who has the disease. Keep the person central.

Notes

1. Of course, it is also true that in many cultures throughout the world, fear, secrecy, and a variety of taboos surround menstruation, pregnancy, and childbirth. One might say that these states are "pathologized."
2. See Zeserson (2001), however, for some of the recent changes in Japan with the greater use of hormone replacement therapy.
3. However, Hochschild emphasizes that many old people are isolated and that poverty reinforces their isolation. She considered Merrill Court, the place she studied, as possibly an exception, "essentially an adjustment to bad social conditions" (1973:139).
4. Murphy also points out the connection with classic rites of passage in which an individual moves from one status to another and in so doing passes through an in-between, liminal phase. See also the classic works of van Gennep (1960), Victor Turner (1967), and Mary Douglas (1966). I have discussed the liminal status of nursing home residents specifically, as well (Shield 1988).

5. Title I of the 1965 Older Americans Act lists ten goals: 1) An adequate income in retirement, 2) the best possible physical and mental health, 3) suitable housing, 4) full restorative services for those who need institutional care, 5) employment without age discrimination, 6) retirement in health, honor, and dignity, 7) participation is civic, cultural, and recreational activities, 8) efficient community services, which provide social assistance in a coordinated manner and which are readily available when needed, 9) immediate benefit from research, and 10) free exercise of individual initiative in planning and managing one's own life (as listed by Carroll Estes 1979:33).

Commentary
The Problem of Elder Abuse
(SMA)

Is it possible, is it even conceivable, that a frail elderly person might be abused by a close relative in this century and age? Yet it was not long ago that society regarded child abuse as an utterly unlikely event. And, as with child abuse, elder abuse does not necessarily leave visible bruises or fractured bones; it might be as slight as a brusque impatience or the treating of grandma, who has a memory problem, as though she were an infant rather than a person deserving of patience and compassion.

The abuse, the withholding of respect, dignity, and care that should have been accorded to parents (and, by inference, to all elderly persons) may take many forms, ranging from momentary indifference, to neglect, to exploitation or, at its worst, even physical abuse and abandonment. Until recently, this shameful act had no name; but in its most flagrant form, we now call it "elder abuse," a phrase whispered rather than shouted since its very existence bespeaks of a profound, moral lapse in interpersonal responsibility.

How common is elder abuse? It is a crime that is neither readily nor easily documented; nor is it a subject that arises spontaneously or willingly in conversations at social gatherings. Some will even deny its existence, saying that elder abuse is unknown in their neighborhood while admitting, begrudgingly, that it may possibly be found in other communities. Police and social scientists, on the other hand, will readily verify its existence in all cultures and all ethnic groups.

According to available statistics, which probably represent a substantial under-reporting, about one person in ten older than sixty-five years is annually the victim of some significant form of elder abuse. Translating this to the Rhode Island community, for example, it would mean, each year, that there are about 7,500 instances of reportable elder abuse in the Ocean State; and in about 3,000 of these instances, the abuse is sufficiently grave to warrant medical intervention or emergency room visit. Extrapolating to the U.S. at large, elder abuse can be seen to be an important social problem of significant dimension.

Most instances of elder abuse, perhaps the great majority, go unreported by the victim for many compelling reasons: fear of not being believed, fear of being "put away," being institutionalized, fear of retaliation by the abuser, fear of being ostracized by the remaining members of the family. Furthermore, many elderly, particularly those who are confused, do not understand either the dynamics or the extent to which they are abused, and they may therefore avoid asking for help because they conclude that they are in some obscure way at blame and hence deserving of abuse.

Elder abuse did not suddenly start when the amendments to the Older Americans Act were approved by Congress, in 1987. It has been part of communal life for millennia; and it must have been a visible element in the lives of ancient communities for its prohibition to have been cited repeatedly in the Bible. Elder abuse may be personal: carried out by someone known to the elder person, usually a close relative. Or it may be institutional: a nursing home perhaps, with the fiduciary responsibility for the continuing care of the elder person. Or, uncommonly, it may be a pathological self-neglect, the behavior or an elderly person indifferent to his or her personal welfare of safety.

In the nursing home setting, abuse of the elderly seems particularly heinous—if only because the old people who are housed there are so severely impaired. In fact, the extreme dependency is part of the reason for the abuse. Fear of retaliation by those living there is often a widespread concern within nursing homes. Insufficient

> staffing, difficult daily routines, patients who are aggressive, and
> the widespread incidence of dementia, all contribute to the prob-
> lem. Patients who forget the abuse or are incapable of telling about
> it also contribute to the magnitude of the situation. Education,
> better training, enhanced teamwork and quality measures, and
> improved screening of employees help. Increased federal and state
> funds for nursing homes would go a long way as well. [RRS]

Elder abuse may assume many legal forms.

1. Physical Abuse—defined as the use of physical force
   causing bodily injury, physical pain or actions leading
   to impairment of function. This may include acts of
   violence (pushing, beating, shaking, slapping), but
   physical abuse also includes the inappropriate use of
   physical restraints or medications (particularly
   sedative agents.)
2. Sexual abuse—defined as nonconsensual sexual
   contact of any kind with an elderly individual. This
   category includes unwanted touching.
3. Emotional abuse—through verbal or non-verbal
   means, the infliction of distress, anxiety, anguish, pain
   or fear upon an elderly person. This form of abuse,
   perhaps the most commonly practiced type of abuse
   and certainly the most difficult to verify, includes
   intimidation, humiliation, harassment, infantilization
   or isolating the elderly person; and in its most subtle
   form, treating the vulnerable elderly as though they
   were incapable of intelligent conversation. They have
   thus been rendered invisible in the eyes of the abuser.
4. Neglect—defined as the failure to fulfill a person's (or
   an institution's) fiduciary responsibility for the care
   and welfare of an elderly person. Specifically, it
   includes neglect of such essentials as water, food,
   clothing, shelter, adequate hygiene, prescribed
   medications, and such other measures as are needed
   for the physical safety of the elder person.
5. Financial exploitation—defined as the illegal use of an
   elder's financial resources, property or other tangible

assets. The forging of an elder's signature is considered a part of this category.

6. Abandonment—defined as the willful desertion of an elderly individual by a person or institution bearing the continuing responsibility for that elderly person.

Who are the abusers? The overwhelming majority are family members (spouse, child, etc.) serving as the designated caregivers.

Physicians may sometimes be the first to suspect the existence of elder abuse when encountering an elderly patient in the home with unexplained cachexia, poor personal hygiene, excessive anxieties, and evidence of bruises.

Institutional abuse is to be considered when such complications as repeated bed sores are encountered. In 2001, newspaper headlines detailed the incidence of abuse rising in nursing homes. The story went on the give details of a congressional investigation that noted that nearly a third of all registered nursing homes, some 5,283 of a national total of about 17,000, had been cited for elder-abuse violations in the past two years.

A curtain of societal shame hides the full measure of elder abuse. And so those elderly incapable of maintaining an independent existence or even of defending themselves continue to be vulnerable to abuse. The words of a sacred decalogue, visibly enshrined on countless walls, go unheeded: "Honor thy father and thy mother" (Exodus 20:12).

Chapter 5

(Negative) Associations to Growing Old
The Elderly Portrayed in Words
(SMA)

"The years of our lives," observed the psalmist, "are three score years and ten ... So teach us to number our years that we may get a heart of wisdom." The biblical words of three score and ten have since resonated in many places; even Lincoln's Gettysburg "four score and seven" is a conscious acknowledgement of this phrase.

In centuries past, few had attained the hallowed goal of seventy years, but not for want of trying nor lack of desire to achieve that elusive objective. Indeed, in the minds of many, to reach this scriptural boundary required a seldom bestowed, but unique endowment of enduring genes, an abundance of wit and, above all, a special grace.

In seventeenth century London, for example, fewer than 2 percent of its citizens entered the rarefied realm of the senior years. By 1990, however, over 72 percent of Americans lived up to and often well beyond the age of seventy years. What had once been an uncommon achievement is now commonplace; where formerly society might have been blessed with an isolated tribal elder, we are now confronted with a substantial political force, a legion of grey panthers, and battalions of retirees populating newly created villages in the southern tier of states. But the elderly person who had once been a venerated patriarch is now disparaged by a younger generation as an exploiter of society's shrinking social security and healthcare resources and an economic burden. Familiarity has bred contempt.

Accompanying the obvious shift in the nation's demographic profile, with more than 12 percent of the population now over seventy years of age, is a disquieting increase in the resentment directed to those fortunate enough to reach these senior decades. Once there were words such as elder, wise man, sachem, patriarch and archivist of tribal legend; now there are such nasty terms as coot, geezer, and crock. And older women who were once revered as tribal mothers, oracles capable of discerning the future and purveyors of curative herbs, are now referred to as witches, hags, and bag ladies.

> *Sorry, but here's the pesky anthropologist interrupting: I worry that you are succumbing to the myth of a glorified past in which the rare elder was revered, trusted, feared, and honored. Do you remember the Grimm's fairy tales where the old women and witches are horrible in their magical abilities? These tales enshrine old European ambivalence about the power that old women often have if they have been lucky enough to survive their child-bearing and child-rearing years. [RRS]*

> *I do not think that the seventeenth century European citizenry were more caring of their elders. I do believe that there were so few elders in those years that the remaining population could be both respectful and magnanimous to them. [SMA]*

> *I think so too. Often, dominant populations tolerate (or are magnanimous towards) people "different" than themselves when the numbers are low. When the numbers go higher, tolerance tends to recede. Do people feel threatened by the proximity of these "others"? When the numbers increase, so do comments about "greedy geezers," old "fogey" drivers, and the like. [RRS]*

> *It is absolutely true that "old fogey drivers" is a terribly disparaging phrase. But it is also true that the highest rates of fatal automobile accidents, per mile driven, are generated by women drivers older*

than seventy-five years of age. These were the findings of a careful retrospective survey of all vehicular accidents in Rhode Island for the years 1977 through 1982 (Nakabayashi et al. 1984). [SMA]

At best, current society has viewed its elderly men and women with mixed feelings, sometimes as wise persons deserving of help, and sometimes as useless, melancholic burdens draining the nation's modest resources. The elderly are just not celebrated the way they had been in the distant past. In recent centuries more festivity accompanies the birth of an infant than when an adult enters the senior decades.

But! It depends on where in the world—and when! It seems that modernization has disrupted patterns of prestige, but not always. In Japan traditional patterns of respect for the elderly, influenced by the Buddhist notion that the elderly are linked to the ancestors and ancient traditions of filial devotion, have been complicated and modified with modernization and the press of greater numbers of elderly that rival those in the U.S. Old age in Japan has traditionally been celebrated at entrance into retirement (inkyo) (Sokolovsky 1997:271), as well as at ritualized birthday occasions, at the sixtieth year, the seventieth year (koki, or "rare old age"), seventy-seventh year (called kiju, or "pleasure age"), the eighty-eighth year (called bei ju or "rice age"), and the ninety-ninth year (haku ju or "purity year") (Palmore and Maeda 1985). But, it's true: even in societies like Japan, where respect for the elderly is ingrained, old patterns have been changing, and ambivalence about age—possibly not new—is clear. [RRS]

Human nature, in general, seems to encourage celebrations at the onset of great voyages but allows only passing acknowledgement of ships that have successfully completed lengthy and perilous journeys. And in Western culture, more reverence is devoted to sunrises than to sunsets.

Abusive Portrayals of the Elderly

The names that are employed in depicting the elderly may range from tender and respectful to abusive and demeaning. The background of some of the more degrading of these names for the aged are worth reviewing.

Hag:

Perhaps derived from an old German word, *Hexe,* meaning witch. Others believe that it stems from the Greek word, *hagia,* meaning holy or saintly (as in hagiography) but by the sixteenth century (and by then spelled "hegge") it signified an aging, ugly, and repulsive female. A 1552 text states: "Hegges or nyght furyes, or wytches like unto old women which do sucke the bloude in the nyght." By some curious alchemy, the hag has been transformed from a wise, elderly matriarch to a dreaded creature of the night.

> *I think the important thing here is that she is powerful. As Brown (1985: 2-3) notes, cross-cultural studies of older women in nonindustrial societies show that for the most part their status improved because of three changes: 1) often restrictions placed on them when they were younger no longer apply; 2) they have authority over younger family members; and 3) they are sometimes elevated to special status. It makes sense to think that when women become more powerful, they are disliked, feared, and shunned—considered witches or hags—as a result.*
>
> *Pitt-Rivers described cultural notions about strong old women in Andalusia, Spain (1977, as noted by Foner 1984b). As old women assumed some of the dominant male roles when their usually older husbands died, younger men chafed at the greater control these women exercised over them. Witchcraft beliefs about older men, as among the Lugbara of Uganda or the Tiv of Nigeria also reveal fear and ambivalence about the old men's authority (see Middleton 1963, Bohannan 1965, Foner 1984b:160-166) [RRS]*

Coot:

The word, colloquially, depicts a querulous, crotchety male, both ancient and bitter of tongue. Formally, however, the word denoted a web-footed, aquatic diving bird (locally *Fulica americana)* with a bill that extends upwards between its eyes to cover its anterior cranium. Thus, from a distance, the bird appears to be bald. The coot, at one time or another, has therefore represented such attributes as baldness, gracelessness, foolishness, and longevity; and, of course, these qualities collectively may define an elderly male (e.g., that old coot.) Other birds also provide disparaging metaphors for the elderly (e.g., old buzzard, old crow).

> *Jenike (1997) tells us that the derogatory term, "baba," means old bag in Japanese. [RRS]*

Crone:

This term describes an elderly, withered woman and may be an etymological descendant of an older Anglo-Saxon term, *croonie,* meaning an old, edentulous ewe. The crone, in some earlier cultures, had been depicted as both the giver and taker of life: as the guardian of medicinal secrets and the art of midwifery, but also as the embodiment of witchcraft and decay.

> *I find it interesting that some activist older women have decided to call themselves "crones" as a deliberate way to expropriate the negative term and make it positively their own. This is a not unfamiliar linguistic strategy that stigmatized groups sometimes make, to wit, African-Americans triumphantly calling themselves "nigger" (to each other) or homosexuals using "queer" approvingly for themselves. To me this means that "crones" aren't sitting back and feeling victimized any more. [RRS]*

Crock:

A common word that is applied insensitively to the cantankerous, senile patient with multiple, but intellectually unchallenging, medical problems few of which are amenable to therapy. The symbol of the fragile crock, or pitcher, to represent the frail, aging person is found in many Western cultures and represents something of no value, something to be discarded. In Ireland, a crock is a derisive word for a person who fancies herself to be ailing or in delicate health. A crock also describes a worthless, infirm horse or a battered, old sea-going freighter.

Father Time:

This is a confusing pastiche of many intertwining myths that incorporate such symbols of impending death as the hour-glass, the enveloping cloak and the scythe. In medieval art, this cloaked figure was frequently associated with an *ourobos* (a winged snake forming a complete circle as it devours its tail), which is a wheel-like symbol representing the interconnectedness of birth, death, and the cycle of life. The grim reaper image can be traced to Chronos, oldest of the Greek gods and the father of Zeus. Saturn, the mythic equivalent of Chronos in the Roman pantheon, is also depicted as a bringer of death. Saturn, depicted astrologically as remote, balefully gloomy and advanced in years, is the name that the Romans gave to the most distant of the visible planets. Saturn is also a synonym for lead, a metal that is weak, sluggish, without resiliency and potentially poisonous.

There are, as well, inanimate objects that symbolize the finiteness of life. In Ecclesiastes the metaphors for advanced age and impending death include the silver cord snapped, the golden bowl smashed, the pitcher shattered, and the wheel broken at the well. In societies that perceive life and death as dynamic elements of a recurring continuum, the wheel is a frequent symbol. The Buddhist wheel of life, for example, with its twelve zodiacal divisions, carries the dual message of involution and death as well as rebirth and maturation.

Yet other common emblems of the dwindling years of life include hourglasses and candles. But, in contrast to derogatory words such as hag or crone, none of these ancient metaphors manage to convey the sense of the malevolent, shriveled soul who exercises some threat to the young and vigorous. Nor do they evoke the sense of a useless, forsaken life, feelings that are associated with such terms as crock or coot.

Geezer:

A word that defines a dull-witted, eccentric, elderly person, usually a male. The word is a dialect variant of an Old English word, *guiser,* meaning a mummer (a person wearing a disguise. Presumably the withered faces of the very elderly were construed as masks.)

> *Jijī means geezer in Japanese, according to Jenike (1997:225), and is one of several terms and attitudes that defy the traditional Japanese notion that reverence for the elderly is desired and expected. [RRS]*

In the private vocabulary of physicians in training, there have arisen some new—and even less ennobling—descriptions of the elderly and the institutions where they are confined.

Gomer:

This is a word popularized in a fairly recent work of fiction (*The House of God* by S. Shem.)

> *See chapter 4 "Is Aging a Problem?" in which I also discuss this word. [RRS]*

Linguists might seek out earlier roots and perhaps identify a Teutonic word, *gome*, meaning old man which is probably cognate with the Latin, *homo*. And scripturalists will remember that Gomer was the eldest son of Japheth, the grandson of Noah and the mythic progenitor of the Celtic people. But the origin of the word, gomer, is far less scholarly. It represents an acronym of the phrase "Get Out of My Emergency Room!" and was probably coined by some hassled emergency-room house-officer who desperately needed a euphemism to hide his frustration and fury when confronted with yet another unresolvable admission to the emergency room at 3 AM.

Lolinad:

This is another recent addition to the unsavory roster of synonyms for the aged, and particularly those elderly women brought to the emergency room, late at night, with a lengthy roster of chronic ailments made worse by a failing memory. Lolinad is an acronym for the frequent clinical observation: "Little Old Lady in No Acute Distress."

Train Wreck:

This whispered phrase is commonly applied to the elderly, demented patient with multiple organ failures who is, in the frazzled mind of the emergency room physician, an island of bare survival surrounded by encroaching mortality.

Inpatient units caring for incommunicative, vegetative, and elderly patients are sometimes scornfully called cabbage patches (cabbage or squash are commonly used synonyms for the head); and nursing homes for the incontinent and sometimes disruptive elderly are often called Haldol Manor. (Haldol is a commonly used sedative agent.)

When viewed from afar and heard in isolation, judgmental words such as gomer or cabbage patch sound insensitive and degrading. Hostile expressions such as these are most commonly voiced by young, overburdened house staff who feel helpless when confronted with human decay which they can neither slow nor reverse. Truly, it is not what they had expected the practice of medicine to be. And the many chronically ill elderly, in their inner thoughts, seem to be abusing the patience of both God and medicine. The hostile thoughts are those of youthful physicians who have not yet learned that medicine, at best, is a holding action delaying an ultimate inevitability. Nor have they begun yet to seek out the aliveness in those elderly with countless impairments. These disabled elderly carry a dual burden: their sickness as well as the disapproval of their younger caretakers. Old people, observed Goethe, forfeit one of the great human rights. No longer are they judged solely by their peers.

> *This poignant passage reminds me how just plain "foreign" the elderly seem to those who are younger. It is strange that when we are young, we feel no connection to those who are old in the sense that we do not see ourselves in their oldness. We can not imagine being old. I remember marveling at the folds of skin in my mother's elbow when I was a child. My elbow didn't have those! Playing with those elbow folds did not teach me that I would one day have them too; only as a person who possesses them now do I recall them as a child. Not only are young physicians surprised to be caring for many old people, they cannot imagine themselves being these old people one day. This astonishing ability to deny ourselves as potentially old is widespread, perhaps universal.*
>
> *Geriatrics as a specialty has been declining for years. Other physicians involved in the training of physicians lament how difficult it is to persuade young MDs to enter geriatrics because it is seen as "depressing" and not well-paid. What a sad commentary, considering the demographics. [RRS]*

Adults, Adultery and Adulteration

And even the word "adult," an allegedly neutral term to define these senior years, seems to have gradually diminished in stature. In the past, the word adult seemed to symbolize those who were no longer dependent children, grown-ups who were now responsible for raising families of their own, voting, taking out mortgages and paying taxes in a responsible manner. To proclaim one's adulthood had been a way of affirming one's visible, accountable role in society.

A small part of this erosion in the dignity of the word, "adult," may be blamed upon the abundant numbers of risqué motion pictures described, with a smirk, as adult. Indeed, "adult entertainment" is now an unambiguous euphemism for anything unabashedly pornographic, particularly motion pictures. Within the lifetimes of most elderly Americans, films have progressed from silents to talkies to unspeakables.

The word "adulterate," meaning to corrupt or make impure by dilution or admixture, helped materially in giving adulthood a very bad name. Did not adulteration imply that growing up in some manner diluted the quality of life? Was adulthood, then, nothing more than an inevitable subverting process where, with the passage of time, the pristine domain of guileless innocence had been progressively contaminated?

> *In Western, Christian society, especially, I think so too. Even with original sin, isn't a baby considered an innocent* tabula rasa *who becomes tainted and scarred with experience as life is lived? Even the word "experienced," especially to teenagers, connotes the prurient meaning of sexual, i.e., "dirty," bad experience. [RRS]*

Things get worse. Society must also confront the word "adultery," a word that has slithered away from the language of the divorce courts and now brazenly appears in family newspapers and daytime television drama. (Byron, no stranger to this act, flippantly stated that "adult'ry is more common where the climate's sultry.")

Might not a child reasonably inquire: "Is adultery something that all adults are expected to do?" There is the story of another child, equally innocent, inquiring of his father: "What's the difference, Dad, between adultery and fornication?" And the father's candid response: "I've tried both, son, and I don't see any difference."

For those who still cherish adulthood as a desirable station in life, the dictionaries provide firm assurance that neither adulteration nor adultery bear any etymological relationship to adulthood. The word "adult," stems from the Latin, *adultus,* meaning grown up and is the past participle of *adolescere,* to grow up (from which is derived the word "adolescent.") Adultery and adulteration, on the other hand, derive from the Latin *ad-alterare,* meaning to change, to modify, to alter, sometimes to defile, and by inference, then, to corrupt. Still another word "adulate," meaning to flatter or to fawn upon, also sounds disturbingly like adult. Fortunately it, too, is unrelated etymologically to adulthood; "adulate" is derived from a Latin word, *adulatus,* meaning to wag the tail.

More than ever before in human history, adults have now expanded the years of their lives into the senior decades. This has in part taken place thanks to the therapeutic advances of modern medicine and the educational efforts of public health agencies. The dramatic increase in the number of living elderly, unfortunately, has been accompanied by a parallel devaluation in the societal merit of these seniors. This depreciation of the elderly, the chronologically challenged of the twenty-first century, has been wrought principally by a generation which, in its youth, had never trusted anyone older than thirty years.

> *I don't know that I'd go so far as this—actually, I know I wouldn't. Each society has to be viewed on its own terms and with specificity. Anthropological example shows some of the complexity of aging.*
>
> *To cite just one, Jenike (1997) described the complexity of filial obligation to parents that continues to endure in Japan. An old folk tale in Japan, Obasuteyama ("Throw Out Granny Mountain") describes the abandonment and death of elderly parents on a mountaintop. Despite tales such as this and disparaging slang and popular cartoons against the elderly—revealing ambivalence at the least—the vast majority of daughters and daughters-in-law (in contrast to the sons) continue to take care of their old mothers at home. [RRS]*

The current generation of active adults now grimly contemplates its own entrance into the retirement years confronting such new and politically charged problems as the possible abridgement of its social security and private sector pension funds.

It is increasingly difficult to say at what age deterioration begins to outpace maturation; or when an admired, assertive adult becomes converted to a querulous, infirm, impatient, intolerant elder. As yet, medicine has no diagnostic test to predict when, if ever, this transformation takes place. Perhaps, as Cicero had once suggested, a man will grow old in body but not in mind if, as a young man, he had absorbed something of the old and, as an old man, retained something of the young. (Cicero probably knew little of the hazards of elderliness since he had lived only through his sixty-second birthday.)

But until an objective test is devised to tell us who amongst us will grow old gracefully and who will grow old awkwardly, the criterion suggested by Ogden Nash will just have to suffice:

> Senescence begins and middle age ends,
> The day your descendants outnumber your friends (1995).

The Poetic Perception of Aging

To death and taxes one might add aging as one of the inevitable confrontations of life. Certainly as the average life span of Americans enters and frequently exceeds the ninth decade of life, more will become intimate with elderliness while fewer and fewer will escape that lamentable state that Shelley had described as:

> A heart grown cold, a head grown gray in vain,
> Nor, when the spirit's self has ceased to burn,
> With sparkless ashes load an unlamented urn. (from Adonais).

Few who live beyond the scriptural seventy years will have been left untouched by the erosions, weariness, and embarrassments of aging. And still fewer will achieve the blessedly unscathed state attained by Moses when he reached the age of one hundred twenty years. In admiration, Deuteronomy declares: "His eye did not lose its luster, nor did his natural force abate."

In more instances the transition from vigorous maturity to irreversible old age is gradual, without any clear boundary beyond which the loss of youthful vigor becomes indisputable. The old, looking back, will say that senility arrives after ten thousand small cuts rather than one bold thrust of the spear. It is therefore naïve to expect that someone awakens one morning to announce that he is irrevocably very old. It is akin to an English laborer awakening on some bright seventeenth century morning and declaring to his wife: "Bring my new shirt, my dear; today is truly special: for today we begin the Industrial Revolution."

No one would deny that there is a measurable trajectory in the decline of human faculties which accompanies increasing age; but the progressive losses involving the various organ systems are usually obscured by the inevitable daily ebbs and flows of human strengths and functions that come about by such mundane happenings as disappointments, economic changes, successes, minor physical traumas, and even upper respiratory infections. These short-term fluctuations, randomly distributed, are often of greater amplitude than the remorseless losses accompanying the aging process. As a result, the magnitude of the aging loss can only be appreciated in retrospect.

There is, though, an interval between full maturity and the decline of aging, a twilight zone, when shadows lengthen and images blur, when time is no longer limitless, when—in the words of one elder citizen—one no longer buys green bananas, and when anxious people confine their leisure reading only to summaries lest they waste their shrinking supply of hours. Somewhere between the states of vigor and crepitude, Turgenev had identified a vague, crepuscular moment, "the time of regrets that resemble hopes, of hopes that resemble regrets, when youth has passed, but old age has not arrived."

Youthful writers have little concept of that incurable disease called aging, viewing it either with bemused wonderment or insincere solicitude. Some, typically the younger ones, suggest that aging is a crowning achievement, much to be sought after and admired; others, such as Dylan Thomas, demand that the act of dying be taken as an opportunity for febrile, aggressive turmoil rather than a time of reflection, reconciliation, and departure:

Do not go gentle into that good night,
Old age should burn and rave at close of day;
Rage, rage against the dying of the light.
(Thomas, "Do Not Go Gentle into That Good Night")

Somewhat more mature writers such as Disraeli, dissatisfied with all ages of life, observed that "youth is a blunder; manhood a struggle; and old age a regret." Still others, acknowledging that some losses are indispensable to the aging process, nonetheless see it as a time when literary productivity seamlessly replaces, and compensates for, sexual vitality:

King David and King Solomon
    Led merry, merry lives,
With many, many lady friends
    And many, many wives;
But when old age crept over them –
    With many, many qualms,
King Solomon wrote the Proverbs
    And King David wrote the Psalms.
(J.B. Naylor, *Ancient Authors.)*

Some, far removed from the aged decades had intermixed adolescent humor with the realities of aging. A thirty-two-year-old bachelor mathematician, once wrote:

"You are old, Father William," the young man said,
"And your hair has become very white;
And yet you incessantly stand on your head –
Do you think, at your age, it is right?"
(L. Carroll, "You are Old, Father William.")

This inspired bit of nonsense was composed by the Oxford don, Charles L. Dodgson, better known as Lewis Carroll. His perception of the old folk seems to require that they be periodically scolded for their imprudent acts ("act your age!"), and that their hair, at least what remains of it, turns white. Whiteness, in many settings beyond hair, is a way of expressing great age. In the Shinto faith, a white gown is reserved for the mourning widow. Among Druids, white signified the rare state of senior citizenship and white robes were then restricted to their older priesthood. (In Welsh, the word *gwyn* variously means white-ness, holiness or advanced age.) Indeed, in most cultures, white, whether in hair or garments, is symbolic of great age or death. It is the color of shrouds, ghosts, and apparitions. Aztec warriors about to undergo ritual sacrifice wore white garments; and in Polynesian cultures, recent widows daubed their faces with white chalk. And while brides and young maidens entering first Communion may also wear white, it then symbolizes submission and surrender rather than youth and innocence.

Beyond the romantic perception of aging, there emerges a more grim reality. Shakespeare comments:

> And all the conduits of my blood froze up,
> Yet hath my night of life some memory,
> My wasting lamps some fading glimmer left,
> My dull deaf ears a little use to hear.
> (*Comedy of Errors*)

And beyond the struggles at the entrance to old age, Shake-speare seeks to describe the final scenes of senility as a time of multiple physiological failures:

> Last scene of all,
> That ends this strange eventful history,
> Is second childishness and mere oblivion,
> Sans teeth, sans eyes, sans taste, sans everything.
> (/*As You Like It*)

An older generation of physicians, educated when antibi-otics and psychotropic medications had not yet been devised, learned many of their skills by watching their professional elders and then taking to heart the many aphorisms that these mentors had distilled from their collective experience. One of these oft-quoted adages was *senectus ipsa morbus* (elderliness is a disease unto itself), but the saying, wisely, avoids specifying when elderliness begins, and when, or even whether, it becomes qualitatively distinguishable from senility. But yet the adage does not totally avoid reality: the conscious experience of being old, for the great majority of people, remains a painful aware-ness of how much has been lost and how little gained.

You've listed the deficits of growing old. What—if any—are the benefits of aging? [RRS]

Admittedly, the benefits are few, and in the eyes of many, non-existent. A small minority of seniors, however, do see some blessings that were not available to them before; but they agree, too, that it takes an abundant imagination, and a willing partner, to find and appreciate these benefits. Let me mention just two of these reserved solely for the very elderly:

First, there is an enlarging awareness that everything—including life itself—is finite. For an old person to finally realize that life is not endless brings a profound sense of visceral relief. (Sartre once wrote a brief play in which hell was pictured as a place where all things go on forever.) Also, there is the bizarre joy in not having to worry, manage, and plan for an endless succession of tomorrows. Furthermore, as we watch young children play in the park and know that the earth has only a limited amount of space for playing, the novel thought arises: "Should it not be their turn eventually? Should it not be inescapable that we all eventually depart so as to allow the children to grow up and have their time on the stage?"

And second, there is the maudlin thought: "My God! I've managed to complete eight decades of life and I'm still here to prattle about it. I've been witness to and participant in a depression, two wars, the turmoil of ensuring civil rights, the Cold War, countless financial retreats and advances, professional successes and failures, yet my partner and I, now weary and old in service, have survived this pilgrimage.

As children we participated in so many games such as hide-and-seek and dodge ball, which involved alternating intervals of acute peril and safety. Entering the senior decades of life is much like entering the safe interval—which is curious since these elder years are far from being safe. But nonetheless there arises a satisfying feeling of having arrived at some plateau in life where little is demanded and even less is expected; and for the brief moment, it feels safe. Elderliness is the final phase of a perilous game almost concluded; and for a short while there is a blessed intermission before the final confrontation with mortality. [SMA]

It seems to me that as time goes on, more is precious and marvelous. I never knew the incredible quality of light that sometimes comes at dusk when the sun is at a particular luminosity and special angle and magically illuminates the inside redness of tulips. I wonder: how does it do that? How come I never saw that before? What makes it so heartbreakingly beautiful? [RRS]

Stamina is certainly lost; hearing fails; a deteriorating vision becomes unreliable; and yet other organ systems function marginally. All of this is part of aging; but the word "senility," is not traditionally applied until there is added a notable loss of orientation and cognitive function. Thus, while advancement in the aging of populations correlates statistically with increased rates of senility, there are sufficient numbers of exceptions to cast doubt on the proposition that age is the sole determinant of that irreversible psychophysiologic state called senility.

Most observers have concluded that the velocity of aging differs measurably from person to person and that the rate of decline is largely an inherited trait. This is not to deny that the retreat of faculties associated with aging can certainly be accelerated by various ambient factors including malnutrition, exposure to certain toxins or radiation, infectious disorders, multiple small strokes and even psychic trauma. Thus, the number of birthdays alone remains an inaccurate criterion of whether or not a person is senile. Furthermore, care must be exercised to distinguish between the tangible pathophysiologic substrates of aging—the atrophies and abiotrophies (diseases caused by the premature death of certain brain cells)—and the *perception* of aging which is, to some measure, a cultural determinant. "I feel old," is not always equivalent to "My body gives functional and structural evidence of advanced aging."

The scriptural patriarchs, at least the postdiluvial ones, lived no longer than the allotted one hundred twenty years. The Hebrew phrase about Moses, that "his eyes were undimmed and his vigor unabated," may more literally be translated as "his secretions did not escape." This is perhaps an allusion to a generalized incontinence of fluids (tearing of the eyes, the nasal discharges, the excessive salivation, and the urinary frequencies) which are often associated with advanced aging. Deuteronomy makes little mention of the diminished affect, slowed cognition, and faltering memory that are currently considered the hallmarks of senility.

The Classical Ages of Man

The Bible offers no sharp divisions of the span of life, nor are numbers of years mentioned except to define the onset of manhood and the limits that God had ordained for the full lifespan of man. Neither do the Scriptures talk of the forces that may alter the velocity of aging—forces that would currently be referred to as risk factors. The Talmud, though, states authoritatively that he who ventures into liaisons with prostitutes will surely be cursed with precocious senility.

Long before Shakespeare's Jacques described man's arc of existence in seven ages, the Romans had already ordained the age-limits of each of six phases of life. *Pueritia* was defined as the interval between viable birth and age five. *Adolescentia* was said to be age six to eighteen years; *juventus*, those years between nineteen and twenty-five years; *majores*, the interval between twenty-six and fifty years; *senectus*, between fifty-one and sixty; and finally, *crepita aetus*, those rare ones who survived beyond the advanced age of sixty-one years. To consider age sixty-one years as the beginnings of advanced senility denies that many in this age range have continued to function actively in society. In the 1996 national elections, South Carolina re-elected its ninety-three-year-old senator despite, or because of, his advanced age. And indeed a review of Senator Thurmond's legislative actions reveals no greater evidence of senility than many of his legislative colleagues one-half his age.

> *Well, on the other hand, in early 2001, there appeared several news accounts of how feeble, both physically and cognitively, the ninety-eight-year-old Senator Thurmond seemed to be. Yet, despite numerous brief hospitalizations and rumors of his demise, he continued to persevere, showing up each and every time to cast his staunchly conservative vote and maintaining the even Republican-Democrat split in the Senate. "Continued to persevere:" meaning, with an aide on each arm, with cue cards in front of him, his every move and wish anticipated and fulfilled. The country and the world watched him with gruesome scrutiny. [RRS]*

Only the old, of course, can possibly distill the inner feelings of being old into poetry. Longfellow boasts of *Oedipus* by Sophocles and *Faust* by Goethe, all written beyond the age of eighty. Yet he knows full well that these are rare exceptions,

> ... but they show
> How far the gulf-stream of our youth may flow
>   Into the arctic regions of our lives,
> For age is opportunity no less
>   Than youth itself, though in another dress.
> (H.W. Longfellow, *Morituri Salutamus.*)

Creativity in the Elderly

Creative people, such as Sophocles and Goethe, have always been our most precious resource. They are the ones amongst us who have explained our surroundings, predicted our futures, enunciated our most authentic feelings, given us continuity and voice, and through art have provided us with rare insight. It has been the creative ones amongst us who have made our world more resonant, more colorful, more understandable.

Bean counters have stated repeatedly that artistic and scientific creativity are talents reserved largely for the gifted young. But there are those older than sixty-five years who cherish the innocent notion that they can still exercise their brains in preoccupations more innovative than jumping to conclusions or wrestling with their consciences. How true is it, then, that creativity is a blessing bestowed solely upon the young?

The yearly Nobel prizes for the various physical and biological sciences have been conferred upon people young and old; but it is indisputably true that the seminal works justifying these prizes were, almost invariably, undertaken and completed well before the age of fifty years. Both Galileo and Newton announced all of their great observations before the age of forty, although one of them lived to be tried for heresy at age sixty-nine and survived to age seventy-eight. Indeed, Galileo's laws of motion and gravity were compiled at age twenty-six. Darwin's theory of evolution was also born to a youth of twenty-six aboard the HMS

Beagle, but it required another twenty-four years of contemplation and refinement before *The Origin of Species* was finally launched. Most of the fundamental contributions to mathematics were offered by persons younger than thirty years.

> *I like this example, to be contrary: John Harrison, born in March 1693 in England, constructed a series of marine timepieces in order to solve the longitude problem of keeping accurate time at sea. He won first prize for it in 1763. Though he completed the first chronometer in 1735, he did not perfect the instrument until his fourth incarnation several decades later in collaboration with his son. Not only did he persevere to devise a creative solution to the longitude problem, he refused to give in to the political struggle that conspired to deny him the prize (see Sobel 1995) [RRS]*

Does a twenty-four-year-old scientist perhaps possess a clearer head, a more acutely conscious mind less cluttered with thoughts of mortgages and morbidities and mortality? Is a younger brain blessed with a greater synaptic plasticity? Does an older scientist accumulate so many contentious theories and false presumptions within his head that there is little space remaining for those outrageous concepts that might some day explain a profound mystery of nature?

How, truly, does creative science work? In a world of abundant scientific data, indeed awash with overlapping information, genius sometimes flourishes by willfully, selectively ignoring data. Science always begins with data, but it is not so beguiled by it that it cannot speculate beyond the raw numbers. Science, creative science, then becomes preoccupied less with facts than with relationships, less with the accumulation of knowledge and more with the extrapolations beyond the accumulated numbers. By inductive reasoning, the creative scientist seeks to illuminate underlying causalities. The intuitive scientist seeks connections between apparently unconnected events in nature under the presumption that no two events in nature are ever totally unrelated. He wants nature to be law-abiding, not capricious or compulsively randomized. He believes, with Einstein, that God will not play dice with the universe. And he therefore gropes for the basic laws that govern these relationships. His starting point, often, is an experiment seemingly gone wrong; a set of results which appears to be internally inconsistent or at variance with prior findings. And from this contradiction in data may eventually come a challenge to an erstwhile accepted axiom of science leading, possibly, to its ultimate rejection and replacement by a newer theory.

A creative theory is of a higher order of thinking than a great discovery. If a particular explorer fails to find the western shores, surely someone else will find it. A theory, on the other hand, is not something fully packaged, merely awaiting discovery. Before it can be realized, something first has to be set aside; and then a new theory, capable of predicting future findings, must be formulated from bare, seemingly unrelated, elements.

Creative scientific discoveries are, by definition, always premature; that is, they are not insights of the very next step in the sequence of scientific revelation; instead, these scientific epiphanies represent immense leaps into the unexplored. They provide us with distant lighthouses, quite discernible from our presently safe position but as yet unconnected with our present knowledge. It is for the more mundane in the scientific community to figure out the more simple, intervening steps.

These paragraphs concur with those of the historian of science, Thomas Kuhn, whose 1962 work, The Structure of Scientific Revolutions, *described the heretical quality of innovative scientific thinking that must struggle to compete with the reigning theories that hold sway in whatever period of time they are dominant. In refuting the notion that science is the tidy and objective accumulation of data and the fashioning of theories to fit the observed phenomena, Kuhn emphasized the culture of scientific inquiry. I don't think Kuhn entertained the notion that youth and impetuousness were necessary factors, but perhaps they are. What Kuhn stressed was how impervious dominant theories are to the steady accumulation of data that don't fit the ruling paradigm of thought that currently is in favor. Dominant theories that scientists of any age share are like cultural beliefs that currently seem unalterable. Maybe energy, boldness, and naïveté that sometimes attach to those who are young are also necessary to shake up whatever ruling culture of thinking is in fashion. [RRS]*

Perhaps this kind of creative science needs both genius and impetuous youth, persons young enough not to be distracted by daily realities, arthritic pains, thoughts of death or even the preciousness of interpersonal relationships. Is it possible, then, that truly creative science is little more than the workings of some post-adolescent hormones upon a substrate of genius?

But what of creativity in the arts: music, literature, and the graphic arts? In music, virtually all of the great classical and romantic works of the nineteenth century were composed by individuals younger than forty years. A major reason for this, obviously, was that so many of these creative geniuses died before age forty (Mozart, Chopin, Schubert, Schumann, Mendelssohn) and we have no access to their postmortem productivity. A handful of composers has created great works beyond the age of sixty-five (Handel, Haydn, Bruckner, Rossini, Wagner, Stravinsky) but with the exception of Verdi's late operas, no truly outstanding works can be ascribed to these later years. Perhaps the well of creativity, once exploited, is not limitless.

What about Aaron Copland (90), Pablo Picasso (92), Marc Chagall (98), de Kooning (93), Edward Hopper (85), Edvard Munch (81), Henry Moore (88), John Cage (80), Voltaire (84), Louis Armstrong (71), Somerset Maughm (91), Nabokov (78), Monet (86), or Duke Ellington (75)? Al Hirschfeld, still working at 98. Did they all peter out years before they died? [RRS]

Yes, these creative ones did survive beyond the eighth decade of life. But I wouldn't confuse longevity with continued creativity. With the exception of Picasso, few on this list, after age 70, did much more than revisit their earlier artistic efforts. [SMA]

Reinterpretation, reworking, refined understanding. I'm thinking of people who continue their work into their older years because they love it and because it remains meaningful and the deepest expression of who they are. Work in this respect is inherently creative even if the works produced are not as "stellar" as those produced earlier. Maybe in many of these cases work is vital for keeping the older person alive and fulfilled. But maybe too, the older worker is genuinely better at what he or she does, having gained important perspective and skill through the years; they understand the essence. The old professors who keep reading, teaching, and writing: unless they are languishing in their tenured sinecures, we have a lot to learn from them still, and their standards can become more exacting rather than less with time. Artur Rubinstein, Pablo Casals and Vladimir Horowitz' performances were legendary in their last years. Hirschfeld's carica-

tures are considered much better now than they were when he was younger. These individuals seem to achieve a greater purity of tone, understanding of the music, elegance of line, or the other media in which they work. [RRS]

In the sphere of great literature, there have been truly great works assembled beyond the age of sixty-five but in quantity, at least, meager when compared with the output from the younger decades. Some writers have continued to be productive beyond age sixty-five: Clemens, Longfellow, Tennyson, Goethe, Tolstoi, Shaw, Eliot. But other writers became acutely aware of their diminishing creativity. Emerson at age sixty-five declared: "It is time to be old. The god of bounds who sets to seas a shore, came to me in his fatal rounds and said: no more!" And Melville, in a letter to Hawthorne, acknowledged that his output was nearing exhaustion. He wrote: "But I feel that I am now come to the innermost leaf of the bulb, and shortly the flower must fall to the mould."

Keats, barely twenty-one years of age, believed that creativity existed in all living creatures but that it emerged only when people were open to its presence within themselves. "The genius of poetry must work out its own salvation in a man; it cannot be matured by law and precept, but by sensation and watchfulness in itself. That which is creative must create itself."

One pays a price for the privilege of growing older. The cumulative pressures of daily responsibilities as well as the accretion of human rust inevitably add up to impediments that discourage all but the most resolute. A seeking after peace and an acceptance of the realities of aging may seem, to the older person, more laudable than the excitement of discovery or the thrill of creativity. The desire, the will to be creative may therefore retreat with time as a more pervasive fatigue takes hold. Society has not as yet seen fit to protect those older adults who still harbor the seeds of inner genius. But when children have declared their independence, when the mortgage is fully paid and the visit to one's physician completed, there is now time to reflect soberly on the fact that the entire universe, with one insignificant exception, is composed of others. And being but one in a countless multitude of others demands both a humility and a need to identify oneself. Somewhere, then, beyond this growing sense of humility, there arises the voiceless cry: I can still contribute, in small measure, to the joy and majesty of life; I can, like Grandma Moses, still paint wondrous scenes.

George Herbert, who died in his thirty-ninth year of life, wrote:

> And now in age I bud again,
> After so many deaths I live and write;
> I once again smell the dew and the rain,
> It cannot be that I am he
> Upon whom the tempests fell all night.
> (G. Herbert, "The Flower.")

Commentary
Anthropological Musings on Dependency
(RRS)

If we do not know what we are going to be, we cannot know what we are: let us recognize ourselves in this old man or that old woman. It must be done if we are to take upon ourselves the entirety of our human state.—Simone de Beauvoir, The Coming of Age.

To the long list of insults attached to the elderly that SMA catalogued in this chapter must be added the attribution of dependency and childlike status. Old people are like children, it is commonly noted, in American nursing homes and other places where elderly congregate or are housed. What crime did old people do to deserve this demotion, this utter reduction of their long lives to such a dubious equation?

Dependency is not necessarily loaded with shame and other negative characteristics everywhere however, although ambivalence seems to be present. Hashimoto (1996) has argued that dependency within the family is still considered legitimate by Japanese, even with modernizing trends that seem to erode this value. Jenike described how Japanese daughters and daughters-in-law continue to feel that it is "natural" to take care of their aging parents at home, though they are not sure how it will be for them (1997). And Lamb (2000) demonstrated how people in West Bengal felt that the obligations between par-

ents and children are reciprocal and last throughout their lifetimes. Older family members can be demanding and insistent
and service is required.

Even where shame may not be evident, however, ambivalence is present in the power relationship of dependency, nonetheless. For example, Lamb writes,

> Providing *sevā* [service] is ironically also a form of power. At the
> same time that *sevā* overtly signifies the superiority of the elder
> being served, more covertly it reveals the elder's declining domes-
> tic power and bodily strength. Many of the acts that constitute
> *sevā* embody this double meaning. As a new, young daughter-in-
> law submissively plucks the gray hairs from her mother-in-law's
> head, she displays at the same time the weakening and aging of
> her mother-in-law's body ... The act of cleaning up an elder's
> urine and excrement marks a junior's hierarchically inferior posi-
> tion, as someone who will accept even the impure (*aśuddha*) feces
> of a superior; but it points sharply as well to the elder's inconti-
> nence, loss of control over even basic bodily functions, and infan-
> tility ... As *sevā* demonstrates the aged moving "up" in a
> hierarchy of older and superior over younger and inferior, it is
> also part of their movement "out" to the peripheries of household
> life, where domestic power and bodily strength have diminished
> (2000:62).

Japanese have also expressed strong feelings against prolonged
chronic illnesses and dependency, and often wish for an abrupt
death (see Plath 1987, for example).

The old person is no longer productive, does not earn a
wage, has reduced power, and instead receives Social Security or
a pension. The asymmetrical balance between the caregiver and
the care-receiver places the dependent person into the debt of
the person providing assistance. The payment for the dependency is acquiescence and gratitude (Dowd 1975). The dependent person knows that assistance can be withheld, grudgingly
given, carelessly delayed, and inadequately performed.

In typical U.S. nursing homes residents are often cajoled,
consoled, and irritatedly made to wait with generic sugary and
blandly affectionate diminutives of all sorts. "Just a minute,
dearie," a certified nursing assistant may intone. "You're not
the only one here, you know," she adds, pretending tolerance of

his passive and needy presence. "Aren't they sweet?" I heard a nurse say about a husband and wife in their nineties who were holding hands. Sweetie, honey, darling—nice terms when they're not condescending put-downs and wait-some-mores—are rotely trotted out for old people and children. Would these terms be routinely used for middle-aged adults? One risks the withering look.

The association between old age and childhood is a common one in the U.S. and Western societies and reveals the liminality of the dependency of these ages. Though age is a continuum, there is a tendency to polarize the extremes and think of comparisons between the beginnings and the ends of the life span. Conglomerate healthcare systems, touting their supposedly all-inclusive care, put up huge billboards of a baby holding the hand of an old person. We get the message: from beginning to end, good care—but also, babies and old people are supposed to go together somehow—dependent, compliant, grateful for the care received.

The status of adulthood, meanwhile, plumply and primly situated between the young and the old, is understood as fully independent, in charge, strong, vertical, active, and powerful. Adults, oblivious of their imminent passage into old age, can barely tolerate the insecurities, vulnerabilities, and dependencies of those already there. Adults believe their physical and cognitive powers are innate to them—their privilege and their right, an earned status—and they do not understand how temporal they are.

What seems to be the most salient linkage between children and old people is dependency. In American society dependency carries associations of shame. Children are forgiven because they are striving for adulthood; their dependencies, the fact that their bodies must be attended to by beneficent others, is a temporary state. They press for adulthood and independence. "I can do it, Mommy!" is the cry of autonomy that parents happily applaud and encourage while they continue to provide the safety net until the child is safely launched.

Another crucial link between children and old people is that neither is considered productive in an economic sense, and cross-culturally, too—demonstrated in examples throughout this book—when older members of many societies no longer control information or resources considered valuable to the others, they become less useful and integral. The fact that the elderly generally leave the work force in the U.S. and Europe may have more to do with negative imagery and terminology surrounding them than the so-called youth cult that seems to glorify those who are young (Hareven 1995).

The cultural position occupied by children is similar to those who are temporarily sick. The sick role gives the ill person a certain license and privilege for a specified amount of time. They can be safely indulged. But when the acutely sick pass into the domain of the chronically ill, a change of status descends on him or her. No longer is the person the deserving recipient of cheerful get-well cards, bouquets of flowers, and animated friendly visits from caring others. Chronicity ushers in a liminal, neither-here-nor-there state of timeless uncertainty with which people are generally uncomfortable. The lack of a specific endpoint in sight is troubling. Are you sick or are you well? Decide, so the rest of us can figure out how to act towards you!

Old age is tainted by its nearness to death and is, in its way, a drawn-out time of liminality between adulthood and death. Common dependencies of old age are reminders of childhood, but without the sweet associations of coos and gurgles and minus the indulgent loving assurances that accompany the holding, feeding, bathing, carrying, and soothing of children. These dependencies are similarly physical—and except in the miraculous domain of physical therapy for acute disease and injuries in which a person often progresses and returns to health and greater independence—in this period of life, they are demeaning.

Lack of control underlies much of the (culturally perceived) shameful moral taint that is attached to adult dependencies. Much of this lack of control involves bodily functions that are considered dirty and polluting (also see Featherstone and Wernick 1995). It is as though the old and young, by exhibiting their lack of control over bodily functions, are highlighting their physically bounded selves, their animality. Adults are supposedly in control of their bodies; adults can use their bodies for pleasure and prowess, and their bodies can be transcended in service of the cognitive. The elderly in many societies who are respected for their knowledge and skills are actually considered more "cultured"—that is, further away from their unpredictable and dangerous animal "natures"—and contrast both with adults and children who know less than they (Amoss and Harrell 1981:19). But when old bodies need attention and cannot be controlled by their old owners, their cultured selves are submerged and dominated by the needs of their physical bodies. It is as though what is human and uniquely individual is sacrificed. Perhaps the lowly status of nursing home nursing assistants in the U.S. can be accounted for by the fact that they are "polluted" by their association with the contaminating substances of urine and feces of the old people in their charge, as Jervis has suggested (2001).

Though the dependent person generally has little recourse, some use various strategies of resistance to protest and to exert control. Behaviors that caregivers call disruptive or disagreeable earn an old person names like "cantankerous" or "curmudgeon." Urinating at particularly inconvenient times can be a strategy against the nursing home staff, Vesperi (1987) maintained. Hockey and James described ways nursing home residents upset routines (like wanting to go to the bathroom just as a meal is announced) to exercise the power of their dependency. "Elderly people, being treated by adults as children, thus empower themselves in a child-like manner in their repetition of the process of infantilization" (1993:175). Or they talk about death as a way to upset the staff, "thus subverting the very process which infantilization is trying to control" (1993:182).

In the U.S. old age dependency seems to carry the moral dimension of shame, but shame is not a necessary cultural association. Posited against this idea is one of old people who have transcended material and physical connections. They are considered free of many of the burdens that weigh on adults and keep them grounded, working, and consumed by everyday concerns. In some cultures they no longer have to observe certain food taboos or conform to rigid behaviors expected of younger people. Along with, or instead of the negative associations often attached to aging, are the more positive ideas that celebrate wisdom, knowledge, and esteemed status.

The "wise old man" is one image that lives alongside the negative ideas in many cultures, particularly in Asia. Maturity through aging is the promise in Japan. Though this concept has changed since the end of World War II, the idea of the old person's wisdom and mental and spiritual maturity is a deep part of the Japanese tradition that endures in their notion of paternalism (Wada 1995). G. Stanley Hall noted that, "there is a certain maturity of judgement about men, things, causes and life generally, that nothing in the world but years can bring, a real wisdom that only age can teach" (quoted in Hareven 1995:119-20).

Whatever one considers the positive aspects of aging, negative stereotyping of the elderly in the U.S. continues. It will be interesting to see if the denigrating images of aging retain their hold as the great numbers of baby boomers become old people or whether they are combated with ideas about the new and wonderful benefits inherent in aging and becoming old. Only time will tell.

Chapter 6

Mobility and Immobility
Stumbling, Tripping, Crumbling,
and Falling Amongst the Aged

[SMA]

How are the mighty fallen in the midst of battle. II Samuel 1:25

There are few functions more cherished by elderly persons than the ability to move about unhindered and at will. Walking when and where they wish is their visible proof that they still possess some measure of autonomy.

> *If I can't shop when I want to, go to the beauty parlor without some damned baby-sitter accompanying me, meet my friends for a lunch wherever and whenever I choose; or visit the grandchildren, there will then be no fun left in my life! [OM]*

With mobility, with freedom of movement both preserved and encouraged, the elderly will inevitably encounter the stumbling, tripping, and falling of late life; and with this new risk will come the many orthopedic and neurosurgical problems caused by falling. Without mobility, of course, these many fearful consequences would virtually disappear. But without mobility so too would independence and the privilege to make choices disappear. Walking carries risks at any age; but for the frail elderly, walking may become a life-threatening activity.

Walking is virtually a biological necessity at all stages of adult existence. It is needed to seek food, to defend oneself against predators, to earn a living, to seek shelter, to revel in the diversity of life, to seek companionship, even to find a mate. Locomotion additionally permits elderly people a real measure of liberation, allowing them to freely choose their venues, to continue to learn, even to make mistakes; and with mobility comes that exhilarating sense of emancipation, however fleeting and however hazardous it may be.

The forelimbs of a quadripedal animal are specialized for little more than ambulation. Biologists tell us that walking on two feet represents a major evolutionary advancement. Certainly, the bipedal stance of *Homo sapiens* frees the forelimbs to accomplish such elegant things as tool making and landscape painting; but it simultaneously creates problems in balance and speed of movement.

A quadripedal creature can maintain its equilibrium more easily since its center of gravity is lower to the ground while remaining within the rectangle of its four limbs. And certainly falling from a four-legged stance is far less traumatic. The upright posture of the bipedal human carries measurable risks of falling since any uncompensated movement that displaces the center of gravity beyond the position of the feet will cause an imbalance that, aided by gravity, renders the person susceptible to a fall. It is this remorseless force of gravity which looms as a major menace to bipedal creatures, particularly the frail, visually impaired, and cognitively diminished elderly ones.

Sooner or later great storms abate, primal human passions eventually subside, but the relentless force of gravity never ceases. To maintain an erect posture, humans are ceaselessly obliged to counteract this unyielding gravitational pull. Postural equilibrium requires such unwavering attention that it cannot be safely assigned solely to a human's conscious will, which is inevitably subject to all manner of casual distractions; rather, protective evolution has relegated the responsibility for this upright stance to a host of subconscious mechanisms. And any lapse in this autonomic postural vigilance makes humans vulnerable to accidental falls. Conscious thoughts, if sufficiently disturbing, may also intervene to cause falls. Even pride in one's ability to sustain the upright posture may increase one's susceptibility to falling. Paul in his epistle to the Corinthians offered this metaphoric admonition: "Let him that thinketh he standeth, take heed lest he fall." Perhaps he was remembering Proverbs 16:18: "Pride goeth before destruction, and a haughty spirit before a fall."

Diminished vigilance, yet another cause of falling, may also arise from intrinsic brain damage, drug-induced states, or even something as banal as momentary distractions. Kataria cites a poem describing what may happen when the essentially automatic act of ambulation is disrupted by a diverting or perplexing thought:

> The centipede was happy quite until the frog, for fun,
> Said 'Pray which leg goes after which?'
> Which wrought him up to such a pitch
> He lay distracted in a ditch
> Considering how to run. —Unknown

Humans are endowed with elaborate neurological systems, operative through their vision, through vestibular signals and by other sensing mechanisms, which inform them of where they are situated in relation to the ground. The vestibular apparatus is that portion of the inner ear that concerns itself with balance. The seemingly simple and easily accomplished acts of standing erect and walking, in truth, are neither simple nor easy; they only seem so when one's undistracted brain is intact and fully functional, receiving accurate messages concerning spatial relationships of the body parts; when the postural reflexes are unimpaired; when the voluntary muscles are fully responsive to autonomic commands from an intact central nervous system; and then uprightness is performed flawlessly, but only after years of diligent post-infancy education. Should any of these integrative elements lapse, as so often happens in advanced aging, then balance falters and upright posture is imperiled; and since gravity will not yield, the individual falls.

Gait

The way an elderly person walks—along with her facial expressivity and the content, pace, and color of her speech—speaks diagnostic volumes about her level of aliveness and the extent to which she is capable of fulfilling the tasks of daily living while simultaneously diminishing her risk of falling.

Her gait, the character and style of her walking, may be hesitant or assertive, erratic or even-paced, expressive or monotonous, ataxic or assured, composed of many small steps *(marche à petit pas)* or of normal strides, courageous or fearful. The length and vigor of each stride certainly reveals much about the integrity of the many integrative elements that govern her body balance and movement; but it also tells the observer much about whether this patient considers life to be a joyous experience, an anxious challenge or a mortal threat.

The epidemiology of falls

Young, healthy people rarely fall unless they are running or at least moving rapidly. And hence when they do fall, the momentum of movement causes them to be propelled forward; and if they are conscious, they will then attempt to break their descent with their upper limbs. Accordingly, in younger people, injuries after falls are generally confined to the upper limbs and head. When, however, a conscious, elderly person falls, the impact, in most cases, is initially restricted to the buttocks and hips. The typical fall in the older person is more an act of stumbling or crumbling. Bone and soft tissue injuries are therefore more commonly confined to the pelvic girdle, its soft tissues and the subjacent pelvic bones.

Falling is a common clinical event; indeed, falling is one of the major reasons why people, young and old, seek help in emergency rooms. While falls are more intimately associated with the frail elderly, adolescents fall just as readily but suffer fewer complications of impact injury such as bone fracture. In an individual whose bones are of diminished density, this type of fall often causes hip or femoral bone fracture.

Some years ago the Rhode Island Department of Health initiated an injury prevention program with particular emphasis upon falling as a major antecedent of injury.

Those studies, based upon a statewide review of death certificates and hospital discharge records, have yielded the following epidemiological insights: falls are the leading etiological agent of serious injury requiring hospitalization, greater even than the injuries caused by motor vehicle accidents. (In a typical year, falls form the basis of 78 percent of hospital admissions secondary to some form of bodily injury.) Falling, particularly in the elderly, is the major antecedent of death accounting for 41.6 percent of all fatal injuries in the state.

The risk of hospitalization secondary to falls, in Rhode Island, is over fourfold greater in older women than in older men largely because bone density in the postmenopausal woman is less than in males of comparable age. Falls in a seventy-five-year-old man will typically result in some bruising (both to limbs and pride). The same fall in a seventy-five-year-old woman will more often result in a life-threatening hip fracture. Eighty-three percent of all hip fractures in Rhode Island are in women for two obvious reasons: First, osteoporosis and diminished muscle mass are more common in elderly females; and second, over two-thirds of individuals older than seventy-five years are female.

There are ethnic as well as gender differences in fall-related injuries. Both osteoporosis and associated hip fractures are significantly less frequent in African-American women. (This observation, noted in numerous retrospective studies on hip fracture, represents one of the very few disease-related advantages in the African-American population.) Hispanic-American and Asian-American women have incidence rates for hip fracture intermediate between white and African-American women. Elderly women who live alone run a higher risk of hip fracture secondary to a fall than do their married counterparts.

Where do serious falls takes place? Largely in the home (68 percent) or in residential (nursing) institutions (11 percent); uncommonly, on the street or in public buildings such as stores. And the physical nature of the fall? Mainly slipping, tripping or stumbling on the same level, occasionally falling down stairs.

The suffering and societal burdens generated by accidental falls are immense. Beyond the obvious institutional costs (estimated to be over 37 billion dollars per year) is the appalling reality that an avoidable fall, followed by weeks or months of institutionalization, often converts a previously independent senior to one who will now require protracted assistance in walking and in fulfilling other basic functions of living. A review of the discharge status of those sixty-five years of age or older who had been hospitalized because of a fall shows that only 11 percent were able to return to their former level of full independence and were competent in resuming such functions as walking without assistance. Many required extended stays in nursing homes; and many never returned to their homes.

It is not that I forgot how to walk after my fall last September. I just didn't seem to have enough strength in my thighs to stand and then to get going on my own. Maybe, too, I was afraid to walk. The world seems to be more threatening now. [OM]

National surveys indicate that about 30 percent of sixty-five-year-olds experience major non-syncopal (i.e., a sudden loss of consciousness, such as a brief fainting episode) accidental falls each year. This frequency increases exponentially as age increases. Such falls may cause soft tissue injury, sprains, dislocations, bone fractures, cerebral contusions and subdural hematomas (blood leakage beneath the dural membrane that envelops the cerebral hemispheres). About one-half of an estimated four million Americans assigned to nursing homes, each year, became victims of recordable falls. About 5 percent of those who fall will have fractured a bone, typically the hip; 10 percent will experience serious soft tissue injury; and 20 percent will show minor lacerations and abrasions.

If the victim's head is struck there is an additional danger of venous bleeding beneath the dorsolateral dural membranes covering the cerebral hemispheres. The resulting hematoma may then compress the underlying brain tissue; and since the bone-encased intracranial cavity is unyielding, critical brain tissues will be compressed, displaced downward—thus compromising vital neural centers within the brain stem—with death a frequent outcome. While the frequency of subdural hematomas parallels the frequency of falls—and thus increases with age, the frequency of *fatal* subdural hematomas tends to diminish after age seventy-five years. The reason for this apparent paradox is as follows: with advancing age, the volume of brain tissue shrinks (senile atrophy) but the intracranial volume (brain tissue and cerebrospinal fluid) remains about the same. There is thus an increasing amount of spinal fluid filled space between the vulnerable brain tissue and the encasing bony cranium. The compressive, and frequently lethal, consequences of a subdural hematoma seen in the younger trauma victim are therefore substantially diminished in the very elderly since it is cerebrospinal fluid rather than vital brain tissue which is displaced by the injury-induced hematoma.

Hip fracture deserves particular societal emphasis since there are more than 300,000 such injuries incurred each year in the U.S. A white woman stands a 15 percent cumulative probability of sustaining a hip fracture by age eighty years; this rate rises to 35 percent in women who survive to their ninetieth birthday. Diminished bone density (osteoporosis) is a major contributing factor. The incidence rate of fracture is higher in thinner women.

Falls carry immediate risks. But they also generate worrisome complications, particularly if the traumatized victim is then bed-ridden. These secondary risks include pathologic dehydration, acute breakdown of injured muscle tissue (rhabdomyolysis), severe anemia due to internal bleeding at the internal site of fracture, pressure sores (decubitus ulcers) and hypostatic pneumonia. Bone fracture in the non-institutionalized elderly remains one of the principle reasons for their assignment to acute care hospitals and then nursing homes.

An unreasonable fear of falling should be added to the list of complications that make life hazardous after an elderly person has experienced an episode of falling.

I used to walk anywhere; and I could go up or down a staircase without clutching a handrail. But after my fall last autumn I am frightened by walking and I sometimes use my walker even when I don't really need it. I especially fear crowded streets with rapidly

*walking younger people who might bump into me. Why do they
have to walk so rapidly? I even fear walking on my bathroom floor
since the rug moves when I step on it. [OM]*

Drug-induced causes of falling

Virtually all drugs that affect nervous system function may
adversely modify alertness, clarity of vision, and balance. Those
medications that significantly increase the risk of falling include
the antihistamines, tranquilizers, sedatives, anti-seizure medications and even diuretics.

The pharmacological agent that most commonly impairs
postural equilibrium, however, is recreational alcohol. And while
the consumption of intoxicating spirits affects both judgment
and sense of balance at all ages, the untoward effects of alcohol
are more pronounced in the elderly person whose proprioceptive
instincts are already compromised.

Certain medications may selectively disrupt vestibular
function thus causing the elderly person to experience dizziness
and hence create a high risk of falling. These drugs include
quinine, aspirin in higher dosage, acetaminophen, and certain
antibiotics such as gentamycin and any of the aminoglycosides.

For the elderly person, anti-depressive medication can often
be a two-edged sword. On the one hand it diminishes his melan-
choly, but by impairing his proprioceptive sense, it increases his
risk of falling. Symptom-abating medications then become a
microcosm of the larger problem confronted by those concerned
with the well being and integrity of the elderly person. Many interventions intended to enhance the person's emotional and physical
capabilities simultaneously intensify the risk of serious injury. A
profoundly depressed, eighty-six-year-old woman, if she is bedrid-
den, is not likely to trip over an uneven sidewalk or suffer a hip
fracture. But compelling this eighty-six-year-old to remain in bed
carries its own grave risks including decubitus ulcers, bladder
infection, pneumonia, and ever-deepening depression.

Environmental causes of falling

The primary care physician attending an elderly patient must be
constantly sensitive to the existence of certain environmental risk

factors that may increase the likelihood of falling. There are the obvious physical risk factors that must be identified and, wherever possible, eliminated: on level surfaces, these include slippery floor surfaces, slippery objects negligently left on secure rugs (e.g., magazines), unanchored rugs, obstacles such as chairs obstructing a late-night path between bed and bathroom, objects that may cause tripping such as children's toys or electrical extension cords, poor or uneven illumination, deceptive patterns on floor coverings; and where there are steps, the absence of banisters, barriers at the head of stairwells and visible markings on step-downs.

These easily solved problems persist because of cultural attitudes too. The building of luxurious assistive housing for the elderly population continues at an astonishing rate. Ironically, the specifications of these new residential units often ignore some of the important sensory deficits catalogued above. We need to ask why this disconnect exists, and why it continues. It certainly is no secret that busily patterned carpets and uneven, insufficient illumination provided by elegant chandeliers distort the way an elderly person perceives his environment and navigates a way through it. Yet, designers create such living spaces fraught with these dangers. Brightly contrasting areas of floor color, for example, are misread as steps by elderly eyes with decreased depth perception. Why, then, do designers persist in installing hazardous floor coverings? Much of this housing is marketed to the younger, more affluent offspring of the targeted elderly population. The developers know that adult children want to see their aged parents housed in upscale apartments outfitted with the comfortable trappings of the good life. Such notions seem to equate with patterned carpeting and wall coverings, glittering chandeliers, and other accoutrements. It is as if these decorative touches are added to help compensate for the loss that the move from the prior home entails. The antique furniture, the potted plants, and the fireplace beckon welcomingly. The elderly, and their adult offspring, are attracted by the decorative symbolism that signify a cozy home rather than a utilitarian warehouse. [RRS]

Pre-existing systemic disease as a cause of falling

Virtually any systemic disease, by increasing the elderly person's weakness, increases the likelihood of falling. Certain ailments, though, increase this risk substantially: disorders of the cardiovascular system (e.g., myocardial insufficiency, cardiac valve disease, bradycardia with arrhythmias, episodic hypotension), disorders of vision (e.g., cataracts, diminished peripheral vision, decreased sensitivity to contrast, macular degeneration), disorders of the vestibular apparatus (e.g., Meniere's disease, labyrinthine disease), primary diseases of the central nervous system (e.g., Parkinson's disease, strokes, seizures, syncopes of any etiology, cerebellar atrophy), impairments of the musculoskeletal system (e.g., atrophies of disuse, peripheral nerve defects, generalized weakness), enduring behavioral disorders (e.g., confusional states, organic dementias), metabolic derangements (e.g., hypoglycemia, uncontrolled diabetes mellitus, excessive dehydration and fluid loss), dizziness of any etiology, and podiatric disabilities (e.g., bunions, ingrown toenails, ill-fitting shoes, untied shoelaces).

Subjectively experienced dizziness is a major precursor to falling. The dizziness described as a spinning sensation is often of vestibular origin. The dizziness appreciated as an imbalance or an unsteadiness is often a sign of some drug-induced, musculoskeletal or neurologic problem. And the dizziness often described as lightheadedness is frequently a sign of cardiovascular disease causing a diminished blood flow to the brain. Patients may state that they feel as though they were about to lose consciousness; and indeed fainting (syncope) in the elderly is most frequently caused by some sudden deficit in the ability of the cardiovascular system to deliver an adequate and oxygenated blood supply to the central nervous system. Some elderly patients volunteer the information that when they turn their head rapidly they experience a feeling of impending syncope. This may represent the effect of an arthritic cervical bone transiently compressing one of the vertebral arteries and thus diminishing the flow of blood to vital nervous system tissues in the posterior cranial fossa (that segment of the cranium that houses the vital brain stem and its attached cerebellum).

"Gram had got up off her knees, struggling up in obstinate sections, one hand clutching her cane, the other the bedpost, rising halfway, and a hand not holding, trying again, and a foot slipping sideways, another try and her cane caught fast in a fold of her gown, and Gram not knowing what was holding her down until she heard a ripping sound, then one major try with what strength

– 141 –

was left to try, and this time Gram standing erect at last, her heart thumping hard, her head shaking a little, her eyes dark-ringed with exhaustion, and her sighs and groans half pain, half exasperation at a body too old to do anything easily." Dorothy West, *The Wedding,* 1995.

The seemingly simple task of walking deserves more ana-lytic study; but even casual observation of the gait of the elderly will sometimes disclose a deterioration in muscular coordina-tion, a diminished muscle-mass, an altered spatial perception and orientation, or hesitancies, tremors, and false steps. The eyes of the old person, once vigilant guardians, may now fail in their surveillance tasks and worse, may send false signals. The paravertebral musculature, once sustainers of the upright pos-ture, now lack the strength to overcome destabilizing forces.

Falling rarely provokes fear in the teenager; indeed, the impulsive behavior of some of them seems intentionally to encourage the risk of falling. Presenescent adults fall less com-monly than do adolescents or the elderly; but the fear of falling, in a typical forty-year-old, stems more from a fear of potential embarrassment than a fear of resulting injury. Only the elderly have a mortal aversion to falling; they know its irreversible, sometimes lethal, consequences. And in some elderly, the fear of falling reaches pathological levels, virtually paralyzing them while restricting their activities, and their lives, to a small room or even a bed.

Surely gravity will not change. Are falls then inevitable or can commonsense preventive measures be undertaken? Certainly each home can be inspected to determine whether there are envi-ronmental hazards such as loose rugs, slippery bathtub surfaces, inapparent objects that might cause a person with failing vision to trip, poor lighting, even confusing floor patterns: environmen-tal factors that might collectively conspire to increase the risk of falling. In addition, there might be medications responsible for episodic dizziness, light-headedness, confusion or slowed reaction time thus imperiling postural integrity. As diligent parents rou-tinely inspect their homes to minimize potential hazards for their children, so too should members of the family critically review the surroundings where their elderly relatives live.

Accidental falling in the elderly is not a randomly distributed catastrophe. The majority of the senior population goes through life without episodes of hip fracture, subdural hematomas or any soft tissue trauma. But if falling is not random, what singular qualities identify the elderly person who is more prone to a fall resulting in serious consequences? Typically she is an asthenic (weak and undernourished), timorous, underweight white woman with ocular cataracts, older than seventy-five, who experiences physical difficulties in rising from a chair or bed, who displays a visible unsteadiness when first walking, who shows increased postural instability particularly when turning or reversing direction, whose gait is shuffling and hesitant, and who is marginally depressed, without a clear agenda for each day, socially isolated, indifferently dressed, and globally apprehensive.

Commentary
When They Fall Down
(RRS)

I sighed deeply while reading this chapter. The sad spiral of events set in motion by the factors described here has the tragic inevitability of a Greek drama. I have been struck so often by the classic way in which a downward course in an elderly person's functioning is triggered by some unforeseen event like a fall and tumbles then in its own trajectory. I have witnessed well-meaning caregivers and family members intervene to stem the spiral, and I have seen how these attempts have frequently led to further problems, unanticipated, yet somehow classically predictable and inevitable. So often the precipitating event has to do with falling.

Take the example of Flora, an eighty-two-year-old recently widowed woman. When Flora's husband suffered a stroke six months before he died, Flora and an aide traveled each day by bus to visit him in the hospital and then the nursing home. Each day they walked several blocks in the frosty New England winter to catch the buses. But after he died, Flora stayed put. She resisted the feeble efforts of the aide to take a daily walk. Her mourning was profound and her bleak outlook was compounded by her increasing forgetfulness. She was stuck, literally and metaphorically.

Within a few months her children had prevailed upon her to move to an assisted living housing unit in a city near them, where she was encouraged to become active, walk, participate in exercise. The months of inactivity following her husband's death had resulted in her becoming very weak, but over several months she received some sessions of physical therapy and slowly adjusted to using a walker and living in the new place. Since meals were provided in the downstairs dining room, she had to walk a long corridor from her apartment to the elevator in order to have her meal.

However, she had difficulty learning the proper way to use the walker. Since she took small steps and became tired, she pushed the walker further ahead of her. After falling several times over a short period (fortunately with no injuries), she was hospitalized for several days for testing, the results of which suggested a thyroid gland dysfunction for her muscle weakness. She was minimally active during this interval.

Upon the advice of the hospital, Flora was then transferred to an elegant rehabilitation nursing center. Her children reminded her that the stay would be brief, and that once she was strong again, she would leave. But Flora forgot the pep talks and was despondent, and physical therapy produced little improvement. She nodded blankly when told she needed to walk better in order to go back home. She dully chanted "yes, dear" to family member encouragement. The therapist issued pessimistic reports, and staff members were doubtful that she would return to her apartment.

When not in these brief daily physical therapy sessions, she sat in a wheelchair or lay on her bed, attached by a safety pin to a device that emitted a horrifyingly loud sound if she stood up on her own accord. However, she regularly unpinned herself, and when her children learned of her actions, they secretly applauded her. They wondered what benefit she gained by being confined in a wheelchair or bed. Wasn't enforced immobility contributing to further weakness? In the middle of the night, when Flora woke up to use the bathroom, she unhitched the safety pin, got up, and walked to the bathroom unassisted. She explained that although she was supposed to press her call button, staff members took so long to respond that she had had episodes of bed-wetting while waiting for them to help her.

The nursing home environment was bringing her down. Though the décor was cheerful, staff members were harried, brusque, and inattentive. Like steady fog horns in a huge gray sky, the resident call buttons beeped dully in the elegant hallways, unanswered—sirens of glum syncopation.

Flora's thyroid test levels gradually came into the normal range and she regained her strength. But the best boost was the physical therapist's brainstorm one day: let us assess her in her own apartment, she suggested. Once there, Flora walked better immediately. Flora walked down her long corridor slowly and with great determination. She was going home. She said, "No," when offered to rest, and continued doggedly down the hallway.

Discharge was arranged immediately. Physical therapy was transferred from nursing home to apartment setting.

Flora's stodgy lack of progress was linked with her gloominess. The nursing home environment was depressing and infantilizing—upscale décor notwithstanding—a sign to Flora that she should give up, no matter the elegance of the carpeting and the cheerful parakeets chirping in the corridors. Central to her lack of progress in the nursing home, if not her deterioration, was the dependency foisted on her by the setting. The safety pin that kept her connected to the wheelchair taught her to stay put, be resigned, ask for help.

Flora's mood was also tied to her ability to move about. Her children noticed that when she first began to have difficulties walking and moving easily months earlier, she often became discouraged and disgusted. She was angry at herself. How could her body abandon her like this? When she momentarily tripped on a piece of carpet or stumbled ever so slightly, she cursed herself and her stupidity. And how was it that now she found herself in an environment—this stupid nursing home—that signaled the end? She would sometimes silently shake her head and wonder out loud how it happened that she had ended up in this place. Truly there could be no hope of improvement. Her inability to walk easily on her own—a symbol of her inability to be independent which she equated with her worthlessness—made her more despondent, and that dreary outlook fueled the heavy passivity that made walking and moving about even more difficult to accomplish.

The Bad Days of Restraints in Nursing Homes

Fear of falling sets off a cascade of events that can be extremely harmful to older people. As noted in chapter 9, until relatively recently, nursing homes routinely tied residents to chairs and beds in order to prevent them from wandering, getting lost, falling, or otherwise hurting themselves. Restraints, such as side-railings on beds and other devices, literally kept people in their places, and psychotropic medications were often inappropriately used to sedate and keep residents manageable. The enforced immobility caused life-threatening bedsores and urinary tract infections. All manner of "disruptive behaviors" or "difficult" behaviors were handled by these kinds of restraints. Restraints caused as many problems as they were purported to solve.

Residents died trying to get out of them. They choked in the bed sheets holding them in a wheelchair or in bed. They suffocated in the side rails of beds when they became stuck in attempting to wriggle through, or they often fell out and injured themselves when they attempted to clamber over the rails. The forced inactivity of being restrained caused muscle atrophy and general weakness, contributed to bedsores and infections due to decreased activity. The heart-rending protests, cries, and screaming led to the overuse of psychotropic medications which caused further problems. Overuse of "vitamin H" (for Haldol, a major tranquilizer) led to medical problems of all sorts. Some of the behavior surrounding restraint use and other management techniques had been for the convenience of staff members. "Wandering" by demented residents was a chief offender.

Many nurses and nursing assistants believed they were preventing harm by restraining the residents in their care. In a profound sense staff members were abused by the system that made them tie residents down and learn to ignore the protests. Several nursing assistants I interviewed in the 1980s expressed their sadness and helplessness in using restraints on residents. However, it also seemed evident that some nursing home staff members used restraints punitively. Restraint use abetted insufficient staffing levels.

As the movement against restraints gained momentum in the 1980s, many nursing home personnel insisted that restraints were necessary. Dire results would ensue, they predicted. Family members would sue if a resident fell and injured himself. Confused residents would wander away from the premises and meet an untimely end. Wandering residents would enter other residents' rooms and invade their privacy, sleep in their beds, take their things.

Restraint use—except when medically necessary—was outlawed in the early 1990s in the OBRA legislation. The dire results predicted have not materialized. Though residents sometimes fall, family members are educated about the risks that accompany both restraint use and non-use, and other safeguards to prevent falling are in place. Identifying bracelets, codes on exits, and auditory alarms alert staff members to residents who attempt to leave a nursing unit. Small individual alarms can be attached by safety pins to residents, like Flora, who are thought to be at risk of falling if they attempt to walk unassisted. The appropriate use of psychotropic medication means anxiety-ridden residents are soothed but not drugged to a level of stupor by the medications. Occasionally a confused resident sleeps on the bed of another resident, but education and tolerance have largely reduced the problems caused by this behavior. Rather than tie a resident into her bed or raise the side rails to keep her in, the bed is lowered closer to the floor so she will be safer. Sometimes, the mattress is put directly on the floor.

The U.S. is a risk-averse and litigious society. At the same time autonomy is highly prized. Autonomous old age carries some risk of falling. It is impossible to safeguard everyone in such a way that independence of movement and spirit are not shackled. Perhaps it helps to acknowledge that the human condition is essentially one of mutual dependence throughout the life cycle. We help one another to be as functional, fulfilled, and as mobile as possible, and together we can also recognize the limitations of this ideal.

Chapter 7

Systemic Diseases of the Elderly and the Problem of Alcoholism
Two Points of View
(SMA)

If youth only knew, and old age only could. —Henri Estienne

Some eighty-five-year-olds are substantially older than other eighty-five-year-olds. Some eighty-five-year-olds function admirably, exercise vigorously, pursue at least two avocations and put in a full day's labor at the office. But in general, those beyond age seventy-five are more frail, are at greater risk for a variety of ills, and even manifest their ailments in ways that are distinguishable from their younger counterparts.

A forty-three-year-old with pneumococcal pneumonia, for example, will typically present with high fever, cough, blood-tinged sputum, and delirium and will look quite ill. Indeed, he will look at least as sick as he really is. An eighty-five-year-old with pneumonia, on the other hand, may give no visible evidence of an acute systemic process and may not even be febrile.

A forty-three-year-old with an expanding brain tumor will suffer from severe headache, may decompensate rapidly, and slip into deep stupor or even coma; an eighty-five-year-old with, for example, an intracranial meningioma, may perhaps simulate a chronically progressive dementia, may have a mild, nonpersistent headache—or may have no neurologic symptoms whatever. A myocardial infarction in an eighty-five-year-old may pass unnoticed without the customary acute chest pains often radiating to the left arm or left face and the cardiovascular collapse typically observed in the active, middle-aged male with coronary artery disease.

The diagnostic guidelines that assist the physician in identifying systemic disease in the ambulatory adult have proven to be less reliable with the geriatric patient; and atypical clinical presentations—or even the absence of outwardly visible manifestations of organic disease—are often the rule with the sick elderly. The geriatric patient, here defined as someone seventy-five years of age or older, is more likely to be organically impaired than someone forty-five years of age; but when sick, will often present with milder, and more idiosyncratic, signs and symptoms than those seen in younger patients.

> In John Adams's and Thomas Jefferson's lengthy correspondence in their last years, Jefferson candidly wrote the following to Adams: "But our machines have now been running for seventy or eighty years, and we must expect that, worn as they are, here a pivot, there a wheel, now a pinion, next a spring, will be giving way, and however we may tinker with them for awhile, all will at length surcease motion" (quoted by Ellis 2000:226). [RRS]

Common Clinical Problems in the Elderly

The manner in which the infant's or young child's body reacts to disease is quite distinctive and makes pediatrics a clearly defined specialty. Similarly, geriatrics differentiates the clinical presentation of the ailing elderly from those in the middle decades of adult life. The older ones, it has been said, are not the victims of diseases unique to the geriatric age range; they merely have many more of these adult illnesses, and they arise in a body already compromised by the aging process.

Safe mobility

To ambulate without personal injury, in a society that cherishes speed over safety, requires much conscious effort by the elderly. It requires that they possess good vision, adequate limb strength, intact proprioception (the capacity of the brain to receive and mediate neural messages from the limbs indicating where one's limbs are in space), an unimpaired sense of balance, a general alertness, an awareness of one's surroundings, and a conscious desire to overcome or bypass the physical obstacles in one's path. And, as problems in ambulation inevitably mount for the older individual—caused by increasing weakness, frailty, and fear— the desire to walk diminishes, a seat by the window replaces the customary stroll to the corner park, and new complications then arise. These include anorexia, increasing muscle atrophy, osteo-porosis associated with a heightened risk of bone fracture, bed sores, discouragement, and involutional depression.

Getting the elderly to move becomes an increasing prob-lem. They will explain their reluctance by pointing to the haz-ards of walking safely on crowded sidewalks without tripping or falling, or negotiating irregularly illuminated corridors and staircases, or even working out safe strategies in finding a secure pathway between bed and bathroom. The physician's task is to identify and exploit whatever mechanisms may be available (including better illumination, handrails in bathrooms and corridors and walkers) in order to keep the elderly person from retreating permanently to the deceptive safety of her bed. "Use it or lose it," is more than an overworked cliché.

> You contribute an entire chapter [chapter 6] to this important sub-ject because of its central role in the life—and incapacities—of the elderly. [RRS]

Control of urination

Loss of control of urination (urinary incontinence) in adults cre-ates problems both social and medical. Untreated incontinence effectively removes the victim from social activities and becomes a guaranteed source of embarrassment and frustration. It is the major reason for the elderly to isolate themselves from the larger community.

> *Incontinence has often been a prime reason for admission to a nursing home or an assisted living facility in the U.S. The shame that attends a family member's incontinence can be the factor that creates the crisis for the family that results in institutionalization. It is as though the family can take only so much evidence of dependency. Even when the older person is living independently, signs of incontinence signal the dependency that seems to demand an intervention. A nursing home resident I once interviewed put it like this: "Pop smells, so into the nursing home he goes." This attitude persists though incontinence can often be treated and managed effectively. [RRS]*

It is not uncommon for the elderly to experience an involuntary loss of small amounts of urine (stress incontinence) following a sneeze, cough, or burst of laughter. The frequently perceived urgency to urinate (and the companion inability to delay urination until a proper facility is found) is also a problem that the elderly will readily admit to; and it is a problem augmented greatly by any pelvic structure inflammation.

> *Urinary tract infection (UTI) in the elderly is another insidious and common problem sometimes associated with incontinence. This kind of infection is often asymptomatic and undiagnosed. Sometimes an elderly person is confused or irritable, "out of sorts" and "out of it." He or she may be more prone to falls or may be disruptive and irascible. What I don't understand is that often this common UTI is unrecognized in the geriatric setting (hospital, assisted living complex, nursing home, etc.). Too often psychotropic medications are used to control the difficult behaviors, which in turn cause other problems—or worse, a fall results in a hip fracture which leads to a hospitalization. The enforced immobility produces muscle atrophy, more disorientation and other signs of a deleterious downward spiral—until later the simple urine test is ordered and the renegade UTI is found, easily treated and cured. Why isn't a urine test ordered when such symptoms first arise, curtailing the above adverse dangerous events and undesirable emergency room visits? [RRS]*

Difficulties in urinary control increase appreciably with age. Effective bladder capacity decreases with age. The number of involuntary contractions of cystic musculature increases in the elderly; and this, superimposed upon a diminished bladder volume, increases both the sense of urinary urgency and its frequency. Laxity of pelvic structures (with diminished tonus of the pelvic floor musculature), is particularly prone to occur in elderly women who had previously undergone multiple childbirths. In males, the enlargement of the prostate gland and an associated instability of the detrusor musculature (urinary bladder muscles) lead to repeated episodes of urinary obstruction or leakage.

Urethro-cystic (the bladder and its conduit to the exterior) infection is more common in the elderly; and the resulting local irritation, conjoined with many of the other factors listed above, cause a distressing frequency of urinary incontinence episodes. In the absence of a neurologic basis for urinary incontinence, however, most of these distressing problems become manageable through simple medical interventions or better scheduling of daily activities.

Amongst systemic factors, cardiac failure and certainly the use of diuretics increases the stresses placed upon the bladder. Acute illness, especially systemic infections such as pneumonia, increase the need to urinate, and if the patient is then immobilized in a hospital bed or is rendered less sensitive to messages indicating the need to urinate, through the use of sedation, urinary leakage will increase substantially. Additional systemic states such as acute delirium or anything entailing body immobility (such as the treatment of hip fracture) will likely result in episodes of temporary incontinence.

Some medications may increase the risk of overflow urinary incontinence, including the opiate narcotics (narcotics derived from opium), beta-adrenergic agents (an important family of heart medicines), some antidepressants, anticholinergic drugs (medications that counteract the actions of the parasympathetic nervous system), and most sedatives.

Urinary incontinence is encountered in about 5 percent of males between the ages of sixty-five and seventy-four; and 7 percent of females in the same age category. In males seventy-five years of age or older, the prevalence of urinary incontinence rises to about 11 percent and in females, to 15 percent (Kane 1989). In the general hospital population, the prevalence of urinary incontinence rises dramatically (documented in about 58 percent of women inpatients over the age of seventy-five years), but this increase may reflect, in part, the stress of acute institutionalization, the existence of some systemic disease causing the hospitalization, and such urinary stress factors as added medications and a systemic overloading with intravenous fluids.

Urinary incontinence in the elderly may be ascribed to local urological disease such as bladder infection, to neurological lesions such as spinal cord trauma or intracranial stroke, to emotional distress (of any etiology) or even to some actions undertaken by the physician such as prescribing a variety of pharmacologically active medications that affect bladder physiology. Cognitive loss, in such states as Alzheimer's disease, may lead to an unawareness of, or perhaps an indifference to, the functional status of the urinary bladder.

Cognitive loss

The human brain is subject to a number of dementing, organic processes, of diverse etiology, which become increasingly common with age. These include such formidable disorders as Alzheimer's disease, Creutzfeld-Jakob disease, diffuse Lewy-body disease and multi-infarct dementia.

Primary memory, specifically short-term recall, does not deteriorate much with age except in instances of organic dementia. Testing such skills as remembering and repeating a sequence of digits or names of objects shows no diminished abilities with aging. It is secondary memory—the storing and retrieval of organized data imprinted in the past—that shows a significant loss with increasing age. An eight-year-old can remember a twenty-stanza poem learned a year or two before, while an eighty-year-old experiences difficulty (and embarrassment) in remembering the name of a single elementary school classmate. A declining and unreliable long-term memory capability is so common and so worrisome in those over the age of seventy-five that physicians attempt to make light of it by calling it a manifestation of benign senescence and ascribe it to an overloading of the storage system. ("You haven't lost that information, Mrs. Brennan, you have merely misfiled it. Undoubtedly you will recall that name, days from now, at 3 AM.")

To me it seems that there is too much information stuffed into too small a space as though it's a vacuum cleaner whose bag is over-filled. [RRS]

Patients with advanced organic dementia exhibit a loss in the precise and effective employment of language whether it be in the accuracy of naming things, the proper phonological use of sounds, or the syntactic coherence of their sentence structure. While there may be some modest decline in verbal fluency with age, a general facility with language is preserved in the non-demented elderly.

Other components of cognitive ability (abstract thinking, attention span, the capacity to conceptualize and the facility to adapt to and manipulate general information in an accurate manner) undergo some modest losses with advanced aging but never to the striking degree seen in the demented.

Much of what seems to be cognitive impairment in the elderly may, in fact, reflect little more than a pervasive discouragement, a reactive depression, and a growing anxiety that they are at the margins of some demeaning organic brain syndrome. The older notion that Alzheimer's disease and aging are intimately intertwined, that Alzheimer's disease is merely an accelerated form of aging, has been effectively disproven.

So, professor, what do you call it when you are old and you don't remember whether it is Tuesday or Friday? Is this a sickness—or something else? When I ran a clothing store twenty-five years ago, I always knew what day it was. Each working day had its own special bundle of worries. Like Fridays when I had to come up with the cash to pay my two salesmen their salaries (which some weeks they didn't deserve.) With that kind of deadline nudging me, I never could forget Friday. But now every day is like every other day, I don't pay anybody anymore, and I can't remember when Friday comes. The chief nurse puts up a sign near her desk, every day, telling us what day it is—just like the school teacher did when I went to public school (the nurse even looks like my old teacher). But I'd rather not know the day than be treated like I was

> *back in kindergarten. I don't remember lots of things that I should remember. But I don't have Alzheimer's disease; I'm just old and maybe just too tired to remember. [OM]*
>
> *I agree with OM. I think the efficacy of memory testing in nursing homes is diluted when it includes questions that ask today's date. When the days are the same, such information is not useful to people. Working people on vacation also often slide into nonconcern about the date. [RRS]*

Frailty

In Elizabethan times, frailty was considered a gender-oriented thing ("Frailty, thy name is woman.") and an alleged companion of wiles, flattery, and coquetry. In a less poetic age, however, frailty looms as a major concern for the enlarging population of the elderly.

Defining frailty in a medical or forensic context may take the genius of a linguist and the caution of a defense lawyer. Yet one glance at some fragile-appearing old person and the phrase "frail elderly" comes forth unbidden. But it is substantially more than the fragile look of certain old persons which clearly identifies them as frail. It is something deeper than their pallid, undernourished appearance; they seem to be more vulnerable to an occasionally hostile environment, susceptible to whatever unanticipated hazards—physical, social or microbiological—may arise.

Frailty is not equivalent to physical impairment; but frailty leads inevitably to an augmented risk of injury and chronic disability. A frail, elderly person, in summary, is a medical disaster waiting to happen.

On a practical level, the frail person with obvious muscular atrophy needs added help in walking, in struggling to complete the sundry tasks needed in daily living, and in coping with any activity requiring physical exertion. Actions taken for granted at a somewhat younger age may present formidable obstacles for the frail individual: activities such as rising from the toilet seat, carrying the groceries from the front door to the kitchen or buttoning a button.

Frail persons, in general, tend to be chronically ill with more diverse disorders such as arthritis, cataracts, and old stroke, than the more robust elderly.

To the physician, frailty looms as a systemic failing. Its existence predicts the imminence of further organic problems as though there were some underlying physiological inadequacy involving many organ systems.

Some geriatricians regard frailty as far more serious than a mere surface fragility. They see it as a palpable organic syndrome, the causes and underlying lesions of which are still unclear. They view it as an abnormal physical state that somehow encourages further deterioration in virtually all organ systems. The phrase, "failure to thrive" is usually reserved for certain maladaptive infants in perilous straits. But it has been used with regularity now when trying to define frailty in the elderly (Guralnik 1991). Investigations of the frail patient have indicted many interval systems: a possibly defective hypothalamic-pituitary-adrenal axis, an insufficiency of growth hormone secretion, an inadequate immune system response, and in general a diminished ability of the body to maintain its homeostatic equilibrium (Winograd 1991).

As increased numbers of adults survive into the senior decades of life, frailty—and the many problems of dependency that frailty creates—will become an increasingly common phenomenon. It will tax the assisted living and nursing facilities of this nation; and it will demand of the biomedical research community a far better understanding of its causes as well as improved means by which its impact upon the elderly may be lessened.

Alcoholism in the Elderly

A neatly dressed eighty-seven-year-old woman seeks medical attention because of loss of appetite, insomnia, and episodes of confusion. To consider alcohol dependency as this woman's initial diagnosis, in the absence of any corroborating evidence, would be imprudent if not rash. After all, she seems poised, reasonably articulate, and volunteers enthusiastic comments about her garden club, her knitting, and her grandchildren. Certainly, in the array of diagnostic possibilities, alcohol abuse does not immediately come to mind. And, indeed, unless there is something specific to incriminate alcohol, it will rarely be included in the physician's list of disorders warranting further exploration, which is why alcoholism persists as a stubborn, but largely hidden, geriatric problem.

And even when the index of suspicion for alcoholism is high and the diagnosis is finally verified either by the patient's admission or by independent laboratory tests, it will often go unreported. "Why deprive Mrs. Williams of her afternoon sips of gin? It does not harm anyone; and it does provide her with something to look forward to. And furthermore, if documented, the family would be humiliated." And so, frequently, the problem is neither confronted nor resolved, while a potentially remediable life-threatening illness goes untreated.

Alcoholism may be difficult to recognize at any age unless the physician operates under the grim presumption that all adults are alcoholics until proven otherwise. Certainly alcoholism in a twenty-six-year-old male is easier to identify than in his eighty-seven-year-old grandmother. The typical twenty-six - year-old has a defined job in the community and a complex social life to maintain. Alcohol-related impairments, sooner or later, will be evident to his family, friends or coworkers; and there will be recurrent episodes of failure to meet family and occupational obligations; his personal health is typically impaired; his work performance is at best marginal; and he runs an increasing risk of auto accidents. The eighty-seven-year-old grandmother, on the other hand, lives in relative isolation, drinks alone, rarely drives a car, is not a menace in the workplace, and uses alcohol more as a private sedative than as a social accelerant. Her drinking is rarely explored in depth, is not regarded as a hazard to others, and her consumption of liquor therefore becomes a source of gentle amusement rather than as a life-shortening disorder. (The image of the neatly dressed biddy guzzling her gin from a teacup is thoroughly ingrained in the British cinema.) And if she shows some cognitive loss, seems depressed or displays an increasing gait disturbance, it will be readily ascribed to the remorseless aging process. Further, if she stumbles excessively, it might then be attributed to one or another of her many daily medications.

*Did the late Queen Mother of England have a drinking problem?
A story reported on the occasion of her death in March 2002 at the
age of one hundred one, relates that at an afternoon tea some years
earlier, the hostess irreverently asked the Queen Mother if she
wouldn't rather prefer gin instead of tea? The Queen Mother is
reputed to have responded that she was not aware that she was
known for liking gin, but indeed, if her hostess was offering it to
her, could she make it a big one? This story is more likely to further endear rather than alarm her fans about alcohol abuse
among the elderly. Many have no doubt attributed her longevity to
her fondness for gin. [RRS]*

*The British have a way of embellishing harsh realities. Virtually
every longitudinal study indicates that daily alcohol consumption
of more than one ounce of gin (or its equivalent in beer, wine or
other spirits) is clearly life-shortening. Perhaps these epidemio-
logic insights don't pertain to the House of Windsor. [SMA]*

Epidemiologists now declare that about 10 percent of those
sixty-five years of age or older have a problem with alcohol. Surveys in some nursing homes and residences for the elderly have
suggested prevalence of excessive alcohol usage to range between
2 percent and 20 percent.

*According to a report from Columbia's National Center of Addic-
tion and Substance Abuse, almost 20 percent of elderly women
abuse prescription drugs or alcohol (Peele 1998). [RRS]*

Two clinical categories of late-life alcoholism are now
recognized. Those whose drinking dependencies began much
earlier in life—often in early adulthood—constitute about two-
thirds of the elderly alcoholics. These individuals are more difficult to treat since their alcohol addiction is more established,
more insulated, and more a part of their daily routine.

*A vivid portrait of elderly homeless men, many of whom include
life-long alcohol abuse among their behaviors, can be found in*
Old Men of the Bowery: Strategies for Survival Among the Homeless *(Cohen and Sokolovsky 1989). [RRS]*

The remaining third of the elderly alcoholics, the so-called late-
onset alcoholics, are usually women who have not been drinking
excessively until some event, late in life, reinforced their lonely

status: the death of a husband, perhaps. Late-onset alcoholism in men, on the other hand, is often connected with enforced retirement or a perceived loss of authority within the home or community. This late-onset group, on average, is more amenable to therapy and less likely to relapse after achieving sobriety. Some have speculated that the elderly women who begin to drink seriously only in the later decades of life may have been married to, and cared for, alcoholic husbands; and when their husbands finally died, they then reverted to the same problem-solving mechanism that had been previously adopted by their husbands.

Recognizing alcoholism in the eighty-seven-year-old widow is not easily accomplished short of routine breath-analysis on all geriatric patients. Addiction physicians will suspect alcoholism when there is a recent, and inexplicable, loss of appetite; when the elderly woman shuns company at particular segments of the day; when she shows excessive irritability while in the prolonged company of others; when she is excessively sleepy at suppertime but suffers from insomnia during much of the night; when she experiences muscle pains beyond the usual aches experienced by the aged; and when there are repeated episodes of stumbling or falling confined to certain times of the day.

Alcoholism, at any age, may cause confusion, ataxic gait, delirium, even confabulation; and any one of these clinical events may be inaccurately interpreted as signifying accelerated aging. No further tests are then undertaken and an opportunity to reverse the patient's cognitive decline is thus lost.

Alcohol has a somewhat different effect upon the elderly patient's body. Less alcohol is needed to achieve the wanted mood-altering effects. This is perhaps related to diminished muscle mass in seniors. Alcohol also interacts adversely with numerous medications commonly prescribed for the elderly including sedatives, antihistamines, psychoactive drugs, and antithromboplastic agents (so-called blood-thinners). Adverse drug interactions are far less commonly encountered in the twenty-six-year-old alcoholic.

Jane Brody (2002) also identifies widely used drugs, such as acetaminophen, aspirin, antidepressants, nonsteroidal anti-inflam-

> *matory medications, digoxin, heparin, hypoglycemics and sleep*
> *aids, as interacting negatively with alcohol. [RRS]*

Seeing an otherwise active person in her eighties enter a non-communicative stupor on a regular basis is neither whimsical nor quaint; nor is it something to be taken lightly. Treatment will require active counseling in a secure alcohol-free environment and the need for benzodiazepine replacement during the withdrawal phase.

> *Of course, we must also recognize that there are health benefits—*
> *even in the elderly—to moderate alcohol consumption. The low-*
> *ered risk of heart disease and perhaps even dementia has been*
> *linked to regular and moderate alcohol use. Furthermore, sharing*
> *drinks among friends is generally festive and positive and there-*
> *fore a benefit. However, since the effect of alcohol on the aging body*
> *is greater than that on a younger body, less alcohol is needed for*
> *the beneficial effect, and more can be destructive in the ways you've*
> *described. [RRS]*

Chemical dependency in the elderly must first be recognized not as a clinical oddity but as a legitimate health menace. When even the barest hint of alcoholism emerges, the abuse must then be search for diligently. And if the diagnosis is firmly established, the elderly patient must then acknowledge, in her heart, that she has a serious problem; otherwise, her therapy will be fruitless. And finally, those professionals who care for the elderly must accept that chemical dependency, to alcohol or other mood-altering agents, is a treatable disorder.

For overcoming loneliness and depression, compassionate care, counseling, and specific therapy work far better than liquor.

From the Viewpoint of Physicians

The university-trained physician thinks of disease in terms of a structural and metabolic departure from something called the normal state. And this training has been distilled over the years into a basic algorithm that insists upon an orderly sequence when confronting a sick individual: list the clinical symptoms and signs; determine the underlying organic lesion(s) held to be responsible for the identified signs and symptoms; verify the existence of these presumed pathological lesion(s) by means of objective tests including chemical assays, radiological studies, microbiological analyses and—considered to be the gold-standard for objective verification—tissue biopsy.

The physician taking a history from an elderly patient needs to recognize certain realities (e.g., shortened attention span, heightened anxieties, marginal confusion, etc.). The conventional sequence of questions should not be slavishly followed with patients in their senior years. Questions should be stated briefly, using commonly understood terminology and should be conveyed in a non-threatening manner. Functional status becomes the crucial element rather than the search for a precise pathophysiological diagnosis. In essence, the geriatrician, in taking a history from the patient, will search for answers to this fundamental question: what can I learn from this interview which will then allow me to intervene so as to increase the quality of life for this sentient human being? And if the answer to a clinical question will have no bearing upon subsequent medical therapy, why ask the question?

If asked to describe the organic diseases of the elderly, the trained physician will properly provide prevalence statistics of each of the major diseases of each organ system, the data segregated by gender, age-range, and perhaps ethnicity. This physician will then relate these data to sundry risk factors to provide the reader with both cause and effect of those illnesses afflicting the aged. Somehow, in this approach, the lesion has become central while the patient's subjective complaints have been reduced to marginal commentary.

There are many ways of measuring the damage to the human body wrought by time. Structurally oriented geriatricians will measure the irreversible metabolic wear and tear upon the internal organs, the degree of senescent atrophy (shrinkage of body tissues accompanying the aging process), regarding these alterations as the most reliable criteria of the ravages of aging. Some physicians will explore beyond the mere quantity of accumulated intracellular rust plus DNA damage in certain organs and determine the frequencies of specific pathologic lesions such as myocardial scarring, involutional deterioration of the glandular organs, cerebrovascular insufficiencies and neuronal abiotrophies unrelated to vascular supply. Still others will contend that aging is better measured by behavioral pathology, by the aggregation of psychiatric abnormalities, whether ennobling or demeaning, and their frequency in a typical population of elderly. And still others, while not denying the significance of underlying pathologic processes, will contend that the most valid—and most meaningful—criterion of aging is the degree to which specific integrative functions are lost; or better, the degree to which these human functions, essential to an individual's continuing place within society, are preserved.

The most obvious criterion of aging, namely duration of life, turns out to be a rather poor measure of functional integrity. There are those who have grown desperately old within a decade of birth, a rare, autosomally inherited disorder known as progyria, which causes accelerated atherosclerosis in the affected child and cellular evidence of advanced aging and DNA vulnerability well before puberty. And then there are those, just entering the fourth decade of their lives who look to be more elderly than people decades older. This too may be the result of certain inherited characteristics but more often than not it also reflects an imprudent lifestyle such as chronic alcoholism causing widespread nutritional and toxic changes within the body. Age, without reference to how those years were lived or how well the body was cared for, says little. (Or, in the words of an anonymous philosopher of vehicular travel, "It ain't the years, stupid, it's the mileage.")

> *To pick up on this point, people look older (and/or age faster) when they are poor and experience more life hardship. People also appear older when they work at physically difficult jobs in harsh conditions. Skin is weathered by outdoor labor, and injuries and wear and tear are more pronounced when work is physically arduous. Treatment for disease may also be delayed or untreated when a person does not have access to a regular physician, and such access problems can be severe among the poor. [RRS]*

Pathologists, when studying the effects of aging upon tissue, have been impressed with a curious paradox: the number and severity of internal diseases increase with increasing age. But beyond about age eighty-five, the number of concurrent diseases in these elderly survivors seems to diminish. A study of the pathology of the extremely aged (i.e., those over one hundred years) was undertaken recently in the Tokyo Institute of Gerontology (Tanaka 1984). Their findings in these autopsied centenarians showed fewer instances of underlying disease such as cancer, while death seemed to be caused by a combination of cardio-pulmonic failure or perhaps, in the words of one pathologist, an exhaustion of the tissues.

Another comprehensive study of the neuropathologic changes in those over age ninety also demonstrated a lowering of vascular disease, the absence of any newly rising intracranial tumors and far fewer instances of organic dementia than observed in the prior decade of life (Peress, personal communication 1981). It seems as though a good measure of healthiness is required to approach one's hundredth birthday.

From the Viewpoint of the Elder Person

A social scientist will claim that there is only an inconstant concordance between underlying organic disease and functional impairment. They will claim that measures of disability say more about the aging process than any roster of polysyllabic pathologic lesions. Certainly, they acknowledge, the state of each internal organ will have a major bearing upon integrative function; but, they assert, the difference from person to person is so dramatic that a reliance solely upon pathological changes to tell us the functional integrity of the elderly population is both naïve and foolhardy. For an elderly person, then, the question is not the degree of oxygenation to the myocardium or whether a cancer is beginning somewhere in the pancreas; rather, the compelling question is: "Do I have the strength to go shopping this morning?" Or, "Can I tie my shoelaces without getting someone to help me?" Or, "Will I be strong enough to meet with my eighty-seven-year-old sister next week?"

It becomes important, then, to find out what fraction of Americans older than sixty-five years can perform those minimally essential tasks that are deemed necessary to survive, with some degree of autonomy, from day to day.

At about five-year intervals the federal government undertakes a lengthy survey of functional impairment, using a representative sample of non-institutionalized U.S. adults sixty-five years of age or older. Those who live in nursing homes, hospitals or homes for the aged are necessarily excluded from this study.

And that's simply because, for whatever reason(s), these individuals have become functionally unable to manage for themselves and cannot carry out the essential "activities of daily living" (ADLs) without the assistance of caregivers. However, this group also consists of heterogeneous individuals whose inability to perform certain ADLs may or may not result in institutionalization. That is, one person must enter an institution because he or she cannot walk unassisted, but another with the same limitations is able to stay at home because he or she has a spouse or a companion who is able to help. [RRS]

The most recent survey of functional abilities involved 53,636 Americans. They were asked a specific set of questions to determine the extent to which these many vital functions remain unimpaired. These data were collated and analyzed by the U.S. Public Health Service, Centers for Disease Control, and by statistical extrapolation now represent the status of American elders, at least those living relatively independent lives, for the year 1999.

Table 6.1 Prevalence Rates of Various Forms of Disability, Non-institutionalized Residents of the United States

Disability	18-65 years	65 years or older
Reading newsprint	2.1%	11.4%
Hearing normal conversation	1.8	12.0
Lifting/carrying 10 lbs.	4.2	22.1
Climbing one flight of stairs	5.6	30.4
Walking three blocks	5.4	30.5
Any of the above	**10.2**	**46.4**

Aids to Daily Living	18-65 years	65 years or older
Eating	0.3	2.0
Dressing	0.8	5.4
Mobility at home	0.9	6.1
Mobility outside of home	1.9	15.1
Light housework	1.6	10.2
Any of the above	**3.2**	**19.7**
Dementia	0.3	3.6
Mental disability	3.6	5.8
Wheelchair use	0.6	3.9
Need for cane, crutches or walker	1.4	13.8
Any of the above	**4.6**	**17.7**

These statistics tell us little about the etiology of the separate impairments. Thus, an eighty-three-year-old woman encountering difficulty in reading a newspaper may be suffering from a variety of causes ranging from the easily correctable to the imminently fatal. She may be burdened with cataracts of her eyes, or visual agnosia (a neurological state characterized by an inability to recognize objects despite intact vision) secondary to an old stroke, or a profound depression rendering her incapable of concentrating on her newspaper, or a global cerebral atrophy of the Alzheimer type, or a basilar meningioma (a slow-growing brain tumor compressing the undersurface of the cerebellum); or she have recently broken her eyeglasses and cannot afford to replace them. Despite this, these raw statistics do tell us that almost 90 percent of the elderly still retain the capacity to read; and, inferentially, to learn.

Is it important to know the cause of the reading difficulty in the 11.4 percent who state that they cannot see newsprint? The answer is an unequivocal "yes," since the problem may extend well beyond a circumscribed reading problem. The underlying cause, such as a hypothetical meningioma (a slow-growing brain tumor more commonly encountered in the elderly), may not sit quietly but may extend to involve other sensory domains beyond vision; and, in time, may even jeopardize the life of this elderly person. To the physician, then, there is a sequence of inseparably linked questions: what is the systemic disease, if any, causing this reading difficulty? Might the reading difficulty be caused by a social rather than medical condition, something such as a long-standing functional illiteracy hiding behind the claim of visual failure? And, assuming that the existence of an organic substrate to the vision problems is duly verified, will it stay as is or will it spread to involve other tissues? Can this process be halted, reversed, even cured? And, since this elderly patient may well have multiple diseases, will the diagnostic interventions to determine the basis for the eye problems also jeopardize the patient's precarious health?

Determining the underlying cause of the problem is therefore important; but at times not as critical as the preservation of a sense of inner peace in the elderly person. The physician's judgment—and discretion—must, at times, overrule the law of medicine that all diagnostic measures must be undertaken to explain any documented variations from the normal. To those burdened with the responsibility of answering the question "what is causing grandma's eye problems? And, whatever it is, will it get worse in the next year or so?"—the resolve to investigate vigorously must then be balanced by an appreciation of how much "investigation" the patient may tolerate without creating problems that had never previously existed. Somehow, and at frequent intervals when such decisions are to be rendered, an informal cost-benefit analysis must be conducted.

A list of impairments such as those summarized in the table above lacks the scientific soundness of a roster of pathological lesions. Yet, in its pragmatism, it will appeal to the practical-minded for at least two reasons: first, it gives us a profile of what proportions of society, for whatever reasons, are so impaired in a particular function as to require some sort of assistance, perhaps even from governmental sources. And second, it may some day provide a better understanding of how certain persons with particular systemic diseases manage to overcome their impairments while others, with the same lesions, have retreated to invalidism. Some recovering from an old stroke will surrender to their worst anxieties and lapse into a state of global helplessness. Others with an identical stroke will strive to overcome their physical impairments by recruiting other skills or strengths. Much can be learned in such a retrospective study to assist others in the future.

A functional analysis is a good beginning when studying both the disabilities and the abilities of the elderly.

Commentary
Practicalities and the Quality of Life
(RRS)

I begin this commentary with a brief summary of the typical biological components of normal human aging to complement the diseases associated with aging described by SMA. Then I speculate on whether all the changes in aging are inevitable. Finally, I expand on the main point concluded above and to repeat the critical sentence: "A functional analysis is a good beginning when studying both the disabilities and the abilities of the elderly."

First of all, the changes to the aging human body are due to processes that are not completely understood and display great variability from individual to individual and between groups (see Hooyman and Kiyak 1993). In addition to genetic components, environmental and cultural factors greatly influence the rate at which a person ages. Though the changes affect many functions, the older person adjusts to some of the decline in capacities in simple as well as in ingenious ways.

In general, skin replaces itself less often, and its springiness and thickness decrease over time. Individual hair strands become thinner, their total volume decreases and is replaced less rapidly, and the pigment in the hair follicles usually decreases. Because of a decline in cell numbers and size, as well as bone mineral, humans become an average of three inches shorter over their lifetimes. Cuts and wounds take longer to heal. Fat and water are retained less well in the lower layers of the skin which result in an individual's slower adjustment to external temperature changes. Muscles become weaker and lose flexibility, ligaments cannot perform as well with decreased elasticity, cartilage in joints thins, and there is less lubricating fluid in the joints. At advanced ages, there is a tendency to lose weight.

Internal organs also vary in the rate at which they show signs of age. Respiratory and circulatory changes are most evident as the organs become less efficient at using oxygen. The amount of air that can be breathed into the lungs decreases, the number of cilia that remove foreign matter diminish, and the decrease in muscle strength makes the lungs less efficient overall. Heart muscle mass and blood vessels decrease, as does the elasticity in the arteries. Fats tend to build up in the passageways. Because the kidney and liver become smaller and lose efficiency in filtering toxins, the effect of medications can increase and cause harm. The bladder generally holds less as it ages. Gastrointestinal organs also decrease in weight, and some of the ability to process foods decreases.

The brain decreases in size and weight over time, and reflexes and reaction times slow. Eyes have less capacity to function in low light, and adjust more slowly to changes in light. The collagen in the lens becomes less flexible and therefore cannot change shape as effectively to adjust focus from near objects to those far away. Reading glasses are an almost universal necessity for people beginning in their mid-forties. It becomes harder to discriminate colors, to see changes in depth and distance, and more light is needed to see. Except for elongation of the external ear, changes in hearing ability vary greatly among individuals and are often due to environmental as well as genetic factors. While the ability to taste does not seem to decline, the sense of smell becomes less intense, and this decrease affects taste. Touch sensitivity declines because of changes in the skin and a reduction in nerve endings. As is described in chapter 6, a decreased ability in the kinesthetic system tends to limit a person's ability to know his or her position in space, which often results in the elderly person using greater caution in moving about.

How Inevitable?

How inevitable are the changes of aging? Can something be done to prevent the ravages of age? Certainly, the currency of the popular phrase, "use it or lose it," conveys the very real importance of exercise for the continued wellbeing of our physical bodies. Qualitative and quantitative studies, personal anecdotes, and clinical vignettes have indicated that people can maintain or maximize health. When they are physically active, eat well, do not smoke, control weight, limit alcohol, maintain friendships, and exercise, individuals can generally maintain their strength, flexibility, and sexual enjoyment; they can improve cardiac function, reduce stress, lower blood pressure, and generally enhance overall good health into their very advanced years. Even those individuals in their nineties can gain muscle mass and strength from physical training with weights.

"Use it or lose it" seems also to apply to our cognitive functions. Our brains are stimulated with use that seems to help keep our mental abilities sharp and functioning. It is easy to allow lazy thinking habits to predominate, and it is difficult to keep ourselves challenged with new ideas and discrepant ways of thinking. A simple test found currency on the Internet recently:

> Exercise of the brain is as important as exercise of the muscles. As we grow older, it's important that we keep mentally alert. The saying; "If you don't use it, you will lose it" also applies to the brain, so...
>
> Below is a very private way to gauge your loss or non loss of intelligence. So take the 6 simple questions presented here.
>
> Q1. What do you put in a toaster?
>
> Answer: Bread ... If you said "toast" then give up now and go and find yourself a shoe box as you can't handle life ... if you said "bread" then please progress on to question 2.
>
> Q2. Say "silk" 5 times, now spell "silk" ... What do cows drink?
>
> Answer: "Water." If you said "milk," then may I suggest that you do not try the next question, as it may seem that your brain cell is over-taxed, you need a holiday ... May I suggest Children's World? If you said "water" then you may go onto question 3.

Q3. If a red house is made from red bricks, a blue house is made out of blue bricks, a pink house is made out of pink bricks, a black house is made out of black bricks ... What is a green house made out of?

Answer: "Glass," If you said "green bricks" then what the hell are you still doing here reading these questions! If you said "glass" then please progress onto question 4.

Q4. 20 years ago a plane is flying at 20,000 ft, over the old country Germany when 2 of the engines fail, the pilot realizing that the last remaining engine was failing, he decides a crash landing procedure, but unfortunately the engine fails before time and the plane crashes smack bang in the middle of "no mans land" the land between East Germany and West Germany in the middle of the Berlin Wall ... Where would you bury the survivors—East Germany, West Germany or in "no mans' land?

Answer: You don't bury "survivors" if you said anything other than the sentence above then please never fly, you may cause more damage should the plane crash! If you said the sentence above then move on to Question 5.

Q5. If on a clock the hour hand moves 1/60 of a degree every minute then how many degrees will the hour hand travel in 1 hour?

Answer: "1 degree." If you said "360" degrees," or anything other than the answer, may I congratulate you on getting this far ... but be honest with yourself, do you think you can handle the last and final question? if you said "1 degree" then please go on to the last question.

Q6. **Without using a calculator**
You are driving a bus from London to Milford Haven (Wales). In London 17 people get on the bus, in Reading 6 people get off, 9 people get on, in Swindon 2 people get off, 4 people get on, in Cardiff 11 people get off, 16 people get on, in Swansea 3 people get off, 5 people get on, in Carmarthen, 6 people get off, 3 people get on, the bus then pulls into Milford Haven Bus Depot ... What was the name of the bus driver?

Answer: "Your name." Read the first line.

Though the test taunts and showcases spelling and grammar deficits, its implicit suggestion to engage with mental puzzles and challenging problems is valid. It seems likely that many older people avoid learning new things—such as how to use a computer—because of the self-fulfilling prophecy of their *belief* that they, as older people, are not capable of learning new technology. However, the saying, "You can't teach a dog new tricks," is not true. What is certainly true is that if people do not challenge themselves because they are certain that they cannot learn, then by definition, they do not learn.

An intriguing account of 678 American nuns between seventy-five and one hundred and six years old from the School Sisters of Notre Dame religious congregation showed a predictive relationship between brief autobiographies that they had written when they were in their early twenties and the development of Alzheimer's Disease decades later. Though the relationship is still not well understood, it appears that those sisters who expressed more emotional and complex thoughts in their autobiographies seemed somehow protected from dementia. On the other hand, some of the nuns with extensive damage from Alzheimer's Disease had performed extremely well on the mental tests, possibly suggesting that some severe dementia may not reveal significant brain damage (Snowden 2001).

More people are taking the message to heart that disuse leads to declining ability, and they are tackling crossword puzzles, brain puzzlers, and other problem-solving tasks in an effort to flex mental muscles and keep them limber. A small industry is developing ways to stimulate aging brains to stay active and vibrant. Some companies (Genco is an example) are designing board games that include mental challenges, such as vocabulary exercises, for aging baby-boomers concerned about mental slippage and eager to jump on preventative band wagons. Researchers are attempting to discover whether strategies for remembering and performing mental exercises of various kinds help improve or maintain the memories of older people. Books that recommend brain exercises and nutritional supplements are becoming numerous (for example, see Carper 2000, Goldman et al 1999, Katz 1999).

Monique Le Poncin (1990) recommends a regimen for the senses and mental abilities that become weak over time. Focusing on perception, long- and short-term memory, and logic, verbal and visual spatial abilities, she has devised routines to strengthen these capabilities. Some of her suggestions to strengthen some of these abilities include the following:

- Observe an object and draw it immediately after seeing it. Then redraw the object at the end of the day.
- Attempt to create a map recreating your route from a place and repeat it over the next few days.
- Practice putting jigsaw puzzles together as quickly as possible.
- Invent a system to replace a shopping list by classifying foods into categories or creating memory aids to help you identify the items you need.
- Switch the games you play to avoid routine. Chess players should refresh themselves by playing bridge, for example.
- Create an anagram of the name of the person you have just met.
- Summarize the book or chapter you have just read by imagining telling someone the gist of it.

Other so-called experts recommend stretching the brain by learning new things. Take up the study of a foreign language. Challenge yourself with an appealing course at a local college that looks stimulating. Be mindful of what you do and how you listen and concentrate because by paying more careful attention, you focus on remembering. The message from these researchers and authors is that though mental decline is not completely understood and is not necessarily preventable, it is also not necessarily inevitable. Each of us can practice methods of maintaining mental agility and flexibility to better our odds.

Function

Whether changes that result with age are mostly inevitable or not, given the above, how an elderly person "functions" reveals how he manages in the world.

The emphasis on function is practical and down-to-earth; it is a notion that transforms knowledge about the diseases and disabilities an elderly person might have into a picture of how the person makes his way through his days. This notion places the emphasis on the person's experiences as well as on her adaptations to the diseases. The questions that this approach asks are pressing to the person experiencing them. Questions about function lead to practical answers. How will I manage this? Who will I need to help me? If I can bend down better with this arthritis medication, maybe I'll be able to get back to gardening again. Maybe the side effects will be worth the benefit.

People are generally interested in what causes the ailments they have. More often, they want to know what to expect from their diseases. Most of all, they want to know whether and how the disease will affect them not only in the present, but in the future. They will do the cost-benefit analysis to determine what course of action is best for them to choose in light of their medical and functional situation.

Furthermore, whether the culprit is primarily this or that organ is not of fundamental importance to an afflicted person. These matters are for pundits. She wants to know the implications for herself. He wants to know if can continue his life in the way that he has lived it. What will be his trade-offs? How limited will she become? Can her symptoms be ameliorated so that she can resume the activities she had to give up previously? Does he have to prepare for new ways of functioning to maintain as much equilibrium in his life as possible? Except as it relates to prevention and eventual outcome, much else seems academic and of little relevance.

Practical matters relate directly to the quality of one's life.

The focus on function reveals whether the person can perform "Activities of Daily Living" (ADLs) and "Instrumental Activities of Daily Living" (IADLs). Can he get out of bed? Get dressed? Prepare his meals? Balance a checkbook? Go shopping? Take a shower? Manage his medications? The demoralizing effect of not being able to tie one's shoes or get up from a chair can be profound. Interventions that improve a person's ability to function are appreciated. As SMA has indicated, the focus on function orients both the physician and the patient on the old person's priorities.

This shift in thinking about the elderly—from looking at the specifics related to particular diseases to appreciating the significance that the ability to function has for the unique person and his or her spouse or loved ones—provides a tool to design practical answers for everyday problems that old people often face.

Unfortunately, however, the healthcare policy perspective that operates in the U.S. today and funds treatments and procedures, does not always match this idea of function and activities of daily living. The patchwork system of medical care and social services places an arbitrary line between the "medical" and the "social" when they are closely related and intertwined in people's actual lives.

It is important to look at a person's situation in a global context. Quality of life is central to the focus on function and raises practical and ethical concerns. Should a medical treatment or test be undertaken when its side effects are too burdensome for the patient? Should a person be denied his cigarettes when he is ninety-one?

Practical management of an ailment can be better than a medical treatment. Ideally, the medical, social, emotional, functional, and the other factors that impinge on the well being of the older person should all be considered together. Sometimes the best option to try is to manage a situation so that its most problematic aspects are better controlled in order to maintain continuity with a treasured way of life.

Chapter 8

Reflections on Retirement and the Concept of "Home"

(RRS)

As people age through the middle years and begin the process of understanding that they are approaching old age, they have choices and they make decisions. Often the first questions arise about whether and how to end or modify work. Other questions concern whether and how to move a residence. This chapter examines some of the ways people adapt to the internal and external processes that prompt some of these important modifications in their lives.

Work and Retirement

How people retire has a great deal to do with how they worked and what they thought about work and how large social programs, such as Social Security, affect them and their communities.

Notes for this section begin on page 189.

Myths surround the idea of retirement in American society. Retirement is often viewed as nirvana: one reaps the reward of a lifetime of work and finally enjoys the fruits of years of labor. The opposing idea to this view is the following: when you are retired, you are at great risk of dying because you are done, finished, used up, and you are a has-been. The cultural idea that work gives a person a purpose (and sometimes a mailbox and a parking space) carries with it the danger of emptiness and anomie when work ends. Much of the literature about retirement consists of prescriptive how-tos about how to fill the time, how to do the financial planning, and how to choose the place in which to live. Much of the literature assumes the existence of problems in retirement and attempts then to offer solutions to these problems. An issue of *Generations* (Spring 1989) focused on dispelling some of the myths of retirement. The issue included cautions about age discrimination, reassurances about Social Security funding, reviews of financial considerations, and discussions of the options and impacts of retirement on individuals and families.

Psychologists and sociologists tend to focus on the dilemmas that attach to this time period when older people often lose roles without replacing them. Jokes in the culture play on these fears and realities. "I married him for sickness and health, but not for lunch," is one heartfelt complaint that uses a trivial irritation as emblematic of the uncomfortable challenges to marriage routines resulting from retirement. What happens when one partner retires and the other does not? (as in the above joke). What happens when one partner retires because of ill health and the other needs or wants to work but also must do some caregiving? What are the expectations of retirement and how do they square with the experienced reality?

Assumptions about the difficulties of retirement are generally taken as given in this literature. The idea that there is role loss that in turn can lead to diminution in social self-esteem is a powerful one (for example, see Rosow 1985). The activity theory is a dominant theoretical model that prescribes continued activity as essential in order to maintain life satisfaction. This theory directly counters that of disengagement theory's notion that mutual disengagement of the elderly from society is natural and ultimately beneficial. The two theories reinforce one another in sharing the assumption about the general decrease in roles and activity with advancing years (see chapter 2).

Work and productivity are greatly valued in U.S. society, and therefore those who do not work or otherwise make themselves worthy (usually, but not always, in monetary terms) find they have some explaining to do. Dowd (1975) maintained that people have less power in society as they age when they have less to exchange that the society finds of value. When their knowledge or skills are not considered worthy, their status declines and they become dependent. This theory helps to explain some of the difficult trade-offs inherent when Americans retire.

Retirement rewards older workers as it replaces them with younger members of the society. As retirement is initiated at earlier and earlier ages, greater choices and the prospects of increasing life expectancy accompany it. Fully one-third or more of our lives can now be spent in retirement. And for those in the military or civil service with retirement options after as few as twenty-three years, they may spend more years in retirement than employment.

While it is now an expected time of life in American society, retirement is a recent phenomenon. Prior to the twentieth century retirement was rare. Retirement was formally introduced to American life through the establishment of Social Security in the 1930s. When the Social Security Act passed in 1935, only 15 percent of workers reached the age of sixty-five whereas in the 1990s more than 80 percent of workers did (Sokolovsky 1997:4). The proliferation of private pension plans in many lines of work has favored early retirement in general. As increasing numbers of people retire at younger and younger ages, retirement as a time of crisis and stress is less and less the case. As time goes on, people who retire do a great variety of things with their extra time, including second careers, part-time work, volunteering, travel, and the development of new skills.

Adjustment to retirement has been a favorite focus of research by gerontologists in recent decades. The assumption that retirement was a time of crisis generated the research questions about how individuals and groups solved the problem of leisure time and dealt with the time of roleless roles. But how people actually fare during the retirement years is turning out to be a question rife with ambiguity and complexity—like everything else concerning the heterogeneous elderly. Factors such as income, health, gender, ethnicity, nature of the work, family situation, and long-held plans affect the decisions that are made. People with satisfying work are often unwilling to retire early and the opposite is true of those who work in jobs they dislike. Certainly, two obvious findings hold true: dissatisfaction during retirement is often due to low income and poor health.

A drop in income almost always accompanies retirement, and there are still large numbers of elderly poor. Social Security was never intended to replace the income of a full-time job. Its main function was to provide a safety net to former workers so that they would not become destitute. In addition, private pensions are available primarily to those who worked in large companies, and they only provide a portion of the income that the worker earned when he or she was working.

Some people resist retiring, and this option—increasingly possible in the U.S.—has also become more common and necessary in the economic slowdown of the new millennium. Legislation that eliminated mandatory retirement in the U.S. for all occupations except those where safety and age are linked was passed in 1986. People now retire at a great variety of ages. The minimum age at which partial Social Security benefits can be collected is sixty-two (and full benefits at age sixty-five). Most people seem to retire when they can afford to.

To penetrate some of the meanings retirement has to retirees, anthropologist Joel Savishinsky studied twenty-six individuals as they prepared to leave work and as they experienced the first years of their retirements. In *Breaking the Watch: The Meanings of Retirement in America* (2000), Savishinsky's long-term intensive fieldwork in an American community revealed some of the pleasures, conflicts, and ambiguities of the retirement experience in the U.S. Though the book did not survey large numbers of people with questionnaires, it reveals the "poignancy and poetry" in the spoken experiences of the people

Savishinsky grew to know over the years of the study. He watched and listened as they learned first-hand what retirement was about for them. He wrote of the contrasts inherent in this time of life:

> In the United States today retirement is the last of life's major active phases, and perhaps the one most mystifying to those who have yet to reach it. The hopes and fears it invites are both fundamental and contradictory. It evokes ideas of freedom and frailty, loss and opportunity, and a sense of time that is either pregnant with possibility or else weighs heavily on the soul. For some, retirement is the promise to fulfill dreams deferred, for others the face of dread. Some people expect from it new forms of life, liberty, and the pursuit of happiness where others envision a failed landscape populated by the workless and the worthless (2000:4).

Comparing the elders of the fictional Shelby, New York with Inuit elders and those in Africa, the Bahamas and elsewhere, Savishinsky provides a cross-cultural framework to his study. Another valuable aspect of this study is how the author considered work together with retirement. How a person felt about work was intimately connected with how retirement was actually experienced. The ways in which people left their workplaces—with a satisfying farewell party or without meaningful partings, for example—proved to be highly significant to them. Savishinsky highlighted the anthropological approach:

> The chance to keep rethinking peoples' experience of retirement was one of the dividends of time—the result of anthropology's emphasis on long-term involvement in community life, rather than hit-and-run survey research. Hanging out with people, rewalking the same paths and revisiting the same topics, sitting with them over teapots and coffee cups, listening to their words and reflections over weeks, months and years—this methodology revealed that retirement is more than just a last day at work, the signing of forms, a farewell party, of the first Monday at home. It is an ongoing process during which people have to get used to being retired, and to coping with it, to establishing a new life, creating a new identity, addressing their dreams and disappointments, developing a sense of purpose, adjusting their relationships, and learning how to look at their past and look into the mirror (2000:244).

Examining aspects of our lives, such as retirement, by keeping our eyes and ears and hearts open to its perplexities and ambiguities, it is possible to begin to understand some of the *chiaroscuro* attending these experiences.

Environments for the Elderly and the Idea of Home

When gerontologists discuss the environment, they refer to both the social as well as the physical aspects of environment. (The special environment of the nursing home setting is considered in chapter 9.) Research has shown how people make communities within the places they live. As increasing numbers of people have moved to retirement communities after they stopped working, scholarly attention has focused on these environments. The interest in retirement communities stems from the general attention social scientists have given to communities of all sorts—attempting to understand how groups of people are similar to and different from their neighbors, how they organize themselves, and what characteristics keep them together or threaten their viability. One of the features of interest has been homogeneous age communities in some of these cultures. Starting in the 1960s anthropologists began to notice and attend to retirement communities in the U.S.[1] The age-segregated environments in which older people live in the U.S. range from exclusive gated communities in the western states to modest trailer parks in Florida and elsewhere.

This work of sociologists and anthropologists in senior communities of various kinds has focused primarily on the factors that influence the formation of community in these settings and create a sense of "we-feeling" (the sense of belonging to a group.) How do people form relationships and devise strategies for managing tasks in these settings?

Other studies have focused on what effect moving has on older people. Early relocation literature concerning the effects of moving from one setting to another determined the stress that accompanied such moves, even positing higher mortality rates for those who move. Later research discounted the inevitability of stress and burdens associated with moving and emphasized the complexity involved. Many important factors had not been considered in the prior research. These included, significantly, the perspective of the person undergoing the move, the amount of control and choice the person had about the move, the kind of environment to which the person was moving, and the circumstances under which the move was taking place.

For example, if the proposed move was planned in advance, was considered by the older person to be a positive step and one in which she had a say in the major decisions surrounding the move, there was often little negative outcomes from the move. A negatively perceived move, with little control over decision-making, had more negative associations and outcomes for the older person. A simple example of the difference is the planned move to a smaller apartment as opposed to an emergency move due to fire or illness.

Architects, interior designers, engineers and others have focused on the physical ingredients that make up the spaces in which older people live, work, and socialize. They are concerned with the sensory deficits and needs of the elderly. For example, psychologists who study visual changes of aging have weighed in on the kinds of lighting and colors that are best suited for elderly eyes for the functions of reading, walking, and other activities. Because elderly eyes require more light to see and have less elasticity to adjust to changes in brightness, better lighting and contrasting colors between walls and floors in buildings for the elderly are some of the most typical and helpful recommendations.

A key theoretical concept dominating much of the work concerning the relationship of older people and the physical places in which they live is person-fit congruence[2]. According to this idea a person's needs should be in equilibrium with aspects of the environment in order for the person to operate at a maximum level. Gerontologists later adapted these notions to theorize how physical factors in the environment can either hinder or support an older person. Architects and designers have been able to use some of these principles in creating good living spaces for older adults.

Much work has concentrated on ways to enhance a person's abilities within a particular environment. Altering physical components in a setting can help a person perform his or her activities of daily living (ADLs) which in turn can aid the person to remain independent. More subtle factors—not necessarily physical ones—are involved, as well. A person who has cherished her privacy in a quiet, rural setting, for example, may respond poorly to a cramped nursing home that is noisy and nosy with intrusive staff members in her room frequently. On the other hand, a person who has been very sedentary who moves into an assisted living building with long corridors may improve his endurance because he has to walk a longer distance to the dining room to get his meals. Similarly, handrails along the corridor may encourage a person to walk further than she might ordinarily and thus increase her strength.

Environmental and personal factors such as these are significant and can actually determine whether an older person is able to remain in his or her residence or not. A person who is hospitalized after a hip fracture may be unlikely to return home if it is a dwelling at the top of three flights of stairs. But a person who lives on a single floor can replace the three steps leading to the front door with a ramp and find she can remain at home. Simple changes can make daily life easier or can render the smallest tasks exasperating. Door levers are easier to operate than doorknobs. Grab bars in showers and by toilets are safety aids simple to install. Many products and elements of home design are being rethought and redesigned by industrial engineers and architects to make doing routine tasks easier for the growing numbers of elderly and physically disabled people in the population. The growing influence of the ideas of "universal design" (such as wider doorways for wheelchair use, ramps instead of stairs at all house entrances, and other standard features of home design) points to the increasing awareness that everyone—whether able-bodied or not in the present—is potentially disabled in the future.

In the nursing home setting various adaptations to the traditional institutional look can alter whether the environment is home-like or hospital-like. Drably-painted walls and vinyl floors, painted and polished to a high sheen to conform to management ideas of hygiene, can be transformed into more appealing spaces with bright colors and warm textures. The typical layout of hospitals and nursing homes in the U.S. places the nurses' station at the center of long corridors that fan out perpendicularly and impersonally. Though many nursing home residents live in a nursing home for long periods, often for years, the notion that these settings are their "homes" has usually been an afterthought in their design. The Western notion of acute medical care has unduly influenced the design of long-term care facilities in the U.S. and has allowed us to forget that these places need to be homes.

Nursing home units can become homey by making them smaller and more human-scaled. The addition of comfortable couches and rocking chairs (with durable, washable cushions made of modern materials) enhances resident as well as staff well being. This kind of furniture even seems to be associated with fewer behavioral problems. Intriguing research from the University of Rochester indicates that the rhythmic motion of the rocking chairs soothes and has led to substantial decrease in the use of some psychotherapeutic medications in some of these units (Watson et al 1998). Music and other appealing sounds have a large bearing on the atmosphere of the facility. Loudspeakers calling nurses or other personnel maintain the impersonal hospital-like quality. Music of Broadway musicals, swing dancing, or 1940s crooners like Frank Sinatra, however, can evoke a mood and a time period often associated with happy times for the residents. This kind of music often helps staff members and visitors feel livelier and more cheery, as well. I have watched the brimming smiles of residents as nurses' aides spontaneously swing their arms in tune with the beat of the music.

Other touches are just as significant in helping to adapt a physical space to human beings living together in a medical setting. Paintings and artwork made by the residents can enliven the walls and help provide meaningful connection to the people living there. Smells are important too. Enticing odors of baking chocolate chip cookies and apple coffee cakes help stimulate conversation about the good scents, provide eager anticipation for the delicacies, elicit talk of memories of home and recipes and domesticity and altogether help make the place an appealing site in which to live or work. Visitors of the residents feel more welcomed by these smells; they may be more willing to return more often because of these favorable associations.

Children, pets, and plants are other additions that increasing numbers of nursing homes are including in their buildings and their activities to help create some delight in the surroundings for the people there. The beneficial effects of these simple additions again help to enhance a feeling of "home" and increase the comfort of those who are there. Children playing with a ball or giggling among themselves are wonderful sights for nursing home residents to witness or participate in. Savishinsky explored the effects of pets in the nursing home in his study of Elmwood Grove (1991) and found that the pets were a stimulus for lively and moving conversation about the homes and families that the residents had. Thomas (1994) has made these ingredients central in the Eden Alternative nursing home where he is medical director. Psychologists have noted the beneficial effects that can occur when nursing home residents take responsibility for the care of pets or plants.

Architects, psychologists, environmental gerontologists, and others have also worked to assist nursing home residents find their way around in these settings. Placing special mementos on the doorway of a person with dementia can aid that person find his room. Other examples of personalizing rooms and spaces help to continue and enhance a person's identity and individuality. Afghans, photos, favorite chairs, cherished figurines, needlepoint—all brighten and enhance the space. This is especially important when nursing home residents have difficulty remembering aspects of their lives that were important. Even when it seems that the nursing home resident is indifferent to these memories, it is often important to family members that these meaningful reminders of a full life are displayed. Furthermore, such clues to past achievements and markers of individuality cue staff members that the nursing home residents were not always impaired.

When people with dementia lose the ability to read, it is useful to create signs with symbols that offer clues to their meaning. A sign with a knife and fork can help a person find the dining room, a sign with a picture of a toilet indicates the bathroom, and so on. Designers have experimented with ideas like color-coding the corridors and naming the units and corridors as other ways to assist nursing home residents find their way through the often-confusing maze of the nursing home environment. Psychologists have emphasized the need for stimulation: decorations on the walls have been designed to create interest in the residents. When items on the walls are made with unusual textures, residents are encouraged to stop and touch. Outside, pathways to walk have been created for safety, familiarity, and interest. Especially for nursing home residents who want to walk a great deal (a common behavior of residents with dementia), such safe and interesting walking paths are extremely beneficial.

In their small-scale studies anthropologists have concentrated on understanding the experiences of the nursing home residents or the inhabitants of other housing situations. Participant-observation can lead to insights that can help alter routines and environmental features positively. William H. Whyte was one of the first people to notice what aspects of outdoor spaces drew people to congregate in them and which elements of the setting seemed to do the opposite. His observations led to design innovations, such as more felicitous placement of benches and plants, for example, that have made these places generally more people-friendly.

Anthropologists have also explored and developed the idea of "home." Jackson (1995) investigated what home and homelessness meant to the Warlpiri of Australia who do not build or live in houses and whose term for house is not the same as that for home. He traveled with them in order to understand how they connected themselves to the world with a sense of home. At one point he felt he understood something of their experience:

> It is to experience a complete consonance between one's own body and the body of the earth. Between self and other. It little matters whether the other is a landscape, a loved one, a house, or an action. Things flow. There seems to be no resistance between oneself and the world. The *relationship* is all (1995:111, italics his).

Clearly, it is important to understand as much as possible about what home means to older adults. What are the ingredients within a dwelling (or without a dwelling in the Warlpiri case) that make it home-like? How can spaces be adapted so that they both support an older person to be as independent and functional as possible and enable a person to feel comfortable and most himself? What are the attachments people have to "things?" How do people make choices about valued things? Understanding what home means to people also entails acknowledging that individuals have varied tastes and preferences. Stafford's experiment in creating "healthy urban environments for older adults" through his Evergreen Project puts into action research into older people's preferences about the places in which they live (see Sokolovsky 1997: xxvi-xxvii for a summary of this project).

Furthermore, it is necessary to question romantic ideas of home and dispel the myths. Idealized notions of family and home are often fictions—that, is, socially constructed and little related to the realities—that are considered opposite to the harshness, impersonality, and anomie of the workplace (see Lasch 1977).

We need to know more about how homes actually work in order to clarify what makes them appealing and comfortable. We need to know more about how spaces help people function better, encourage sociability, and allow people to feel most fully themselves. The interdisciplinary study of these and other questions should yield answers that can improve the lives of older people.

Notes

1. Some of the work on trailer parks and public housing is summarized in Rhoads and Holmes (1995). Some of the community studies of public housing and senior centers include Hochschild (1973), Francis (1984), Teski (1981), Jerrome (1992), and Johnson (1971), among others.
2. Lewin (1935), Murray (1938), Kahana (1975), and Lawton (see for example, Lawton, Windley and Byerts 1982) were key developers of the concepts that led to this theory.

Commentary
Vagrant Thoughts on Retirement
(SMA)

Retirement—along with the transition from infancy to childhood, the entrance into sexual maturity, and the onset of economic and residential self-sufficiency—represents one of the major steps in the lives of humans. Except for retirement, each of these transitions, in a sense, symbolizes a step in the direction of greater independence, greater access to more varied choice, and more freedom to explore the unknown. The levels of accompanying hazard, of greater vulnerability, obviously rise with each new venture into uncharted territories.

Retirement clearly represents a retreat from the abrasive parts of competitive life; and many of the daily dangers of the workplace are now past and retirement becomes a haven of relative safety; but, much as it may be portrayed otherwise, retirement also represents, for most, an abject retreat from the joys of discovery and the creation of new enterprises.

What, other than income, is lost when an active person retires? Certainly a feeling of authentic participation in daily events of significance, and certainly the capacity to make meaningful decisions that determine the future of self, family, even community.

And as the retired person steps back from this decision-making position, as this sixty-five-year-old retreats to the observer galleries, a curious thing then happens. His voice somehow becomes reduced to an inarticulate whisper; his suggestions (now, no longer commands) are either unheard, or if heard, treated condescendingly. And the most curious event of all in the transformation to retirement, is that his body no longer seems to be opaque, no longer seems to occupy space. Many a retiree notes, ruefully, how he is no longer noticed when he ventures through the erstwhile familiar corridors of the workplace, how he has now become totally transparent. The eyes of former colleagues, in these familiar corridors, no longer focus on the face of the retiree; rather, they seem to peer through him as if focused upon the far wall of the corridor.

As one former executive described it: "I no longer made decisions. I am now allowed, encouraged, to sit quietly, think about life, amuse myself with harmless pastimes, discuss golf, read obituaries, rue my past indiscretions, contemplate the increasing wrinkles in my skin and watch in awe the enhanced efficiency of the organization coincident with my retirement. Like a child, I am allowed to be seen but not heard."

Most who currently retire from positions of authority are male. But as women assume an increasing degree of control in the executive chambers of industry and government, they too, in years to come, will confront that feeling of loss (akin to bereavement) when they are required to face a powerless idleness. It is possible, though not certain, that they will handle retirement with greater equanimity and understanding than do their male counterparts.

Hard to believe that women will fare particularly better than men at retirement, but who knows? Many people experience the "non-person" treatment described above. Women after a "certain age" learn that they are invisible to others, and this age occurs increasingly early. Various groups of unprivileged people, such as the poor, the disabled, and the homeless are often treated as non-persons, and the treatment seems unrelated to age.

Here is an excerpt from another man's perspective after a year of retirement offered as contrast:

"Though my story is just one of 1.7 million (the number of workers who retire each year, according to the Social Security Administration), I can say this much with confidence: retirement is a hard thing to plan. My reaction toward just about everything has been to slow down. It turned out that I did not need to do most of

what I had thought was essential. I certainly did not need to do it quickly ...

But what, really, is retirement? It is more than what you do or don't do. It is an attitude ... Oh, I teach a couple of writing courses because I enjoy them. I judge a newspaper contest, write a few articles. But I turn down as much work as I accept. To me, working was often doing things you didn't particularly want to do because you thought you had to. Retirement is saying you don't have to do anything unless you want to.

Isn't retirement lonely and unstructured? I had that fear. I thought I would miss the intellectual stimulation I used to get from workmates. But then I realized that I got more stimulation reading at home ...

I do things I have wanted to do for years, like helping my ninety-one-year-old mother with her memoirs.

I have some markers to the future. My father was retired for thirty years when he died at ninety-two. He loved retirement, never looked back. Had a million hobbies and acted as a caretaker for my ill grandmother. My mother, I suspect, will be starting Book 2 of her memoirs at any time ..."(Volz 2001). [RRS]

Chapter 9

Some Social
and Ethical Implications
of Dementia

(RRS)

As the numbers of old people in the world increase at a rapid rate, the incidence of those with dementia has gone up accordingly. Physicians and social scientists, including anthropologists, have been among those to examine dementia from diverse points of view. Most people with dementia in the U.S. eventually end up in nursing homes.

Dementia

The understanding of dementing diseases has broadened in recent decades in the U.S., propelled in great part by the sense of urgency of our rapidly aging population and the increase of those with dementias. Most of the investigation into Alzheimer's disease and other dementias has been undertaken by physicians, epidemiologists, biologists, geneticists, physiologists, neurolo-

---

The note for this section can be found on page 204.

gists, and others trained in the hard sciences. Their work has led to increasingly significant findings, helpful psychotherapeutic medications, genetic clues, and a growing understanding of the neuropathology of the disease. Epidemiologists help plot the incidence of dementias, reveal where suspicious geographical clusters occur, and point the way for further research opportunities and causal relationships. As a result of their work, more is known about what dementing diseases are, what factors increase their risk, and where they are located.

Other researchers in dementia are those most concerned about the treatment and management of persons with the disease. Social workers and therapists have proposed theories and interventions designed to ease some of the more problematic and troubling behaviors that arise with the disease. Some of the problems include mood changes, aggression, wandering, paranoia, passivity. Different kinds of professionals from various fields have devised special strategies that help caregivers in a variety of situations.

Treating people with dementia raises perplexing questions. Should caregivers attempt to anchor people with dementia in the here and now realities (an approach termed "reality orientation") or should they go along with a demented person's rendition of events to provide a reassuring form of therapeutic intervention? Should we train in special communication techniques that may decode the "real" meaning of what people with dementia are talking about (e.g., "validation therapy" [Feil 1993])? Most dementia units are predicated on the widely accepted notion that intellectual stimulation is a beneficial "treatment" for those with dementias. Therefore, activities designed to stimulate the mind via word games, trivia questions, and so forth are the mainstay of many of these programs.

These regimens that are based on an assortment of sociological and psychological research are rooted in the assumption that active brains work better, last longer, and resist atrophy. The "use it or lose it" philosophy underlies much of the caregiving rationale. It is a particularly North American approach. Whether these therapies accomplish what they set out to do in dementia treatment is far from certain, but the idea is popular in the U.S.

As the incidence of dementias rises, the ripple effect spreads far beyond the affected person. The toll in the loss of productivity of work (both in the affected person and the family caregivers who must alter their work lives) and in the lives of family members seems to be great. Dementia is spoken of as the endless death, the endless mourning, the endless night, and the thirty-six-hour day (see Mace and Rabins 1981).

Anthropology's interest in dementia takes many forms. Henderson (1995) has noted how the marketing of special dementia units in nursing homes only barely masks the more basic "veterinary" care of the residents housed there, and Lyman maintains that daycare centers for those with dementia that focus on more social aspects of behavior seem better for the clients than the more medicalized settings (1993).

Cohen (1998) identified contradictory cultural forces related to Alzheimer's disease. His work in India stressed the culturally relative definitions of dementia. For example, in the Indian city of Varanasi, "weak" or "hot brain" and anger are some of the explanations for the crazy behavior of old people.[1] Senile-type behavior is considered to be caused by insufficient support from or abandonment by family members. "Bad" families caused by poverty, the caste system, problems between mothers- and daughters-in-law, as well as other Indian social conditions were partly responsible for how "crazy old people" behaved—and were not encompassed by Western biomedical conceptions of dementia. Cohen observed that people in the part of India he studied were more likely to blame the decline in the well-being of old people on the decline of the "joint family" because of modernization and Westernization rather than on memory problems or dementia.

These kinds of analyses show us the arbitrariness—or the cultural nature—of some of the conditions we label dementia. They show us how much we assume and how little we share and know.

Some anthropologists focus on the experiences of the people affected by dementia themselves. A field study by Lyman (1996), for example, revealed the "unexpected identities" of people in the U.S. with moderate cognitive impairment. Though such people were expected to "experience diminished 'person-hood,'" Lyman found that people with dementia did not talk about themselves or their experiences with the dread and gloom that others expected. The following example reveals the contrast in perspectives.

An eighty-two-year-old woman with dementia seemed undistressed by her growing inability to remember. She cheerfully answered her son's queries on the phone about what she did that day with a singing, "What did we do today, dear?" question called out to her husband in the next room. He patiently related where they had gone and what they had eaten and she in turn recited that information into the mouthpiece of the phone. Whatever inkling she had of her progressive memory loss seemed not to cause any distress to her. This loving husband—who explained to others that his patience and forbearance would be offered to him by her were the tables reversed—made her comfort possible. He, as well as she, seemed little perturbed by her growing dependency. Though she had little or no short-term memory, they enjoyed one another's company, did pleasurable things, and seemed content. As the cliché has it, they "lived in the moment."

Once her eighty-five-year-old husband died, however, she was unable to live by herself. Her inability to cook, shop, pay bills, keep or make appointments now became noticeable. She and her situation were now problems that needed to be managed. "You can't stay here," "you have no one here," "you need someone to help you" were her children's mantras at once real and urgent that eventually convinced her to move to assistive housing near them. Once she moved, her deficits seemed still more apparent. Was this decline due to a progression of her disease, to the loss of her husband, to the loss of her home, or to all of these? Over a short few months she had lost her husband, her home, her city, her strength, and her formerly agile mind. The loss of her husband and her home made her less willing and curious to embrace new experiences. Mourning seemed to develop into clinical depression. Finally, her gradual accommodation—to a new residence, to a life without her husband, to the necessity of accepting a certain amount of help from caregivers—became an accommodation to her new reality. She was making sense of her life—composing it anew. Dementia in her old age would be a part of her and her new experiences, but only a part.

Nursing Homes

Nursing homes are discrete institutions created to house and meet the needs of aged individuals who are physically and/or mentally unable to care for themselves and function with a sufficient degree of independence. Not all countries utilize nursing homes, and they are structured differently in different places. In Scandinavia, for example, nursing home rooms are constructed like separate, independent living places where assistance is available, more akin to American assisted living housing. The use of nursing homes varies by ethnicity, as well. African-Americans, for example, are far less likely to institutionalize a family member than are white Americans.

Many people mistakenly assume that great numbers of elderly people live in institutions such as nursing homes while only a small proportion of elderly live in them for long periods of time. Some 5 percent of those over the age of sixty-five live in nursing homes. The proportion of those in nursing homes rises steeply over the age of eighty-five, however: at any one time about 20 percent of those over this age reside in nursing homes. A greater number still spend some shorter stays in nursing homes for short-term rehabilitative stays.

Nursing homes in their self-contained buildings are like societies onto themselves. Usually separate from whatever community in which they are physically planted, their administration, employees, residents, intermittent doctors, and visitors occupy predictable niches and interact with one another in certain ways.

Or do they? Highly regulated, closely overseen by federal and state mandating authorities, they are each nonetheless different at the same time that they share significant features and house individuals with familiar and predictable diseases.

Researchers have focused on what actually goes on in these places, why they seem terrifying and forbidden, and how to sep-

arate myth from reality about them. Government studies have
chronicled their shortcoming and mandated reforms over the
years. Anthropological studies—often small, comparative, and
conducted over a long term using open-ended interviews and
lengthy conversations—have helped illuminate some of the
ambiguity, nuance, and complexity of these spaces. The cross-
cultural framework challenges the acceptance of the status quo
because societies organize care for the elderly and think about
being old in various ways.

Gubrium's classic account of the world of Murray Manor
showed the vivid differences between the various groups of people who work in the institution. Laird (1979) described her own
experience living in and surviving one. Pet therapy programs in
one nursing home stimulated anthropologist Savishinsky (1991)
to explore how pets elicited reminiscences of domestic life and
families. Anthropological interest in narrative and personal history has spurred several to probe the histories of nursing home
residents. My *Uneasy Endings* (1988) was an examination of
how the nursing home created a liminal existence for its residents adrift from the community in which it was situated.
Foner's *The Caregiving Dilemma* (1994) and Diamond's *Making
Grey Gold* (1992) concentrated on the excruciatingly difficult
work of the nursing assistants. Henderson and Vesperi's (1995)
edited volume described different aspects of doing ethnography
in nursing homes and the kinds of insights long-term research
reveals. Kayser-Jones (1981) showed the vast differences in philosophy and attitude between the Scottish and American nursing homes that she studied, and Cohen's (1998) study revealed
contrasting ideas about nursing homes in India.

Some researchers focused on the management of difficult
behaviors within nursing homes and helped usher in reforms.
For example, the widespread use of restraints in nursing
homes—for those who yelled, disturbed others, bit, spit, wan-
dered, were at risk of falling—generated debate, controversy,
and changes.

Investigation of the use of restrains eventually led to the
almost complete reversal of this less-than-ideal treatment.
Reform came in the Omnibus Budget Reconciliation Act (OBRA)

of 1987 (spurred by the Institute of Medicine's 1986 critical report on nursing homes). New regulations mandated that restraint use had to be justified. Similar reasoning pertained to psychotropic medication use. Standardized assessment forms (the Minimum Data Set and the MDS+) came into widespread use and helped clarify goals of care, created uniform ways to initially assess and continue supervision of ongoing care and helped to target specific problematic treatment areas (such as guidelines for bedsore prevention and treatment). Emphasis on resident autonomy is now a central feature of assessing the quality of nursing homes. This is a big change from years ago.

The staffing and training of nursing home personnel remain a chronic problem. OBRA '87 mandated the training and certification of nursing assistants, but the availability of certified nursing assistants (CNAs) relies on the labor market and the overall economy, and the hourly rate of pay remains low. A CNA told me in 2001 that her eighteen-year-old son found a job in a warehouse store for $10 an hour, a marked contrast to her $7/hour job in the nursing home after training and ten years experience!

The way nursing homes are funded reflects the profound flaws in how healthcare for the elderly is paid for in the U.S. Because Medicare pays primarily for acute hospital care and doctor visits, chronic, long-term care is not reimbursed except for a specific amount of time (about 100 days) following at least a three-day hospitalization for skilled nursing care. Most nursing home care is unskilled. If clients can afford it, nursing home care is paid from private funds. When a person runs out of money or has insufficient funds, nursing home care is paid by Medicaid, a healthcare program for the needy that is funded by federal and state monies. Medicare cuts exacerbated the funding problems of nursing homes and many nursing homes, including for-profit chains, filed for bankruptcy protection. Nurse and CNA shortages continue in the industry.

How nursing homes have changed in the environment of managed care is of continuing interest and concern (Mor, Banaszak-Holl, and Zinn 1996; Shield 1997). In response to changing Medicare reimbursement policies that result in the discharge of sicker and more impaired residents, nursing homes have specialized in more acute and high-tech nursing as well as in rehabilitative care (Zinn and Mor 1994). Comfort care and hospice for dying residents occurs in many nursing homes (Miller and Mor 2002). Though nursing homes still house many non-acute, non-technological and very long-term residents with dementia, new assisted living environments—often with specific dementia care wings—are being built for the growing numbers of elderly who need supportive care. However, these housing solutions are costly and not currently reimbursed by federal or state funding programs.

Architects and designers have looked at how space can be utilized and transformed to help people live and function better, as described in chapter 8. Though nursing homes are burdened by the voluminous regulations of building, fire, and other regulatory codes, designers are finding creative ways to make these environments more people-friendly and supportive. Designers devise plans that make impersonal spaces individual and unique and welcoming. Recessing a doorway a small amount and framing it with contrasting color can transform a drab entrance to a nursing home room into a space that suggests the entryway to a house. Beyond ramps and grab bars, these ideas hint at the limitless possibilities inherent in creative design.

Ethical Issues

As technology enables more people to live, more questions are raised about the quality of life that they are leading. Ethical questions about the rights of people with dementia are important and pressing. Decisions about medical care and daily life in nursing homes—rights of residents to sexual partners and activity, choices about meal time and privacy, the right to eat unhealthy foods, the rights of residents' children versus those of their parents to make decisions, the freedom to move about beyond what is considered "safe," whether or how to withhold or withdraw treatments for dying persons and how to incorporate comfort care for residents into the highly task-oriented routines of the facility—these are examples of some of the issues that confront nursing homes.

Ethics committees in nursing homes are likely to discuss issues of "everyday ethics" (Kane and Caplan 1990; Shield 1995; see also *Generations* winter 1995/6) as well as life and death concerns. The ethnicity of those on the board can make a difference to the outlook of the committee. One ethics committee discussion in which I participated was influenced by a Ghanaian nursing assistant committee member's perspective on elder care in his native community.

Ethical quandaries are numerous within and beyond the doors of the nursing home as well. Whether a person should be told he probably has Alzheimer's disease is a question that physicians have grappled with for years. End-of-life questions are staples for physicians. Should a ninety-eight-year-old have surgery? When does dialysis stop making sense? Should CPR be administered to a demented and frail older person? Whose wishes should be followed when a demented person does not want hospitalization? Should the stops be pulled out for relief of pain if these medications hasten death? Can physicians order nursing home residents to submit to constraints in lifestyle in a medical setting that is also the resident's home? Should a widow with dementia be corrected when she speaks about her husband as alive? Do the adult children of a confused nursing home resident have a say about the consensual sexual relationship she develops with another resident? Who makes decisions about these lives?

Traditionally, ethical issues in the U.S. are the bailiwick of philosophers. But people in all their variety do not necessarily think like Western philosophers. Furthermore, how people actually conceptualize questions and behave in relation to situations is often very different from what they say they do. Similarly, the ethical premises guiding physicians are sometimes different than those for social workers, nurses, and anthropologists, not to mention those of their culturally diverse clients. Anthropologists critique the rationalist assumptions inherent in most philosophical discussion.

As anthropologists question underpinnings of Western philosophy, they sometimes bring in non-Western notions of ethical decision-making. A prime example of the Western assumption is the primacy of the individual and his or her rights vis-à-vis society and others. Eastern religions and philosophies are conceived in terms of totalities and harmonies rather than in the polarities and oppositions of the Cartesian thinking of the West. Typically the individual is subsumed within the group. These differences lead to other ways of understanding and resolving ethical issues. While medical practitioners may consider an autopsy a straightforward medical decision, many cultures prohibit practices that destroy the integrity of the dead body because such actions are understood to prevent a peaceful afterlife. Cultural beliefs can similarly reject the possibility of organ donation (see Lock 1993).

Throughout the world people who are viewed as less than adult have fewer rights than adults. Children, and in many places, women, conceived of as property or under the guidance of adults, are told what to do and are expected to do what they are told. Adults usually make the important decisions for these individuals. When adults consider other adults incompetent, the important decision-making powers of the noncompetent individuals are removed from them as well. When aged members of society are considered decrepit, non-contributing, and either mentally or physically incompetent, others start speaking in their behalf. When that happens, the integrity of their selves is also in question. Less than adult, they are somehow less than human as well. All of these definitions and notions are also contested and negotiated.

Technological prowess and the proliferation of devices and procedures that can extend and prolong life complicate the picture. Physicians, philosophers, and anthropologists probe the fine points and subtle ramifications of what makes a person competent, who can make decisions and how do individual rights balance against those of the family, the community, the state. The use of advance directives and the passage of the Patient Self-Determination Act (PSDA) of 1991 attempt to make patient preferences in care explicit, but these documents cannot ensure that the wishes are carried out. Should people in persistent vegetative states be allowed to die? By whose wishes should they be continued on life support? How do those in control ascertain what the patient wants or would have wanted, and how different are those two tenses in our idea of what the self is? How is an advance directive to be interpreted in each highly specific case?

Philosophy and law have dominated much of the discussion about withholding care and the termination of treatment. The debates about euthanasia at the end of life have been framed in terms of whether it is passive or active. Political arguments polarized by language about right to life and murder inflame and cloud the debate rather than help to clarify the complicated questions involved in it. Medical researchers and physicians have tried to understand and describe normal physiological processes involved in dying. Their work has suggested that losing the desire to eat and drink is not experienced as painful hunger and thirst, for example. Psychiatrists have helped clarify whether a patient who wishes to end his life has a clinical depression that could be treated with medications and talk and possibly result in a renewed wish to live. Anthropologists enter the discussion with description and explanation about how death, suicide, and the beyond are understood by people throughout the world. For example, the "Eskimo on the ice floe" idea of how some cultures dispose of their elderly masks how the Inuit perceive such rare "altruistic suicide" (Savishinsky 2000) which occurs in dire circumstances.

Ethical issues concerning autonomy are important, particularly in North American society where individual rights are a traditional and a cherished foundation of the culture. Autonomy carries with it ideas of independence and self-reliance. When rights are embedded in a self-contained individual, and autonomy is considered so important, any threat to autonomy is viewed as shameful. Ideas of interdependency and dependency without the connotations of sick role or disgrace are notions less familiar and comfortable for North Americans. But these are ideas that more North Americans are struggling with as the proportion of elderly grows and as more and more people live full lives despite debilitating disability or chronic conditions of all sorts.

Philosophers have tended to frame healthcare debates about decision-making and autonomy in terms of traditional

Western principles such as beneficence, autonomy, and paternalism. Lawyers talk about competency in relation to guardianship. Can a person handle money, hold sustained opinions over time? That North Americans value their privacy is an accepted tenet of modern life in the U.S. Furthermore, the wish for privacy is individual and culturally determined to a great extent. Moreover, the value on privacy conflicts with a medical culture with respect to which it takes a decided back seat to medical urgency, medical teaching, and other concerns.

As the entrenched routines and mandates of medical culture come under increased scrutiny, it is to be hoped that more individualized care, more reflective thinking about what is automatically considered right, and increasingly sensitive attitudes about the nuances and ambiguities of life and death will be developed and incorporated into humane care-giving.

Note

1. Sarah Lamb says that in the city of Mangaldihi, India that she studied, "such changes in the mind—though noted at times—were not commonly stressed as constitutive of old age" (2000:44).

Commentary
The Expectation of Sorrow as Anticipatory Grief
(SMA)

L oss and reactive grief are experienced by all who have lived beyond childhood. Caregivers such as nurses, social workers, and physicians are certainly not immune to immediate grief in response to some grave reality. But, in addition, they also may grieve for things that have not as yet happened, something called anticipatory grief. This curious reaction has particular relevance when working with and caring for those in the premonitory phases of Alzheimer's disease.

Immediate grief is a solitary passion, experienced as a mourning for that which is lost and a despair that life can provide nothing to replace that which has been taken away. Anticipatory grief, on the other hand, intrudes at a time when the sky is not yet darkened and the feared storm, if indeed there will be a storm, is at the far margins of visibility.

Most people agree that providing necessary solace is a vital part of the unwritten covenant between patient and caretaker; but support, of course, will be rendered by whomever can willingly offer it. The sharing of grief that is not one's own is a rare capacity that requires neither formal training nor certification for its fulfillment.

The caring physician, in staying with a grieving person, inevitably feels the margins of that person's sorrows but, typically, will not share the unrelieved sense of despair that immediate grief so often generates. In these tragic encounters the physician's personal sadness arises from his/her greater familiarity with the many faces of tragedy. It is tempered not only by his/her sure knowledge that life is stronger than grief, but also the deep awareness that true grief is not a commodity to be transferred.

Yet there is a form of grief—anticipatory grief—that is peculiar to the caregivers of society. Since knowledge about the mechanics of disease necessarily provides the physician with a small window to the future, the burden of anticipating terrible things becomes inevitable.

A century ago medicine was capable of curing very few diseases. Yet the profession was more than the mere placating of the patient while nature provided an occasional cure. Physicians were skilled in a number of technical interventions such as setting a fracture; and, with medications, reducing pain. In addition, through their intimacy with the kinetics and trajectory of diseases, they were able to offer reasonably accurate forecasts of each patient's future.

Western medicine has placed great emphasis on the nosology and etiology of systemic disease. The separateness of each illness was repeatedly verified by objective criteria, named, and then classified. To this day much of formal medical education is invested in precise identification (diagnosis) and clarifying the natural history (prognosis) of human disease. Beyond its expanding capability of providing comfort and occasional cure, contemporary Western medicine has refined, albeit imperfectly, the art of predicting the future. In many ways, this has been the profession's greatest accomplishment: to confront the aggregate of organic sufferings and to perceive within this population of distressed persons separate maladies each with its own risks, histories, etiologies, therapies, and future courses.

Two elderly people may seek medical help, each because of a severe headache. In one, the physician recognizes the characteristics of tension headache and may then offer the patient reassurance that the ache will readily respond to simple medication. But in the other person the physician may detect the subtle hints of an underlying brain tumor as the cause of the headache, and then foresee in a seemingly healthy person the remorseless inevitability of more headaches evolving into seizures, blindness, and coma. The trained physician perceives more than that which is apparent to the intelligent but untrained eye. The physician's skills in diagnosis allows him or her to review the fragments of information and to arrive at some explanation that will account for the various signs and symptoms offered by the patient.

Physicians therefore invest much of their energies in establishing a firm diagnosis. But the path toward achieving this is typically strewn with discarded alternatives. Each lump looms as a cancerous node and each chest pain as the harbinger of coronary artery disease until ruled out by further studies. In each excursion into the dark realm of diagnostic possibilities, the physician is compelled to anticipate the consequences to the patient should the more serious possibility turn into reality. The sixty-three-year-old married accountant, the father of three children, and the sole support of his elderly parents, visits the office because of intermittent rectal bleeding. The likeliest cause is benign hemorrhoids, but the possibility of an underlying colorectal cancer must be diligently investigated. Between the time of conjecture and the time of verification, perhaps a few days, the physician is the bearer of a terrible weight: the knowledge that this currently functioning family may soon face serious problems. During this interval of anxiety before the diagnosis is established, the prudent physician keeps the many possibilities behind a bland facade. Nature is generally kinder and most lumps are eventually shown to be benign and most chest pains turn out to be of non-cardiac origin. This interval of diagnostic doubt is usually unavoidable and it becomes a matter of tender charity to withhold from the patient all of the various clinical possibilities. If indeed the worst scenario is verified, there is sufficient time to share the truth; and if no cure or specific treatment is available then the patient's future path must be jointly appraised by patient, family, and physician.

The skilled physician accepts anticipatory grief as a near-constant companion, a necessary part of his or her professional duties. Ninety-nine negative tests do not provide the emotional compensation to balance but one positive screening test that predicts some human tragedy in the future of a single patient. When this happens, the physician's grief is increased by the inevitable conflict that arises between the desire to give the patient some peace of mind and the obligation to provide the patient with the unmanipulated truth. Sometimes the truth must be unfolded slowly, otherwise much harm may be done. Emily Dickinson once said that the truth must dazzle gradually, or else every man be blinded. The heartache borne by the concerned physician cannot be discarded without also discarding his humane instincts and commitments. The physician knows that giving the patient truth without mercy is a cruelty; whereas providing mercy without truth demeans both patient and physician.

There are times, many times, when the diagnosis remains elusive despite all efforts and the patient continues to deteriorate, when neither truth nor mercy can be served, leaving the patient to endure his/her own personal grief alone. This sadness, mixing both immediate and anticipatory grief, is a hazard within the care-giving professions and may be the basis for their little-publicized high rates of emotional impairment and chemical dependencies.

Anticipatory grief also accompanies the surgeon who must envision what the patient will feel as a result of the removal of an important body part. Knowing that the procedure may be lifesaving will not lessen the emerging grief. The woman facing mastectomy for breast cancer must confront the threat to her life, but also the parallel assault on her sexual identity. Dismemberment rather than death, then, may also provoke anticipatory grief in the physician.

Certainly the physician's license to see beyond today deprives him or her of some peace of mind, whereas this intimacy with aging allows for few comforting illusions. Aging is sometimes a graceful event, a work of art, with much wisdom and insight replacing the inevitable loss of certain faculties. More often, though, aging is a poignant, demeaning, and graceless thing, filled with memories that are both bitter and failing.

As a larger fraction of the American population survives beyond the age of seventy-five years, an erstwhile rare disease is becoming increasingly frequent, creating what has been described as the next great epidemic. This illness, Alzheimer's disease, by its nature, is a source of great anticipatory grief. It is a lengthy, progressive illness that finally deprives its victims of memory, orientation, clarity of thinking, and the capacity to attend to basic everyday needs. Ultimately there is a loss of spirit and identity with the individual reduced to a mean, vegetative existence, surviving for years in a nursing facility. At the moment there are no proven therapies to prevent or even halt the desolate course of the disease. Imagine the grief in the physician when detecting the earliest hint of memory lapse or cognitive misjudgment in an otherwise vigorous, healthy person. It requires little imagination to envision the stretch of years ahead with its destructive effects on spouse and children.

At this sad moment in the patient's dementing course the physician can offer little more than his diagnostic conclusions and prognostic projections. But as a compassionate human in society, the physician may offer solace as well as advice to the family as they begin to learn how to cope with the problem; but in the privacy of his or her mind, the physician may anticipate and experience the full dimensions of grief that will surely arise as the disease progresses.

> *I have wondered: what is the self? As the dementia takes over the person whom I know so well, with whom is she being replaced? [OM]*

Interlude
Some Joys: My Personal Ode to Aging Thus Far
(RRS)

Perhaps it is naïve for me to say—at this point, fairly early on in my aging—that I am finally beginning to find my stride— or at least, a stride that suits me pretty well. I think this is a good thing about my aging. I have lived in my skin and on this earth for enough time by now to become comfortable and famil- iar with who I am. [But I also know I am not *really* old, and I know that I do not know what lies ahead. Admittedly, in many places of the world, and by many definitions, I am already old. And I have been lucky so far. I seem to be healthy, and I still have energy. I have the privilege to know that my body has been a mostly dependable friend.]

It takes a long time—at least for me—to inhabit oneself fully. It is simply not possible when one is young. The self, what- ever that elusive notion is all about, has slippery and complex visions to which a person only gradually becomes accustomed. After years of fighting certain traits and of developing and strengthening other aspects of a personality, a person fits some- what more compatibly on him or herself than before.

The reflection I see is familiar and generally friendly. I see my mother looking back at me—and though her look is a disori- enting glimpse of my old age—it is also warmly reminiscent of a view so intimate, so connected with my essence as to be profoundly confirming. My mother in my face looks back at me, and I see her in a look of my mouth or in the shape of my eyebrow. Recognizing her in me links me to my younger—not just my older—self. Somehow, the look of my mother makes me feel ageless while it clues me to my aging.

The newness of youth *is* rough and rude, I see now. The young are essentially clueless. What do they know of elemental things such as aging and irretrievable loss or so many other things that are important? They struggle with knowing, but what a pose it is. How they scramble to piece together the world, to attempt to know how things work, how to trust, whether to ask, how to simply gauge what is. How can they know with so little experience that which we have taken many years to figure out? The things that happen with the accretion of years cannot be collapsed into prescriptions, crammed into formulae, or preemptively studied. Friendships, work, loves, accidents, tragedies, encounters, coincidences, amazing events, deep sadness—these experiences make us who we are. We react individually—unlike anyone else—and we react predictably—just like everyone else. Learning to live with the tension of this sameness and difference from and with other human beings is part of what imparts the richness to the long-lived life.

Young creatures are not only rude, bumbling, and unable to grasp the disparate elements of experience into some meaningful whole—their acute sensitivity to sensation and events makes them too vulnerable to fully understand. Of course they are also resilient and pliant, wonderfully quick to heal and to bounce back from danger with neither damage nor insight. But profoundly, their skin—like that of a newborn—is too exquisitely delicate to touch. The skin of a newborn's fingers peel away in those first few days; one can literally see the new layers of tougher epidermis getting set down, rapidly trying to add cushioning where none exists. The young child cannot tolerate hot water, cannot abide strong flavors, does not have a necessary toughness. The young child craves predictability, routine, assurance that stability will anchor him in a world of swirling stimuli. This emotional reassurance is necessary for the child because the incessant cacophony of new things—the riotous sights, sounds, experiences, knowledge—does not fit together into any kind of pattern that makes sense to the child without history to provide context and order. A child generalizes to simplify and to reject the extraneous noise of experience that confuses and defies understanding.

In contrast, the recognition of aging in middle age, carries the sad acknowledgement that life is brief—but also the joyful clarity that life is unbelievably precious and rare. How do we know this with any kind of awareness of life's richness and layers without having lived the intense contradictions, the agonizing confusions, and the bitter disappointments—as well as the exquisitely brief, happy highs?

Increasingly, in this aging world where more and more of our population is over sixty-five—indeed, over one hundred—there are greater numbers of fabulous role models for us younger and middle-aged people to emulate. Many of us have old people in our families or neighborhoods who work, create, travel, tell the greatest joke, make the best dessert, and embody a vitality more pungent than any slouching teenager. Increasing numbers of old people doing wonderful things are out there for the rest of us to witness. How many of us know old women with attitude—ATTITUDE!—that does not suffer fools, and that revels in the certain knowledge of who each one of them uniquely is? For many women—and men—the development of this confidence simply takes years to achieve and is the best prize of all.

Enchantment with life in its myriad and complex forms invigorates us and mitigates the insults that our aging bodies also deliver to us. We understand the trade-offs better. We know that anything in life is possible, and we shock less easily. We know what we know and we know what we like. We can distinguish the small stuff from the important stuff a lot of the time. We sometimes know not to fight the stupid stuff. We know that young people will also grow old—and we are sad for them because of it—even if, and because, they do not yet understand this fundamental fact. We see how young people also struggle with the brevity of fast-elapsing time. We savor our long-lived marriages and our ancient friendships; they are indescribably precious because they are old, and the years have been literally woven into them. We are reassured to know that we are *not* the center of the universe, that the things that happen in life are *not* necessarily personal. Sometimes we are even wise.

Yes, the joints ache, the energy sometimes wanes, and I feel nauseated on a swing; but the smell of fall leaves and the sharp muscular pleasure of my limbs moving on a brisk walk imparts a joy I had been less intensely aware of when I was younger.

But how I hate the presbyopia, and how I can never find my reading glasses!

Chapter 10

Conclusion
The Face in the Mirror
(SMA)

When we strive to understand the texture and substance of aging, and to appreciate what it feels like to be irreversibly old, we must first avoid the scholarly discourses on geriatrics. Instead, we should direct our inquiries to those who speak solely from personal experience, those who have already entered the community of the old. The received answers will inevitably vary from person to person, and even from season to season; but certain enduring themes will appear and reappear with disturbing regularity. These themes include such commonplace issues as decaying self-image, the vulnerability of memory, the preoccupation with death, and how the elderly construe such primal passions as hope and loss.

> *But as we have seen from the reflections in this book, it is important also to understand some of the universals of aging, the physical substrate of how human bodies pass through time. We need the dialectic of hearing from individual elderly as well as understanding some generalizations about the group of elderly. One old person who tells us how rotten it is to be old sheds valid light only on a sliver of the total experience of what it is like to be old. [RRS]*

Self-image

It is difficult to stroll along a city street or through a shopping mall without encountering full-length reflecting surfaces as part of some storefront façade. And when elderly people are asked to look back upon their lives and consider the accuracy or authenticity of their self-image, they will frequently mention these confrontations with outdoor mirrors as metaphors of how they view themselves. This might be the essence of their response:

> *I'm walking down Wickenden Street and I see a stranger reflected in a storefront mirror. He is much older than I am, perhaps by ten or twenty years, but he bears a disturbing resemblance to my father, even my grandfather. This alien face in the mirror clearly shows some curiosity but also a look of dismay tinged with a touch of horror. There is then a suspenseful interval, perhaps two or three seconds, before a chilling sense of recognition sets in. Yes, this is me, but only the visible part of me, not all of me. That somewhat stooped, elder citizen with monochromatic grayness of hair and complexion and anxious face, is only my outer image; because deep inside of me there is still color, vitality, an erect posture, even sly humor.*
>
> *As I continue my stroll past further stores, I now consciously avoid the many reflecting surfaces since my one daily encounter with unsettling reality is quite sufficient.*
>
> *I now recall distant childhood experiences with distorting mirrors in amusement parks, and how we children would marvel, and nervously laugh, at how short or how wide or how distorted we had suddenly appeared. The laughter was nervous because at some level of awareness there was the disturbing thought that mirrors don't lie, that the fleeting image is the true reality while the inner self-image is the transient and insubstantial one. But thoughts, especially the troublesome ones, never seem to loiter in young people; they are quickly replaced by other, more urgent, thoughts. Only with the old people do thoughts, especially the painful ones, persist. They hang on like low-grade headaches, never in the forefront but never totally gone. [OM]*
>
> *I know OM is talking for himself, but I want to disagree! How relentlessly angry we can be of our vulnerable selves when we are young! Even when one remains dismayed with one's limitations, with time they become familiar and known. In some ways a person learns to accommodate his or her constraints, like a blind person becomes better at making his way down the street or across a room. [RRS]*

I walk more slowly now, trying to reconcile my childhood memories, my current perceptions of myself, and the uninvited reflections of my outer self. The improbable thought crosses my mind that I have been allowed a prophetic glance at what I might look like some decades hence. But since epiphanies are not commonplace in Providence, I discard this thought and return to the satisfying illusion that a truly vigorous soul occupies the innermost recesses of my body.

Some vagrant doubts however persist. A few more minutes pass before the inner turmoil abates. Perhaps, just perhaps, both images are valid; perhaps the aging process is really not a uniform one, with both interior and exterior body elements in lockstep degeneration. Maybe, I speculate, some parts age quite rapidly while the core parts of the body remain more resistant to the aging process. Yes, I suppose I am older on the outside but, I still claim, substantially younger on the inside. This reconciling thought, I am dimly aware, is about as logical as the old Westinghouse refrigerator advertisement widely seen on television programs of the 1950s: "Smaller on the outside and bigger on the inside."

And even when I finally accept that both my inside and my outside are equally corrupted by age, there is always the enterprising thought, taken from some childhood catechism, that the innermost soul, never withers, never decays, never grows old. [OM]

I agree that we retain an idea about our self that somehow stays constant. The person we are to ourselves has frozen in time and is jarred by the reflection in the mirror. The portraits in Sharon Kaufman's The Ageless Self describe this unending internal image of ourselves as persistent vitality. As one of her seventy-year old informants notes, "I just saw some slides of myself and was quite taken aback. That couldn't be me. That's a nice looking woman, but it couldn't possibly be me. Even though I look in the mirror all the time, I don't see myself as old."[RRS]

I conclude by accepting this innocent illusion, not as the ultimate truth but as an anodyne to lessen the ache of a persistent and fear-ridden sadness. In centuries past, older people had enough sense to die shortly after the onset of some grave illness. But the science of modern medicine now keep so many of us alive with our decrepitudes, giving us time to view ourselves in the mirror and reflect upon the wonder and absurdity of life. [OM]

The Unreliability of Memory

For the cognitively intact, memories have always been sources of wonderment and satisfaction. They comfort us in times of uncertainty and strengthen us in happier times by allowing us to relive past accomplishments, savor former victories, and relive cherished moments. But for the elderly, memories become both more precious, and, sadly, more fragile: first, because there are so many more memories to confront, and second, because memories have assumed an increasingly important element for older persons; their lives are fulfilled more in recollections than in active engagements. Memories for the elderly, whether accurate or reconfigured, then become their substitute for newly created happenings; and more than ever before life is lived vicariously in past recollections despite the fact that these remembrances may be dim, distorted or at substantial variance with reality.

A young man may forget the name of a distant relative, and people will shake their heads disapprovingly at the flightiness and irresponsibility of youth. ("Had he just taken the trouble, he would have remembered.") A lost memory to an adolescent is rarely troublesome since there are always erotic thoughts pushing to fill the void. A middle-aged woman may forget an appointment and people will nod understandingly, saying, "She has so much on her mind." But when an eighty-year-old woman forgets the name of one of her eleven grandchildren, the younger relatives glance at each other and the unspoken specter of Alzheimer's disease taints the atmosphere.

I think when the fifty-four-year-old woman forgets her train of thought, she sees her grown children shoot knowing looks at one another. They are unaware of how much is on her mind. [RRS]

The sad reality, of course, is that memories, both the trivial and priceless ones, are indeed lost at an increasingly greater rate with advancing age. Those elders who undergo this loss hope that it represents little more than a benign senescent forgetfulness and not a prelude to something more ominous. They pray that it is a misfiling of information rather than an irretrievable loss, an error in circuitry rather than the destruction of data-storing neurons. Younger persons can afford to forget a name or the technical details of a past experience, for they can look forward to countless replacing memories. A much older woman, her world rapidly shrinking to the solitude of the bedroom and a mind vainly clutching the remnants of eight decades of past happenings is not as indifferent to this loss of memory.

To an elder citizen each memory loss represents a shrinkage of the whole with little hope for replacement; and lurking behind thoughts such as, "What was the name of that hotel I went to on my honeymoon?" is the grim fear that a devastation called Alzheimer's disease, with its unrelenting dementia, will convert a vibrant life of awareness and struggle into an unraveling existence. When you say that a young woman is forgetful, at worst you are hinting at capriciousness, but with an older woman, the hint carries a more threatening message.

A fine, and aging, neurologist named Oliver Sacks, in his book entitled, *The Man Who Mistook His Wife for a Hat and Other Clinical Tales* (1985), quotes Luis Buñuel, as follows: "You have to begin to lose your memory, if only in bits and pieces, to realize that memory is what makes our lives. Life without memory is not life at all...Our memory is our coherence, our reason, our feeling, even our action. Without it, we are nothing."

> *As for me, if I don't make a note to record what I want to remember right now when I'm thinking of it, whether it is an idea for this book, or a reminder to buy an eggplant and garlic, I know I may lose the thought. It is a nuisance with a worrisome undertone.*
>
> *More than that, of course, memory is the repository of the idea we call the self. Without it, we lose the notion of ourselves. Who we are in the present is merely the thin skin of who we are to ourselves and others. Without a way to connect to the layers comprising our personal trajectory through time, we become indistinguishable beings among many others. [RRS]*

The Daily Obituary Review

Younger people are convinced that any elder, in his right mind, would earnestly avoid the obituary pages of the daily newspaper. Older ones certainly read many sections of the daily paper but rarely do they bypass the biographical descriptions of the recently departed. In many a nursing home the residents refer to the obituary page as their daily comic strip. It is a common bit of gallows humor for an aged one to declare: "I get up each morning, count my arms and legs; then I check the obituary page, and if my name is not there, then I decide that I'm alive and ready to go down for breakfast."

> *I also scan the obituaries, intensely interested in why the person died and what age he or she was. I have on my bulletin board a New Yorker cartoon of a person looking at the obits that are labeled, "Two years younger than you," "Five years older than you," "The same age as you," and so on. [RRS]*

There are, of course, other reasons why the elderly scan the obituaries. With mixed feelings, they seek out the names of friends, people of their generation. And if they encounter the name of someone known to them, the fugitive thought may pass through their mind: "By God, I've outlived them!" There is grief, too, but it loses its singularity when it merges with still other laments; and when that happens, and many such laments have been accumulated, people then call it senile depression and think that it can be treated with a medication.

And then there are the obituary notices of the erstwhile famous personalities, a glamorous movie actress, perhaps, from the motion pictures of the early 1930s. The elderly will avidly read the obituary and then smile briefly while reliving in their minds the cinematic splendor of the recently departed. Newspapers are not known for displays of sensitivity. But they regularly show great compassion in their published obituaries by displaying photographs of the deceased taken some forty or more years before her death. Readers who respond to the name of the deceased would not readily recognize her current photograph. Printing a more recent photograph, showing the ravages wrought by age, would be in bad taste; but it would also break a fundamental rule of idolatry: never show the blemishes or wrinkles of those still in the ranks of the worshipped.

> *Saddam Hussein dyes his hair black and only displays photos of his young and vigorous persona. To reveal his aging self would show a vulnerability that could risk his overthrow.*
> *I never thought I'd become old enough that I could say, as I heard my parents say, "I haven't seen that person for at least twenty (or thirty or forty) years!" Hearing this, I would think to*

my eight-year-old self, how could one think back that amount of time when I'm not even close to having experienced that many years myself? Now, of course, I tell stories that are forty years old, and I occasionally have a reunion with a person from thirty or more years ago. I still retain the disbelief that such time travel is possible. [RRS]

Youth possesses all the advantages of life but one: the old ones can always say "We were there before you were even born." And this is yet another reason why the elderly compulsively scan the obituaries: it is their curious way of validating that they were contemporary with the recently deceased, that they too had participated in such historic events as the speakeasies, the roaring twenties, the depression, voting for FDR or serving in World War II. In lives that are increasingly bereft of meaning and agenda, it is comforting for them to say: "There may be little that is outstanding in our lives but yes, we too were there."

The Hope for a Future

Chesterton had once declared that hope is the last gift given to man, and the only gift not given to youth. An older person will strenuously disagree with this contention. To all but the population of elders there is always hope. It encourages the young, sustains the middle-aged, while the old find it merely an amusingly quaint deception. Hope, they will declare, is allowed solely for those with sufficient expectation of future years such that, by random chance alone, something good might happen.

I really don't believe this. I think this trait has much to do with individual, socio-economic, as well as other factors than age. Does the five-year-old whose parents have just died have hope? Does the family of a young, unarmed, African-American teenager killed by the police feel hope? Am I naïve? [RRS]

Your rejoinder does not differentiate between transient and permanent loss of hope. Certainly a five-year-old feels a profound sense of loss but he knows, if not consciously, then instinctively, that there is a world of time in front of him. It is the difference between being five runs behind in the first inning and five runs behind, with two outs, in the ninth inning. On the surface, the dif-

ferences seem merely quantitative but in truth the "ninth inning hopelessness" is substantially different; and to compare the two, I think, trivializes what a thoughtful elder citizen really feels (as he rapidly learns the true meaning of finiteness) and all that this elder can say is: "Wait until you have been there; then you will see the difference." And I don't see the analogy between the African-American rage and disgust with the system and the elder whose life is draining and whose timespan for repair and rerouting is vanishing. [SMA]

I don't want to trivialize the experience of being old. I do not mean to equate the five-year-old's perceptions with those of the older person. They are fundamentally different. The young child's lack of perspective—his or her inability to live other than in the moment—is exactly what makes his hopelessness so total. Perhaps he or she cannot imagine—does not have the capability or experience to understand—that hope and new beginnings will eventually replace some of the terrible feelings of the present. He doesn't know that he's in the second rather than the ninth inning, and that runs can still be made up. The old person's grasp of perspective, on the other hand, lends tremendous poignancy to his or her understanding of finiteness. As for my African-American example—that was meant to suggest another kind of fundamental hopelessness that is not connected to age. Hope is not merely linked to temporal situation. [RRS]

The Meaning of Loss

Loss, even loss of innocence, is never happily accepted at any age. A child loses a front tooth and for an hour or so is inconsolable. A teenager loses a baseball game and becomes convinced that the world joins him in mourning. An adult's business loses money and he wonders why the radio stations still play happy music and the traffic lights continue to alternate. But an old person absorbs losses silently, almost willingly, knowing that loss is the lingua franca of seniority and rarely comes singly. Losses, intruding almost on a daily basis, no longer loom as shattering experiences. Losses, to the old one, are therefore more like confronting new riders entering an already filled city bus. As the bus becomes increasingly crowded, its occupants may resent the new riders collectively, but not individually. They expect the arrival of these new strangers and are prepared, if somewhat reluctantly, to yield a bit more of the meager space allotted to them.

> *Losses? That's another word for growing old. Everyday we lose something, a bit of hair, a memory, maybe, a friend, or even an enemy sometimes. When you are young you say that the neighborhood changes and then you shrug. But when you are ancient, a lost neighborhood means a loss, too, of remembered stores and neighbors and cherished happenings. [OM]*

Little is expected of older persons in the final stretches of their lives as their organic losses accumulate and their lives become reduced to a group of rudimentary biological functions. The elderly have become increasingly transparent since people regard them either as impediments or, more rarely, as something iconic to be preserved and revered. They neither fulfill tasks assigned by others nor give commands to complete projects. They have finally been transformed from living people to objects needing to be sustained.

> *There is great resiliency to the old also, no? Many individuals promise themselves they will never enter a nursing home, never move to supportive housing, never accept a few hours of help from a home health aide—yet when personal circumstances change and the intimate world shifts in response, many individuals suddenly—even if reluctantly—reassess and make new choices. Such a person's ability to make these modifications of expectations and his or her practical decision to mentally disconnect assistance with shame makes many an old person look agile in his or her reorientation to new realities.*
>
> *In some cultures the old people know things that younger people do not. Their knowledge is valuable for the continued survival of the group. Biesele and Howell tell us how the nomadic !Kung people of the Kalahari Desert of southern Africa valued the old people in their society because they remembered where to find water. Other practical information that they had collected over the years was useful to the group as a whole (in Amoss and Harrell 1981). [RRS]*

But Maybe Some Losses Are Not Losses

Old people find that aging has often deprived them of admirable skills that they had once possessed. An eighty-year-old cannot run as rapidly, sketch as accurately, speak as assertively or think as swiftly or assuredly as someone half his age. The eighty-year-olds, with diminished abilities, are no longer competitive; nor, after a while, do they wish to compete.

Can a loss, perhaps, be a gain? Can having less sometimes bring forth new or latent talents? Some years back there was an endearing story appearing in many newspapers:

On November 18, 1995, Itzhak Perlman, the great violinist, came on stage to give a concert at Lincoln Center in New York City. Just as Perlman finished the first few bars, something went wrong. One of the strings on his violin broke. The snap of the broken string could be heard throughout the auditorium. Perlman waited a few moments, closed his eyes briefly, and then signaled the conductor to begin again. The orchestra began, and Perlman played from where he had left off. And he played with such passion and such power and such purity as they had never heard before. The audience could see him modulating, changing, recomposing the piece in his head. Of course, everyone knows that it is impossible to play a symphonic work with just three strings. Everyone knew that; but that night Perlman refused to know that. When he had concluded, the audience, briefly silent, then rose to cheer.

Perlman smiled, wiped the sweat from his brow, and then said in a quiet, pensive tone: "You know, sometimes it is the artist's task to find out how much music you can still make with what you have left."

Old people know this too: they may ignore the wreckage and work with what is left. And if they are lucky, maybe, just maybe, some good things will come out of their labors.

What do the elderly really want in the end? No one asks them this question and rarely do they ask it of themselves. The end, they hope, will be without embarrassment and without messiness. Shaw once said that while youth is forgiven everything, it forgives itself nothing; and old age forgives itself everything but is forgiven nothing.

I suppose that in the end we want the full orchestra playing; not just making incontinent noises but really playing together and concluding with a joyously triumphant blast. Instead, it is often like that symphony by Haydn in which, toward the end, players leave the stage, one by one, until finally there is but one solitary violinist quietly providing the last breath of musical life. Some want their end to be calm and tranquil; but most of us want to end with a stirring anthem, not a whimper.

Concluding Thoughts

(RRS)

We grow too soon oldt and too late shmart—Yiddish saying

Youth, large, lusty, loving—youth full of grace, force, fascination,
Do you know that Old Age may come after you with equal grace,
*   force, fascination?*
Day full-blown and splendid—day of the immense sun, action,
*   ambition, laughter,*
The Night follows close with millions of suns, and sleep and
*   restoring darkness*—Leaves of Grass, Walt Whitman, 1881

Today I misplaced a key that I wanted to copy. My husband and I looked for it and quizzed one another about its whereabouts. We both remembered that I had asked for it and he had given it to me. We both remembered where we thought the key had been placed. It was not there. We were both thinking, but did not say, that the other is getting more forgetful and distracted.

The feeling of vulnerability about the passing years seems inappropriate to a baby boomer nestled safely in her mid-fifties. Yet, I am entering the frightening decades of cancers, heart disease, and who knows what else. Those fortunate ones who make it to their eighties are the hearty survivors who have demonstrated their ability to live even longer.

I asked Stan if he had concerns about his memory when he was in his fifties and he scoffed: "I was too busy!" and then he added that knowledge of dementing illnesses was so scanty and new that people never considered it. I know that the absented thought, the discarded commitment, the lapsed pledge to do something, call someone, or recall that important idea—these annoying interferences in our daily lives—were easily discounted and swiped away when we were in our twenties or younger, but they nag now. Could this be ...

Baby boomers make nervous jokes all the time about their "half-zeimers." We hear those ten years older poke gently and forgivingly at their so-called "senior moments." Many of us are poignantly aware first-hand about the deterioration of aging as we witness it in our long-lived parents and relatives and neighbors.

In one basic sense we are cushioned with a continued ability to deny our own aging because it is still happening to those "above" us. Older people in our families are still our "ceiling," and it is hard to tell how much of a psychological barrier they are for us acknowledging our own aging. In fact, when I complain about what I think may be an age-related ailment—some forgetting, a creakiness, the wrinkles and sags—my older relatives shush me up with hasty protectiveness. "You're too young to be thinking about that," they protest, and if I persist, insistent on proving my point, then they look a little crushed that I am beginning to join their ranks. I see I have disappointed them. And they understand at the same time that my valid complaint means that indeed, I am aging, which in turn means that they are that much older than they usually let themselves know.

My husband and mother-in-law were visiting together at her assisted living complex. She sighed and shook her head and told him she never ever expected to end up in a "home" such as this. Deciding not to protest that her assisted living place was certainly not a nursing home, he instead offered that he himself wonders if in the next twenty or thirty years, a place like this one is where he will be. Immediately, she reared up to contest this vision—not him! No. One's child doesn't get old!

The presence of those who are older creates a wall of deniability for those who are younger. Our older relatives and our parents, after all, have always been "old" to us. And we who are younger in age, do we join them in understanding aging or do we maintain our positions in parallel lockstep, separated and thereby immune from our acknowledgement of age? When I try to understand—as I have professionally attempted to understand—I see the connections between old people and me. I feel what I think is the continuity—it can be frightening at times. I know I am well on my way, vigorous and healthy and active though I may be now.

What I think I see is the evidence of continuity. No longer do I safely hold the illusion that old age begins in the distant future. I see, I feel, I witness the beginnings of it now.

The flickers—those hints and notices that I have been on this earth for over five decades—are there. Healing is slower, elasticity is gone, more light is needed to read, reaction time is more prolonged—regrettably, the list is long. Most of the time the changes proceed invisibly; whatever insidious developments are brewing, are imperceptible right now—at least to me. Then the startling awareness of change slams my consciousness. Acknowledgement is rude.

Denial is a strong muscle that refuses to understand. It is also easily underrated for just this trait. The reality of finiteness and end is too huge to comprehend. Yet death is a mundane, simple, commonplace fact. Perhaps the simplest fact of all.

At fifty-four I also know that I do not really "get it." I think old people—or many of them—do "get it." As my eighty-five-year-old uncle walked with some difficulty down a street, he told me how in his childhood he used to regard an old lame man walking jaggedly in his neighborhood. Now here was my uncle reflecting upon this memory: this old lame man! My uncle was telling himself how he did not get the connection back then. He was trying to teach me that he was once young, and I might one day be old. I understood his message, but know it is hard to grasp the meaning he intended.

Older relatives confer and joke about the dues that must be paid. They teach the next generation what they have learned. We constitute the younger audience as they compare notes, do the calculus of the trade-offs, the price they pay to continue to live. They joke, they turn the complaints into funny spoofs, they know we are listening, they think we are learning. Now many in my generation practice the same thing. We complain about the insults of age that we find so galling and so inconvenient. We find community in those of our own age who are bothered by the same evidence. My friends and I are disgusted by our reading glasses. We turn our complaints into jokes as we have been taught, but our complacency is disturbed.

* * *

The key turned up on the ledge by the fireplace. Neither of us knows how it ended up there, and we've left it at that.

* * *

How do you convey the inner, intimate, diversely-felt, experiences of aging? I agree with Stan that the best way is to ask the old to speak and to listen to what they have to say.

Jonathan Rosen recalled an encounter with his ninety-two-year-old grandmother. His wife asked her why she had had only one child and she answered that in fact she had had a second child, but stillborn. She added that she thought of him everyday. Rosen relates his surprise:

> Hidden beneath the surface of her seeming contentedness was a seed of perpetual sadness. And I learned something more than that, about myself. I felt I knew her so well ... My grandmother had seemed as fixed and constant as a planet—what more could she have to teach me at this late stage in our relationship? What I discovered was that I had been only half aware of her (Rosen 2000:126).

We who study aging and old age describe the outer contours but not the essence. But it is also necessary to know the physical substrate of age, to understand senescence, these processes by which the human body changes over time and deals with the challenges of internal deterioration and external threat.

In so doing we participate and must not avert our eyes. Those of us who are young and middle-aged may fool ourselves that we can gain the knowledge without the experience. Maybe we think we have inoculated ourselves by studying age? If we "know" about aging when we are young, maybe we can avoid its unpleasantness, even its end? Maybe we become even more adept at denying the idea of inevitability? Maybe we can discover the secret elixir that exists someplace? Maybe we can unearth the silver lining and discover that getting old enriches our lives, provides wisdom, gives rewards.

Would we want to be in our twenties again? No. We have a perspective and an appreciation of cycles.

And yet … as I see some of the connections and the signs of aging in myself, I also avert my eyes and momentarily mourn. I sometimes see myself in the mirror or my reflection in my children's eyes, and I recognize age, the division in years, the difference in generation, the gap. Pictures from the 1960s—my youth!—now look as ancient as those of the 1880s, the 1920s, and of my parents' photo albums from the 1940s. I see signs in myself of becoming old, and I see how these small signs—only slightly exaggerated or merely continued—are what will turn me into an Old Person. Then I flee from this acknowledgement and tuck it aside. I deny the connection and go on with my day and my enduring, reassuring, timeless, endless sense of myself as me.

* * *

My mother-in-law and I overheard a couple of women talking on the patio of their assisted living apartment complex on one of the first warm spring days of the season. Ethel spoke about an event that had happened a long time ago. Agnes listened intently, interested and engaged in the story. Ethel wound up her tale and added the refrain, "But of course, they're all gone now." "Yes," murmured Agnes, "Of course they are." "They're all dead," continued Ethel, "I'm the only one left of all of them." "Yes," confirmed Agnes, "Me too." "I'm the only one left. I've lived too long," Ethel said, smiling and nodding. Agnes agreed. "That's right," she concurred amiably, also smiling and nodding. "We've lived too long." "*Way* too long," added Ethel agreeably.

We watched the women nodding and smiling, alternating their pleasant mid-day responses with each other. My mother-in-law commented to me, "I know just what they mean." "But," I asked, too quickly—confused and protesting—"Do you want to keep living?" She snapped her head around to me briskly, surprised by my question. "Of course!"

She understands—as I do not—that a basic fact of old age is the accumulated loss of many people close to you. These losses add up. A dreary complacency of sadness hangs heavily. This understanding does not mean that she is ready to die or that she no longer wants to live. Is not living amidst loss worth it?

Some old people do not relent. They shrug the losses aside, impatient, businesslike. They have life to attend to. Deaths are commonplace, they are typical, they cannot be indulged. These old people know they are implicated, and they hurry to squeeze more life in before the door shuts. You live, you love, you die. Get over it.

The 85-year-old matriarch, Pearl Tull, in Anne Tyler's *Dinner at the Homesick Restaurant*, is dying and (the young author) Tyler tells us her thoughts.

> She'd been preoccupied with death for several years now; but one aspect had never before crossed her mind: dying, you don't get to see how it all turns out. Questions you have asked will go unanswered forever. Will this one of my children settle down? Will that one learn to be happier? Will I ever discover what was meant by such-and-such? She had also supposed that there would be some turning point, a flash of light in which she'd suddenly find out the secret; one day she'd wake up wiser and more contented and accepting. But it hadn't happened. Now it never would. She'd supposed that on her deathbed ... deathbed! Why, that was this everyday, ordinary Posturepedic, not the ornate brass affair that she had always envisioned. She had supposed that on her deathbed, she would have something final to tell her children when they gathered around. But nothing was final. She didn't have anything to tell them. She felt a kind of shyness; she felt inadequate. She stirred her feet fretfully and searched for a cooler place on the pillow (1985:30).

* * *

This book's conversation about old age comes from two professionals in different fields who have wrestled with some of the important questions in aging for a number of years. During the twenty years that we have known one another, our positions in the life span and our perspectives on age have changed. SMA was on my dissertation committee and was nearing retirement as the first dean of Brown University's School of Medicine. I was embarking on a career of anthropology in healthcare and nursing home settings and raising my children. Twenty years later as we write about aging and age, Stan's grandchildren and my four children have reached adulthood.

In these twenty years the predictions of a rapidly aging society have come true—and more. Dementing diseases are now commonplace. Everyday conversation among strangers in the U.S. just as easily concerns the difficulties of caring for old relatives as it does the weather, El Niño, terrorism or global warming. People who are in their eighties, nineties, even over one hundred years of age are becoming more prevalent in U.S. society. Entrepreneurs are taking advantage of the vast marketing opportunities that the demographic realities suggest while federal and state governments struggle with the implications of shrinking revenues and the increasing need for more services.

More professional recognition and respect need to be paid to the importance of old age. This is a vital time of the life span which exhibits great uniformity as well as stunning diversity in its expression. We need—somehow—to teach our young people that they too will grow old. But this acknowledgement seems to be the most difficult barrier of all to be overcome. The current shortage of geriatricians is critical, and if current projections hold, the shortage will become more acute. Professional organizations lament the dearth of people willing to be trained in this field and some estimate that the U.S. currently has one-third the number of geriatricians it needs to provide the proper care for the elderly of the country. Some medical schools do not offer geriatrics in their curricula. Young physicians rightly assess the field to be out of sync with modern medicine. Concepts such as quality of life, palliative care, prevention of disease, maintenance of function, and enhancement of autonomy seem foreign to a medical system that values prompt diagnosis and relies on the notion of cure.

Nonetheless, our two fields are in the forefront of understanding age. Anthropology informs our knowledge of age by showcasing the people who age, exploring the variety of ways in which people age, and abhorring generalizations that erase differences between individuals, cultures, and time periods. While anthropologists describe the diversity that springs from the common basis of being human, geriatrics places more focus on the physical basis and manifestations of age, attempting to understand the vagaries in the universals. Both approaches are necessary and valuable.

Our two fields have a great deal to offer one another. We must read the research emerging from one another's professions. We must write so that others outside our professions can understand what we say. We must pay attention to the growing body of knowledge about the "envelope" that encases us, the body that houses us. Most of all, we should be talking with one another, discussing what it means to be old, and what it means to live in a society and in a world in which more and more old people are living longer.

We have a lot to learn from one another—and most especially from those who are old—and we need to launch these vital conversations now.

> *So? This is it? After all of these words, this is what we think we know about being old? A rabbi once told me that if you can't explain something while standing on one foot, the explanation was not worth listening to. Maybe. So, you ask me: what really is aging? And my answer, while standing on one arthritic foot, is: Listen to the old ones. They will say that no road is endless; and nothing, even pain, goes on forever. And I think, now, you are beginning to hear me. So let's talk again in twenty years; by then, I bet, we'll be in total agreement. [OM]*

References Cited

Abel, Emily K. 1991. *Who Cares for the Elderly? Public Policy and the Experiences of Adult Daughters.* Philadelphia: Temple University Press.

Adams, W., Cox, N. 1995. "Epidemiology of Problem Drinking among Elderly People." *Int. J. Addict. 30:* 1693-1716.

The *American Heritage Dictionary of the English Language.* 1992. Third edition.

Amoss, Pamela T. and Stevan Harrell. 1981. "Introduction: An Anthropological Perspective on Aging. In *Other Ways of Growing Old: Anthropological Perspectives,* edited by P.T. Amoss and S. Harrell. Stanford: Stanford University Press.

Angel, J.L. 1972. "Ecology and Population in the Eastern Mediterranean." *World Archeology 4*: 88.

Aronson, S. and Okazaki, H. 1963. "A Study of Some Factors Modifying Cerebral Tissue Response to Subdural Hematomata." *J. Neurosurgery 20*: 89.

Bar-Josef, O. 1970. *The epi-paleolithic cultures of Palestine.* Ph.D. dissertation. Hebrew University (as quoted in Hassan, F.)

Bateson, Mary Catherine. 1989. *Composing a Life.* New York: Atlantic Monthly Press.

Beall, C. 1987. "Studies of longevity." In *The Elderly as Modern Pioneers,* edited by P. Silverman. Bloomington: Indiana University Press.

Beauvoir, Simone de. 1972. *The Coming of Age.* New York: Warner Books.

Becker, Gaylene. 1980. *Growing Old in Silence.* Berkeley: University of California Press.

Becker, Gay. 1997. *Disrupted Lives: How People Create Meaning in a Chaotic World.* Berkeley: University of California Press.

Bengtson, Vern L., Tonya M. Parrott, and Elisabeth O. Burgess. 1996. "Progress and Pitfalls in Gerontological Theorizing." *The Gerontologist 36* (6): 768-72.

Biesele, Megan and Nancy Howell. 1981. "'The Old People Give You Life": Aging among !Kung Hunter-Gatherers." In *Other Ways of Growing Old: Anthropological Perspectives,* edited by Amoss, Pamela T. and Stevan Harrell. Stanford: Stanford University Press.

Black, Helen K. and Robert L. Rubinstein. 2000. *Old Souls: Aged Women, Poverty, and the Experience of God.* New York: Aldine de-Gruyter.

Blythe, Ronald. 1979. *The View in Winter: Reflections on Old Age.* New York: Harcourt Brace Jovanovich.

Bohannan, Paul. 1965. "The Tiv of Nigeria." In *Peoples of Africa,* edited by James L. Gibbs, Jr. New York: Holt, Rinehart, and Winston.

Brody, Jane E. 2002. "Hidden plague of alcohol abuse by the elderly." *New York Times:* D7. April 2, 2002.

Brown, Judith K. 1985. "Introduction." In *In Her Prime: A New View of Middle-Aged Women.* Brown and Kerns and contributors.

Brown, Judith K. and Virginia Kerns, and contributors. 1985. *In Her Prime: A New View of Middle-Aged Women.* South Hadley (MA): Bergin & Garvey.

Callahan, Daniel. 1987. *Setting Limits: Medical Goals in an Aging Society.* New York: Simon & Schuster.

_____ 1993. *The Troubled Dream of Life: In Search of a Peaceful Death.* New York: Simon and Schuster.

Carper, Jean. 2000. *Your Miracle Brain.* New York: Harper Collins.

Cattell, Maria. G. 1997. "African Widows, Culture and Social Change: Case Studies from Kenya." In *The Cultural Context of Aging: Worldwide Perspectives,* edited by Sokolovsky, Jay. Second Edition. Westport (CT): Bergin & Garvey.

Clark, Margaret M. and Barbara G. Anderson. 1967. *Culture and Aging: An Anthropological Study of Older Americans.* Springfield: Charles C. Thomas.

Cohen, Carl I. and Jay Sokolovsky. 1989. *Old Men of the Bowery: Strategies for Survival among the Homeless.* New York: The Guilford Press.

Cohen, Lawrence. 1994. "Old Age: Cultural and Critical Perspectives." *Annual Review of Anthropology 23*:137-58.

_____ 1998. *No Aging in India: Alzheimer's, the Bad Family, and Other Modern Things.* Berkeley: University of California Press.

Cole, Thomas R. 1992. *The Journey of Life: A Cultural History of Aging in America.* New York: Cambridge University Press.

Cotrell, Victoria and Richard Schulz. 1993. "The Perspective of the Patient with Alzheimer's Disease: A Neglected Dimension of Dementia Research." *The Gerontologist 33* (2): 205-211.

Cowgill, Donald O. 1986. *Aging Around the World.* Belmont (CA): Wadsworth.

Cowgill, Donald O. and Lowell D. Holmes, eds. 1972. *Aging and Modernization.* New York: Appleton Century Crofts.

Cumming, Elaine and William Henry. 1961. *Growing Old: The Process of Disengagement.* New York: Basic Books.

Curley, Richard T. 1973. *Elders, Shades, and Women: Ceremonial Change in Lango, Uganda.* Berkeley: University of California Press.

Davis, Dona L. 1997. "Blood and Nerves Revisited: Menopause and the Privatization of the Body in a Newfoundland Postindustrial Fishery." *Medical Anthropological Quarterly 11* (1): 3-20.

Deary, N.S. et al. 1999. "Physicians Newly Licensed in Rhode Island during 1998." *Medicine and Health/Rhode Island 82*: 360-64.

_____ 2000. "The Practicing Physicians of Rhode Island: Medical Schools Attended." *Medicine and Health/Rhode Island 83*: 245-48.

Diamond, Timothy. 1992. *Making Gray Gold: Narratives of Nursing Home Care.* Chicago: University of Chicago Press.

Douglas, Mary. 1966. *Purity and Danger: An Analysis of the Concepts of Pollution and Taboo.* London: Routledge and Kegan Paul.

Dowd, J.D. 1975. "Aging as Exchange: A Preface to Theory." *Journal of Gerontology 30*: 584-594.

Ellis, Joseph J. 2000. *Founding Brothers: The Revolutionary Generation.* New York: Knopf.

Estes, Carroll. 1979. *The Aging Enterprise: A Critical Examination of Social Policies and Services for the Aged.* San Francisco: Jossey-Bass, Inc.

Fabian, Johannes. 1983. *Time and the Other: How Anthropology Makes its Object.* New York: Columbia University Press.

Fabrega, H. 1975. "The Need for an Ethnomedical Science." *Science 189*: 969-75.

Farmer, Paul. 1999. *Infections and Inequalities: The Modern Plagues.* Berkeley: University of California Press.

Featherstone, Mike and Andrew Wernick. 1995. *Images of Aging: Cultural Representations of Later Life,* edited by M. Featherstone and A. Wernick. New York: Routledge.

Feil, Naomi. 1993. *The Validation Breakthrough: Simple Techniques for Communicating with People with "Alzheimer's-Type Dementia."* Baltimore: Health Professions Press.

Foner, Nancy. 1984. Age and social change. In *Age and Anthropological Theory,* edited by David Kertzer and Jennie Keith, eds. Ithaca: Cornell University Press.

_____ 1984b. *Ages in Conflict: A Cross-Cultural Perspective on Inequality Between Old and Young.* New York: Columbia University Press.

_____ 1994. *The Caregiving Dilemma: Work in an American Nursing Home.* Berkeley: University of California Press.

Foucault, Michel. 1973. *The Birth of the Clinic: An Archaeology of Medical Perception.* New York: Vintage Books.

Francis, Doris. 1984. *Will You Still Need Me, Will You Still Feed Me, When I'm 64?* Bloomington: Indiana University Press.

Frenkel, Eli and Stanley Aronson. 1986. "Family Income and Mortality Rates: An Analysis of the National Mortality Survey." *Rhode Island Medical Journal 69* (4): 165-70.

Fries, J. F. 1984. "The Compression of Morbidity: Miscellaneous Comments about a Theme." *The Gerontologist 24*: 354-359.

Gennep, Arnold van. 1960 [1908]. *The Rites of Passage.* Chicago: University of Chicago Press.

Geron, Scott Miyake. 1997. "The Role of Clients in the Assessment Process." *Generations 21* (1). Spring 1997: 10.

Giddens, Anthony. 1976. *New Rules of Sociological Method: A Positive Critique of Interpretive Sociologies.* New York: Basic Books.

Glascock, A.P. and S.L. Feinman. 1981. "Social Asset or Social Burden: Treatment of the Aged in Non-Industrial Societies. In *Dimensions: Aging, Culture, and Health,* edited by Christine Fry. South Hadley (MA): Bergin & Garvey.

Glass, D. and Revelle, R. 1972. *Population and Social Change.* London: Edward Arnold.

Goffman, Erving. 1963. *Stigma: Notes on the Management of Spoiled Identity.* Englewood Cliffs (NJ): Prentice-Hall, Inc.

Goldman, Bob et al. 1999. *Brain Fitness: Anti-Aging Strategies for Achieving Super Mind Power.* New York: Doubleday.

Goldstein, M. 1999. *Alternative Health Care: Medicine, Miracle, or Mirage?* Philadelphia: Temple University Press.

Gubrium, Jaber. 1975. *Living and Dying at Murray Manor.* New York: St. Martin's Press.

_____ 1986. *Oldtimers and Alzheimers: The Descriptive Organization of Senility.* Greenwich (CT): JAI Press.

Guralnik, JM et al. 1991. "Morbidity and Disability in Older Persons in the Years Prior to Death." *American Journal of Public Health 51*: 443.

Hareven, Tamara. 1995. "Changing Images of Aging and the Social Construction of the Life Course." In *Images of Aging: Cultural Representations of Later Life*, edited by M. Featherstone and A. Wernick. New York: Routledge.

Harrington, Charlene, Christine Kovner, Mathy Mezey, Jeanie Kayser-Jones, Sarah Burger, Martha Mohler, Robert Burke, and David Zimmerman. 2000. "Experts Recommend Minimum Nurse Staffing Standards for Nursing Facilities in the United States." *The Gerontologist 40* (1): 5-16.

Hashimoto, Akiko. 1996. *The Gift of Generations: Japanese and American Perspectives on Aging and the Social Contract*. New York: Cambridge University Press.

Hassan, Fekri. 1981. *Demographic Archeology*. New York: Academic Press.

Havighurst, R.J. 1963. "Successful Aging." In *Processes of Aging,* edited by R. Williams, C. Tibbitts, and W. Donahue. New York: Atherton.

Hawley, J.S., ed. 1994. *Sati: The Blessing and the Curse*. New York: Oxford University Press.

Hazzard, WR et al. 1994. *Principles of Geriatric Medicine and Gerontology*. New York: McGraw-Hill, Inc.

Henderson, J. Neil. 1995. "The Culture of Care in a Nursing Home: Effects of a Medicalized Model of Long Term Care. In *The Culture of Long Term Care: Nursing Home Ethnography*, edited by J. Neil Henderson and Maria Vesperi. Westport: Bergin & Garvey.

Henderson, J. Neil and Maria Vesperi, eds. 1995. *The Culture of Long Term Care: Nursing Home Ethnography*. Westport: Bergin and Garvey.

Henry, L. 1976. *Population: Analysis and Models*. New York: Academic Press.

Hochschild, Arlie Russell. 1973. *The Unexpected Community: Portrait of an Old Age Subculture*. Berkeley: University of California Press.

_____ 1976. "Disengagement Theory: A Logical, Empirical, and Phenomenological Critique. In *Time, Roles, and Self in Old Age,* edited by J. F. Gubrium. New York: Human Sciences Press.

Hockey, Jenny and Allison James. 1993. *Growing Up and Growing Old: Ageing and Dependency in the Life Course*. London: Sage Publications.

Hooyman, Nancy R. and H. Asuman Kiyak. 1993. *Social Gerontology: A Multidisciplinary Perspective*. Third Edition. Boston: Allyn and Bacon.

Hrdy, Sarah Blaffer. 1999. *Mother Nature: A History of Mothers, Infants and Natural Selection.* New York: Pantheon.

Hu, Y.-H. 1995. "Elderly Suicide Risk in Family Contexts: A Critique of the Asian Family Care Model." *Journal of Cross-Cultural Gerontology 10* (3): 199-217.

Hurt, R. et al. 1988. "Alcoholism in Elderly Persons: Medical Aspects and Prognosis in 216 Patients." *Mayo Clin. Proc. 64*: 753-760.

Hyde, Alvin S. 1996. *Accidental Falls: Their Causes and Their Injuries.* Key Biscayne (FL): HAI Publisher.

Institute of Medicine. 1986. *Improving the Quality of Care in Nursing Homes.* Washington, D.C.: National Academy Press.

Jackson, Michael. 1995. *At Home in the World.* Durham (NC): Duke University Press.

Jenike, Brenda Robb. 1997. "Gender and Duty in Japan's Aged Society: The Experiences of Family Caregivers." In *The Cultural Context of Aging: Worldwide Perspectives,* Second Edition, edited by Jay Sokolovsky. Westport (CT): Bergin & Garvey.

Jerrome, D. 1992. *Good Company: An Anthropological Study of Old People in Groups.* Edinburgh: University of Edinburgh Press.

Jervis, Lori L. 2001. "The Pollution of Incontinence and the Dirty Work of Caregiving in a U.S. Nursing Home." *Medical Anthropology Quarterly 15*(1): 84-99.

Johnson, Harold R. 1995. "Claiming Boundaries: The Foibles and Follies of Gerontological Imperialists." *Generations 19* (2): 23-24.

Johnson, Sheila. 1971. *Idle Haven: Community Building among the Working Class Retired.* Berkeley: University of California Press.

Kahana, Eva. 1975. "A Congruence Model of Person-Environment Interaction." In *Theory Development in Environment and Aging*, edited by M. Powell Lawton. New York: Wiley.

Kane, RI. 1989. *Essentials of Clinical Geriatrics.* Second edition. New York: McGraw Hill, Inc.

Kane, Rosalie A. and Arthur L. Caplan, eds. 1990. *Everyday Ethics: Resolving Dilemmas in Nursing Home Life.* New York: Springer Publishing Company.

Kataria, Mohan, ed. 1985. *Fits, Faints and Falls in Old Age.* Lancaster, UK: MTP Press Ltd.

Katz, Lawrence. 1999. *Keep Your Brain Alive: 83 Neurobic Exercises.* New York: Workman Publishing.

Kaufman, Sharon R. 1986. *The Ageless Self: Sources of Meaning in Late Life.* Madison: The University of Wisconsin Press.

_____ 1998. "Intensive Care, Old Age, and the Problem of Death in America." *The Gerontologist 38* (6): 715-25.

_____ 2000. "In the Shadow of 'Death with Dignity': Medicine and Cultural Quandaries of the Vegetative State." *American Anthropologist 102* (1): 69-83.

Kayser-Jones, Jeanie. 1981. *Old, Alone, and Neglected: Care of the Aged in Scotland and the United States.* Berkeley: University of California Press.

_____ 2000. "A Case Study of the Death of an Older Woman in a Nursing Home: Are Nursing Care Practices in Compliance with Ethical Guidelines?" *Journal of Gerontological Nursing.* September 2000: 48-54.

Keith, Jennie. 1982. *Old People as People: Social and Cultural Influences on Aging and Old Age.* Boston: Little, Brown and Company.

Kerns, Virginia. 1983. *Women and the Ancestors: Black Carib Kinship and Ritual.* Chicago: University of Illinois Press.

Kertzer, David I. 1995. "Toward a Historical Demography of Aging." In *Aging in the Past: Demography, Society, and Old Age*, edited by David I. Kertzer and Peter Laslett. Berkeley: University of California Press.

Kleinman, Arthur. 1980. *Patients and Healers in the Context of Culture.* Berkeley: University of California Press.

Koenig, Barbara A. 1988. "The Technological Imperative in Medical Practice: The Social Creation of a 'Routine' Practice." In *Biomedicine Examined*, edited by Margaret Lock and Deborah Gordon. Boston: Kluwer.

Konner, Melvin. 1987. *Becoming a Doctor: A Journey of Initiation in Medical School.* New York: Penguin Books.

Kramer, Peter D. 1993. *Listening to Prozac.* New York: Viking.

Kuhn, Thomas S. 1962. *The Structure of Scientific Revolutions.* Chicago. University of Chicago Press.

Laird, Carobeth. 1979. *Limbo: A Memoir about Life in a Nursing Home by a Survivor.* Novato (CA): Chandler & Sharp.

Lamb, Sarah. 2000. *White Saris and Sweet Mangoes: Aging, Gender, and Body in North India.* Berkeley: University of California Press.

Lasch, Christopher. 1977. *Haven in a Heartless World: The Family Besieged.* New York: Basic Books.

Laslett, Peter. 1995. "Necessary Knowledge: Age and Aging in the Societies of the Past." In *Aging in the Past: Demography, Society, and Old Age*, edited by David I. Kertzer and Peter Laslett. Berkeley: University of California Press.

Lawton, M. Powell, Paul G. Windley and Thomas O. Byerts, eds. 1982. *Aging and the Environment: Theoretical Approaches.* New York: Springer.

Le Poncin, Mónique. 1990. *Brain Fitness.* New York: Ballantine Books.

Lewin, K. 1935. *Dynamic Theory of Personality.* New York: McGraw-Hill.

Lock, Margaret. 1993. *Encounters with Aging: Mythologies of Menopause in Japan and North America.* Berkeley: University of California Press.

Lopata, Helena. 1973. *Widowhood in an American City.* Cambridge (MA): Schenkman Press.

_____ 1996. *Current Widowhood.* Thousand Oaks (CA): Sage.

Luborsky, Mark R. 1995. "Questioning the Allure of Aging and Health for Medical Anthropology." *Medical Anthropological Quarterly 9* (2): 277-81.

Luborsky, Mark R. and Andrea Sankar. 1993. "Extending the Critical Gerontology Perspective: Cultural Dimensions." *The Gerontologist 33* (4): 440-44.

Lyman, Karen. 1993. *Day In, Day out with Alzheimer's: Stress in Caregiving Relationships.* Philadelphia: Temple University Press.

_____ 1996. "Unexpected Communities and Unexpected Identities: The Creation of Meaning among Persons with Dementia." Paper presented at the Gerontological Society of America annual meeting, Washington, DC, November, 1996.

Mace, Nancy L. and Peter V. Rabins. 1981. *The 36-Hour Day: A Family Guide to Caring for Persons with Alzheimer's Disease, Related Dementing Illnesses, and Memory Loss in Later Life.* Baltimore: Johns Hopkins University Press.

Mann, A.E. 1975. "Some Paleodemographic Aspects of the South African Australopithecines." *University of Pennsylvania Publications in Anthropology, Volume 1.* Philadelphia: University of Pennsylvania Press.

Marcus, J. 1976. "The Size of the Early Mesoamerican Village." In *The Early Mesoamerican Village,* edited by Kent Flannery. New York: Academic Press.

Middleton, John. 1963. "Witchcraft and Sorcery in Lugbara." In *Witchcraft and Sorcery in East Africa,* edited by John Middleton and E. H. Winter. London: Routledge and Kegan Paul.

Miller, Susan and Vincent Mor. 2002. "The Role of Hospice Care in the Nursing Home Setting." In *Journal of Palliative Medicine 5* (2): 271-277.

Moody, Harry R. 1988. "Toward a Critical Gerontology: The Contribution of the Humanities to Theories of Aging." In *Emergent Theories of Aging,* edited by James E. Birren and Vern L. Bengtson. New York: Springer.

Mor, V., Banaszak-Holl, J. and Zinn, J. 1996. "The Trend Towards Specialization in Nursing Care Facilities." *Generations,* Winter: 24-29.

Mullen, Patrick B. 1992. *Listening to Old Voices: Folklore, Life Stories, and the Elderly.* Chicago: University of Illinois Press.

Muller, Jessica H. 1994. "Anthropology, Bioethics, and Medicine: A Provocative Trilogy." *Medical Anthropology Quarterly 8* (4): 448-467.

Muller, Jessica and Barbara Koenig. 1988. "On the Boundary of Life and Death." In *Biomedicine Examined,* edited by Margaret Lock and Deborah Gordon. Boston: Kluwer.

Munoz, Eric. 1983. "Economic Costs of Trauma." *New York Medical Quarterly 4*: 103.

Murphy, Robert F. 1987. *The Body Silent.* New York: Henry Holt.

Murray, H.A. 1938. *Explorations in Personality.* New York: Oxford University Press.

Myrianthopoulos and S. M. Aronson. 1966. "Population Dynamics of Tay Sachs Disease: Reproductive Fitness and Selection." *American Journal of Genetics 18*: 313.

Myerhoff, Barbara G. 1979. *Number Our Days.* New York: EP Dutton.

Nakabayashi, K., S.C. Aronson, M. Siegel, W. Sturner and S.M. Aronson.1984. "Traffic Fatalities in Rhode Island, Part 1— Descriptive Epidemiology." *Rhode Island Medical Journal 67*: 25-30.

Nash, Ogden. 1995. *The Selected Poetry of Ogden Nash.* New York: Black Dog & Leventhal.

Nason, James D. 1981. "Respected Elder or Old Person: Aging in a Micronesian Community." In *Other Ways of Growing Old: Anthropological Perspectives,* edited by Pamela T. Amoss and Stevan Harrell. Stanford: Stanford University Press.

National Center for Health Statistics, Division of Vital Statistics, 1966/68 (magnetic tape).

Palmore, Erdman B. 1975. *The Honorable Elders: A Cross-Cultural Analysis of Aging in Japan.* Durham: Duke University Press.

_____ 1984. "Longevity in Abkhazia: A Reevaluation." *Gerontologist 24*: 95-96.

Palmore, Erdman B. and Daisaku Maeda. 1985. *The Honorable Elders Revisited: A Revised Cross-Cultural Analysis of Aging in Japan.* Durham: Duke University Press.

Peele, Stanton. 1998. "Alcoholism and the Elderly—The New Epidemic?" *The Star Ledger.* July 29, 1998: A19.

Peress, N. 1981. Personal correspondence.

Pitt-Rivers, Julian. 1977. *The Fate of Schechem or the Politics of Sex: Essays in the Anthropology of the Mediterranean.* Cambridge: Cambridge University Press.

Plath, David. 1987. *"Ecstasy Years—Old Age in Japan."* In *Growing Old in Different Societies: Cross-Cultural Perspectives,* edited by J. Sokolovsky. Acton (MA): Copley Press.

_____ 1998. "The Last Confucian Sandwich: Becoming Middle Aged." In *Japanese Society Since 1945,* edited by Edward R. Beauchamp. New York: Garland Publishing.

Preston, S. ed. 1980. *Biological and Social Aspects of Mortality and the Length of Life.* Liege, Belgium: Ordinn Editions.

Providence *Journal.* 1 November 2000: A13.

Quadagno, J. 1982. *Aging in Early Industrial Society.* New York: Academic Press.

Quam, Jean K. and Gary S. Whitford. 1992. "Adaptation and Age-Related Expectations of Older Gay and Lesbian Adults." *The Gerontologist 32* (3): 367-374.

Rapp, Rayna. 2000. *Testing Women, Testing the Fetus: The Social Impact of Amniocentesis in America.* New York: Routledge.

Ray, Ruth E. 1996. "A Postmodern Perspective on Feminist Gerontology." *The Gerontologist 36* (5): 674-680.

Rhoads, E. and L. D. Holmes. 1995. *Other Cultures, Elder Years,* second edition. Thousand Oaks (CA): Sage.

Rigler, S. 2000. "Alcoholism in the Elderly." *Am. Fam. Physician 61*: 1710-16.

Rosen, Jonathan. 2000. *The Talmud and the Internet.* New York: Farrar Strauss Giroux.

Rosow, Arnold. 1985. "Status and Change Through the Life Cycle." In *Handbook of Aging and the Social Sciences,* second edition, edited by Binstock, R.H. and E. Shanas. New York: Van Nostrand: 62-93.

Rosten, Leo. 1968. *The Joys of Yiddish.* New York: Pocket Books/Washington Square Press.

Rowles, Graham D. 1983. "Between Worlds: A Relocation Dilemma for the Appalachian Elderly. *International Journal of Aging and Human Development 17* (4): 301-14.

Sacks, Oliver. 1985. *The Man Who Mistook His Wife for a Hat.* New York: Summit Books.

_____ 1995. *An Anthropologist on Mars: Seven Paradoxical Tales.* New York: Random House.

Salber, E. 1983. *Don't Send Me Flowers When I'm Dead: Voices of Rural Elderly.* Durham: Duke University Press.

Savishinsky, Joel. 1991. *The Ends of Time: Life and Work in a Nursing Home.* Westport: Bergin & Garvey.

_____ 2000. *Breaking the Watch: The Meanings of Retirement in America.* Ithaca: Cornell University Press.

Scheper-Hughes, Nancy and Margaret M. Lock. 1987. "The Mindful Body: A Prolegomenon to Future Work in Medical Anthropology." *Medical Anthropology Quarterly 1*(1): 6-41.

Selzer, Mildred M. and Suzanne R. Kunkel, eds. 1995. "What it Means to be a Professional in the Field of Aging. *Generations 19* (2).

Sheehy, Gail. 1995. *New Passages: Mapping Your Life Across Time.* New York: Random House.

Shem, Samuel. 1981. *House of God.* New York: Dell.

Shield, Renée Rose. 1988. *Uneasy Endings: Daily Life in an American Nursing Home.* Ithaca: Cornell University Press.

_____ 1995. "Ethics in the Nursing Home: Cases, Choices, and Issues. In *The Culture of Long Term Care: Nursing Home Ethnography,* edited by J. Neil Henderson and Maria D. Vesperi. Westport (CT): Bergin & Garvey.

_____ 1997. "Managing the Care of Nursing Home Residents: The Challenge of Integration." In *Focus on Managed Care and Quality Assurance: Integrating Acute and Chronic Care,* edited by Robert J. Newcomer and Anne M. Wilkinson. Annual Review of Gerontology and Geriatrics, Volume 16. New York: Springer Publishing Company.

_____ 2002. *Diamond Stories: Enduring Change on 47th Street.* Ithaca: Cornell University Press.

Simmons, Leo. 1945. *The Role of the Aged in Primitive Society.* New Haven: Yale University Press.

Snowden, David. 2001. *Aging with Grace: What the Nun Study Teaches Us About Leading Longer, Healthier, and More Meaningful Lives.* New York: Bantam Books.

Sobel, Dava. 1995. *Longitude: The True Story of a Lone Genius who Solved the Greatest Scientific Problem of His Time.* New York: Penguin.

Sokolovsky, Jay. 1997. "Starting Points: A Global, Cross-Cultural View of Aging. In *The Cultural Context of Aging: Worldwide Perspectives,* second edition, edited by Jay Sokolovsky. Westport (CT): Bergin & Garvey.

_____ 1997a. "Aging, Family and Community Development in a Mexican Peasant Village." In *The Cultural Context of Aging: Worldwide Perspectives,* second edition, edited by Jay Sokolovsky. Westport (CT): Bergin & Garvey.

Sokolovsky, Jay and Carl Cohen. 1997. "Uncle Ed, Super Runner and the Fry Cook: Old Men on the Street." In *The Cultural Context of Aging: Worldwide Perspectives.* second edition, edited by Jay Sokolovsky. Westport (CT): Bergin & Garvey.

Stegner, Wallace. 1976. *The Spectator Bird.* New York: Doubleday.

Sudnow, David. 1967. *Passing On: The Social Organization of Dying.* Englewood Cliffs, NJ: Prentice-Hall.

Tanaka, Y. et al. 1984. *Pathology of the Extremely Aged.* St. Louis, MO: Ishiyaku EuroAmerica, Inc.

Teno, Joan. 2001. "Advance Care Planning in the Outpatient and ICU Setting." In *The Transition from Cure to Comfort,* edited by R. Curtis and G. Rubenfeld. New York: Oxford University Press.

Teski, Maria. 1981. "Living Together: An Ethnography of a Retirement Hotel." Washington, DC: University Press of America.

Thomas, William H. 1994. *The Eden Alternative: Nature, Hope and Nursing Homes.* Sherburne (New York): Eden Alternative Foundation.

Turner, Victor. 1967. *The Forest of Symbols: Aspects of Ndembu Ritual.* Ithaca: Cornell University Press.

Tyler, Anne. 1985. *Dinner at the Homesick Restaurant.* New York: Knopf.

Valois, H.D. 1960. "Vital Statistics in Prehistoric Population as Determined from Archeological Data." *Viking Fund Publications in Anthropology, no. 28:* 186-222.

Vatuk, Sylvia. 1980. "Withdrawal and Disengagement as a Cultural Response to Aging in India." In *Aging in Culture and Society: Comparative Viewpoints and Strategies,* edited by Christine Fry and contributors. New York: Bergin.

Vesperi, Maria. 1987. "The Reluctant Consumer: Nursing Home Residents in the Post-Bergman Era." In *Growing Old in Different Societies: Cross-Cultural Perspectives,* edited by J. Sokolovsky. Acton (MA): Copley.

Volz, Joe. 2001. "After a Year in the Slow Lane, Life is Good." *New York Times.* Special section: Retirement. 21 March, 2000: E11.

Wada, Shuichi. 1995. "The Status and Image of the Elderly in Japan: Understanding the Paternalistic Ideology." In *Images of Aging: Cultural Representations of Later Life,* edited by Mike Featherstone and Andrew Wernick. New York: Routledge.

Watson, Nancy, Mary Hauptmann and Carol Brink. 1998. "As Elders Rock, Emotional Burden of Dementia Eases." Press release of paper presented at the Eastern Nursing Research Society, April 12-25. Rochester, New York.

Weidenreich, F. 1943. "The Skull of Sinanthropus Pekinesis." *Paleoontologica Sinica, ns. No 10.* Peiping.

Weinberger-Thomas, Catherine. 1999. *Ashes of Immorality: Widow-Burning in India.* Chicago: University of Chicago Press.

West, Dorothy. 1995. *The Wedding.* NY: Doubleday.

Wetle, Terrie. 1995. "Ethical Issues and Value Conflicts Facing Case Managers of Frail Elderly People Living at Home." In *Long-term Care Decisions : Ethical and Conceptual Dimensions,* edited by Laurence B. McCullough and Nancy L. Wilson. Baltimore: Johns Hopkins University Press.

_____ 2000. "Living Longer, Living Better: Public Health and Aging." Talk presented in the Department of Community Health, Brown University, October 25, 2000.

Whitman, Walt. 1992. *Leaves of Grass.* New York: Barnes & Noble.

Winograd, C. et al. 1991. "Screening for Frailty: Criteria and Predictors of Outcome." *Journal of the American Geriatrics Society 39*: 778.

World Health Organization.1996. *Investing in Health Research and Development.* Geneva.

Zeserson, Jan Morgan. 2001. "How Japanese Women Talk about Hot Flushes: Implications for Menopause Research." *Medical Anthropology Quarterly 15* (2): 189-205.

Zinn, J.A. and Mor, V. 1994. "Nursing Home Special Care Units: Distribution by Type, State, and Facility Characteristics." *Gerontologist 34:* 371-377.

Index